Navigating Globotics at the Semi-periphery

International Comparative Social Studies

VOLUME 61

The titles published in this series are listed at *brill.com/icss*

Navigating Globotics at the Semi-periphery

Public Management and Governance Shifts in the Visegrád Group under Globalisation and Technological Change

Edited by

Michał Możdżeń
Marcin Zawicki

BRILL

LEIDEN | BOSTON

Cover illustration: Castle of Visegrad, where the Visegrad Declaration of cooperation was signed in 1991. © Andrzej Kozina

This project was funded by Ministry of Science and Higher Education of Poland within "Regional Initiative of Excellence" Programme for 2019–2022. Project no.: 021/RID/2018/19.

Library of Congress Cataloging-in-Publication Data

Names: Możdżeń, Michał, editor. | Zawicki, Marcin, editor.
Title: Navigating globotics at the semi-periphery : public management and
   governance shifts in the Visegrád Group under globalisation and
   technological change / edited by Michał Możdżeń, Marcin Zawicki.
Description: Leiden ; Boston : Brill, [2025] | Series: International
   comparative social studies, 1568-4474 ; volume 61 | Includes index.
Identifiers: LCCN 2024048014 (print) | LCCN 2024048015 (ebook) | ISBN
   9789004711945 (hardback) | ISBN 9789004711952 (ebook)
Subjects: LCSH: Globalization–Czech Republic. | Globalization–Hungary. |
   Globalization–Poland. | Globalization–Slovakia. | Visegrád Group
Classification: LCC HF1365 .N385 2025 (print) | LCC HF1365 (ebook) | DDC
   337–dc23/eng/20250103
LC record available at https://lccn.loc.gov/2024048014
LC ebook record available at https://lccn.loc.gov/2024048015

Typeface for the Latin, Greek, and Cyrillic scripts: "Brill". See and download: brill.com/brill-typeface.

ISSN 1568-4474
ISBN 978-90-04-71194-5 (hardback)
ISBN 978-90-04-71195-2 (e-book)
DOI 10.1163/9789004711242

Contents

Acknowledgements

The research for this book was funded by the Polish Ministry of Science and Higher Education as part of the Regional Initiative of Excellence Programme for 2019–2022. Project no. 021/RID/2018/19; total funding: 11 897 131.40 PLN. We would like to express our gratitude for the funding, and for the constructive feedback provided by the reviewers of the project proposal.

We would like to thank the following experts for their cooperation in the research: Pavel Horák, Assistant Professor, Department of Social Policy and Social Work, Masaryk University (Czech Republic); Máté Hajba, Director of the Free Market Foundation (Hungary); and Martin Reguli, Senior Analyst at the F. A. Hayek Foundation (Slovakia).

We are also grateful for broadening the interpretations of the research findings to the panellists and other participants in the Conference Mechanisms of Collective Action Management held on 21 September 2022 at Krakow University of Economics: Katarzyna Śledziewska, Eva Pavlikova, Ignacy Święcicki, Krzysztof Izdebski, Marta Musidłowska, Przemysław Pałka, Kazimierz Ujazdowski, Katarzyna Baran, Maria Libura, Bartosz Paszcza, Tomasz Rychter, Joanna Erbel, Maciej Grodzicki, and Jan Zygmuntowski.

We are grateful to Wojciech Paprocki, full professor at the Warsaw School of Economics, for his constructive comments throughout the project.

Finally, we would like to thank Rafał Śmietana and Marcin Kukiełka for their assistance with the translation, proofreading, and editing of the manuscript.

Figures and Tables

Figures

Tables

Notes on Contributors

Bartłomiej Biga
is involved in the economic analysis of law and public policies. His primary focus is on issues related to intellectual property, especially copyrights and patents. He believes in the efficiency of business models based on extensive conditional sharing.

Maciej Frączek
holds a PhD in economics and works as an assistant professor at Krakow University of Economics (Department of Public Policy). His research focuses on labour market issues, social policy, public administration.

Tomasz Geodecki
holds a PhD in economics and works as an assistant professor at Krakow University of Economics. His research and articles focus on industrial and innovation policies, global value chains, institutional economics and public administration.

Máté Hajba
(1989), Director of Free Market Foundation, Hungary. He is the author of several books, and he publishes research and articles on digitalization, economics, the history of ideas and human rights.

Pavel Horák
is an assistant professor at the Department of Social Policy and Social Work at Masaryk University in Brno. His research focuses on public administration and implementation of public policies, especially labour market, family, and social service policies.

Marcin Kędzierski
holds a PhD in economics and works as an assistant professor at Krakow University of Economics. His research focuses on public policy, global public goods and European integration. He has worked as an advisor to many Polish public institutions.

Andrzej Kozina
is a habilitated doctor and PhD in management. He works as associate professor of management in Department of Public Policy at Krakow University of

Economics. His research focuses on socio-economic negotiations, managing organizational relationships and change.

Stanisław Mazur

habilitated doctor in political science. Works as associate professor at Krakow University of Economics. First Deputy Mayor of Krakow since 2024, Rector of the Cracow University of Economics (2020-2024). He specializes in i.a. decentralization, public policy analysis, public management, governance, organizational learning.

Michał Możdżeń

holds a PhD in economics and works as an assistant professor at Krakow University of Economics. His research focuses on political economy, macroeconomics, fiscal policy, public administration and labour market issues in CEE countries, with emphasis on Poland.

Marek Oramus

holds a Ph.D. in political science and works at Krakow University of Economics. His research focuses on new trends in public management and the use of innovative solutions in public administration, especially at the level of local government.

Marcin Zawicki

habilitated doctor in policy sciences and PhD in economics. He works as associate professor at Krakow University of Economics. His research focuses on public management and governance, public policy and public administration.

Michał Żabiński

holds a PhD in economics and works as an assistant professor at Krakow University of Economics. His research focuses on public governance, propaganda and disinformation, local governance and collective actions in CEE countries, with particular emphasis on Poland.

CHAPTER 1

The Visegrád Group at the Threshold of the Fourth Industrial Revolution

Marcin Zawicki

1 The Fourth Industrial Revolution as a Catalyst for Change in Public Management and Governance

The Fourth Industrial Revolution (4IR) taking place today affects every aspect of state, economy and society as the boundaries between the public, private, and non-profit sectors are becoming increasingly blurred. The search for innovative ways to increase efficiency by public authorities leads to the growth of a mixed economy involving public, private, and non-profit providers of public services, as well as increased participation of private and non-profit actors in addressing problems traditionally considered to be the domain of public policy (Barber, Levy and Mendonca, 2007).

Due to the complexity and interdependence of the challenges faced by states, national governments are increasingly inclined to engage in international, regional, and judicial forums to address them (KPMG, 2016). Global shifts in international balances (Z-Punkt, 2021) and rising international tensions (PTPS, 2021) are giving rise to political (dis)order (Z-Punkt, 2021), a crisis of democracy, and the emergence of new governance models (PTPS, 2021). In the European Union, on the other hand, integration processes are underway to consolidate a European centre of power at the expense of the eroding sovereignty of EU member states. Christopher Bickerton aptly captured the essence of this transformation as leading "from nation-states to member states" (2016).

The Fourth Industrial Revolution is an era of learning, acquiring, and integrating knowledge (Puncreobutr, 2017). It provides strong incentives for the convergence of research disciplines, sciences and technologies, systems, information and communications technologies, production technologies or manufacturing systems (OECD, 2017). The technological revolution is also an era of creativity and innovation (Puncreobutr, 2017), which triggers profound changes in the work environment (Z-Punkt, 2021) resulting from the digitisation and automation of work (PTPS, 2021). These developments have been accelerated by the rise of remote work (Linthorst and de Waal, 2020) amidst lockdowns and employer decisions in response to the COVID-19 pandemic (Gupta, 2020; Leonardi, 2020), and the spread of flexible employment (Linthorst and de Waal, 2020).

It is also becoming increasingly clear that as 4IR proceeds, its centre of gravity is shifting towards high-tech firms. Its ramifications affect not only the economy, but also the social and political spheres. A handful of big technology businesses are gradually and steadily eclipsing the traditional dominance of governments (Tan and Shang-su, 2017).

Demographic shifts are at the forefront of social transformation (Z-Punkt, 2021; PwC, 2016). Their most prominent manifestation is the worldwide population growth (UNDESA, 2019; PTPS, 2021) resulting from increasing life expectancy (KPMG, 2016; PRB, 2021) and high birth rates in Africa and other developing countries. According to the 2021 edition of the World Population Data Sheet (PRB, 2021), the global population is expected to reach 9.7 billion by 2050.

At the same time, the mean age of populations in developed countries continues to rise (UNDESA, 2019; PTPS, 2021). The number of senior citizens worldwide is projected to increase from 901 million in 2015 to 1.4 billion in 2030 to 2.1 billion in 2050 (UNDESA, 2015). This major shift has already started to undermine the viability of many social welfare systems, such as pensions and health care (KPMG, 2016).

Population movement is also intensifying (UNDESA, 2019; PTPS, 2021; Wahba et al., 2021). Increased migration of skilled and unskilled labour creates new challenges for both sending and receiving countries (Wahba et al., 2021; Linthorst and de Waal, 2020). Migration and demographic changes lead to significant shifts in workforce composition (Rudolph et al., 2018), whereas growing disparities and social polarisation result from technological advancement and migration dynamics (Z-Punkt, 2021; PTPS, 2021).

The Fourth Industrial Revolution presents enormous challenges that all the countries worldwide are trying to meet to the best of their abilities and resources. This is true for the core countries, i.e. the most developed, prosperous, and industrialised ones, as well as the middle- and low-income ones, also known as semi-periphery and periphery countries, which continue to rely on economic assistance. The challenges posed by 4IR will also be felt faced by the Visegrád Group, comprising the Czech Republic, Hungary, Poland, and Slovakia, all of which are located in Central and Eastern Europe and have comparable political and economic aspirations.

2 The Origins and Aims of the Visegrád Group

In his work entitled *The singularity of Central Europe?*, Jacek Purchla notes that "The history of the Czech, Hungarian, Polish and Slovak states is built upon the foundations of Western European civilisation: the tradition of antiquity, Christianity, self-government, and respect for the rights of individuals," and that "the character of the relations between the states and nations in Central Europe was formed by the distinct historical experience of this part of the continent, and in no small part by the lessons of the twentieth century" (Purchla, 2020).

The events of the first half of the 14th century served as the historical backdrop for the establishment of the Visegrád Group. In 1335, the kings of Poland, Bohemia, and Hungary met at Visegrád Castle, which was at the time a prominent seat of Hungarian rulers. The meeting led to an agreement on policy and trade as well as a prosperous future for Central European cooperation. After more than six and a half centuries, the memory of this event was rekindled by the fall of the Iron Curtain in 1989–1990, which also opened up new prospects for collaboration among Central European countries. The Visegrád Declaration, which established the Visegrád Triangle, was signed on 15 February 1991 in Visegrád, northern Hungary, by then Czechoslovak President Václav Havel, Hungarian Prime Minister József Antall, and Polish President Lech Wałęsa. Due to the largely parallel histories of these nations, it was possible to identify the following objectives of the newly formed cooperation forum (www.Visegrádgroup.eu):

- full restitution of state independence, democracy and freedom,
- elimination of all existing social, economic and spiritual aspects of the totalitarian system,
- construction of a parliamentary democracy, a modern law-governed state, respect for human rights and freedoms,
- creation of a modern free market economy,
- full involvement in the European political and economic system as well as the system of security and legislation.

After the break-up of Czechoslovakia in 1993, the name of the forum was changed to the Visegrád Group (shortened to v4). Its current members are the Czech Republic, Hungary, Poland, and Slovakia.

Prior to the Visegrád Declaration, systemic reform initiatives in the v4 countries had already been launched in the late 1980s and early 1990s. In the Czech Republic, Hungary, Poland, and Slovakia, the communist system was replaced by a democratic one based on the tripartite distribution of power, and local self-government was restored. The withdrawal of Soviet troops also contributed to the demise of the totalitarian system. The economic transition attempted to institute a stable and convertible currency, expand the private sector, marketise prices, and privatise state-owned enterprises, all of which marked important steps towards the post-socialist nations' incorporation into the global economy. The Czech Republic, Poland, and Hungary joined NATO in 1999 (Slovakia did so five years later), and all the V4 countries became members of the European Union in 2004.

The events of the 20th century, particularly World Wars I and II and the communist era from 1945 to 1989, as well as the resurgence of democracy after 1989 were the major determinants of the development of the current forms of public governance in the Visegrád countries. Piotr Kopyciński identified 6 stages in the development of the public governance model in the V4 countries (Kopyciński, 2020):

- Foreign-power control (until 1918), marked by the dominance of the bureaucratic model imposed by foreign rulers.
- Independence (1918–1939), involved establishing autonomous state structures based primarily on bureaucratic ideas.
- Soviet dominance (1945–1989), characterised by the forced adoption of the Soviet form of government.
- The first stage of reforms (1989–1997), which incorporated components of new public management.
- Preparation for and admission to the EU (1997–2004) with reforms including components of new public management and public governance.
- Post-accession and the 2007/2008 crisis (starting in 2004) based on the hesitant institutional convergence model, which combines modern public management, public governance, and the concepts of the neo-Weberian state.

The Visegrád Group's thirty-year collaboration record has not been entirely positive. Because of their shared identity, these countries are a powerful representation of the Central and Eastern European region in the arena of European politics. Yet, their cooperation flourishes best in times of calm, with each subsequent crisis heightening political tensions that expose the disparities between the individual countries and erode the strength of their single stance (Patyk, 2022). Technological change, globalisation, and other momentous modern political changes, particularly the ongoing war in Ukraine since February 2022, have spurred a rethinking of the V4 Group's rationale for collaboration. According to experts, this organisation needs to establish new development goals based on similarities rather than differences among the individual nations and the policies pursued by their governments, including building a regional community, economic development, and the promotion of Central and Eastern Europe (ibid.). However, the adoption of new institutions and techniques for public management and governance that enable these nations to respond to the realities of 4IR may also serve as an example of convergence. In any case, the challenges brought on by dynamic technological change and globalisation will likely trigger other changes in the public management and governance paradigm in the V4 countries over the next few years.

3 The Economic and Social Potential of the Visegrád Group

In economic terms, the Visegrád Group countries are considered to be semi-peripheral. As a result, they currently do not play decisive roles in the system of global value chains, although they constitute an important component of the so-called Factory Europe. Their economies are mostly engaged in manufacturing processes that do not generate the most added value. The latter is realised in the core countries with the highest level of development at the initial and final stages of global value chains.

Worth (2009) argues that the very term semi-periphery is sometimes contested and remains essentially undefined in world-systems theory. However, it provides a much-needed link in the 'core–periphery divide' and expands the possibilities for exploring the complexity of institutional structures at the expense of introducing classical sociology-inspired theoretical tensions into this paradigm. In an attempt to define the semi-peripheral countries, the author notes that they usually exhibit the following set of characteristics:

- more or less balanced levels of basic and advanced production forms,
- GDP per capita somewhere between the richest economies of Europe/USA and underdeveloped countries,
- strong reliance on manufacturing as a production base,
- relatively weak state capacity,
- relatively high and growing inequality,
- increasing urbanisation.

Fairly affluent countries controlled by a major economic power, which participate in international alliances that enable the exploitation of developing countries can also be categorised as semi-peripheral, according to the author.

Although the Visegrád countries have recently witnessed tremendous growth, prompting Bohle and Greskovits (2012) to label them as 'semi-core,' they have met practically all of the above-mentioned qualities for decades. In fact, it was Immanuel Wallerstein, the concept's creator, who classified them as semi-peripheral along with other Eastern European countries (Wallerstein 1976). Following the global financial crisis, the literature on international political economy generally did not question their membership in this group, despite attempts at new definitions emphasising the role of global capital in national economic policy (transnational state; Shields 2009), market-driven structural dependency (dependent market economies; Nölke and Vliegenthart 2009), and demand-driven dependency (export led growth model; Grodzicki and Możdżeń 2021, Baccaro and Hadziabdic 2023). Indeed, most studies in the field of international political economy devoted to the Visegrád Group, or more broadly CEE, underscore the structurally incomplete economic and political autonomy of these countries.

Nevertheless, the importance of the Visegrád economies in Europe is increasing. Taken together, they represent the sixth economic powerhouse and the third largest consumer market in Europe. Between 1991 and 2019, their combined GDP at current prices increased by 155 per cent to €996 billion in 2019. Poland stood out from the region in terms of growth dynamics, with its economy growing more than threefold in the stated period. In 2019, GDP per capita in the V4 countries accounted for nearly 72 per cent of the so-called old EU countries.

Between 1995 and 2019, the value of exports of manufactured goods increased more than 19-fold, imports surged 16 times, and investment in fixed assets grew three times faster than in the EU-15. Because of the region's investment appeal, the V4 economies have been able to integrate into global value chains. The V4 countries have particularly strong trade and economic ties with Germany. The volume of trade between the V4 and Germany is 1.5 times bigger than that between Germany and China.

When compared with Western Europe, the V4 economies have low unemployment rates, but one of their main problems is an ageing population. While the population of the EU as a whole has grown by 12% over the past 30 years, it has fallen by 1% in the V4. The region's demographic outlook was made worse by the exodus of young, educated residents in the years immediately following EU accession (Ambroziak et al., 2020). Despite some encouraging trends in the V4 economies since then, they have not yet attained the average EU level of economic development. Table 1.1 shows the most recent growth statistics for the V4 economies.

One of the factors determining the pace and ease with which countries adapt to the challenges of 4IR is the sophistication of their digital economies. According to the 2022 Digital Economy and Society Index, the Czech Republic, Hungary, Poland, and Slovakia score below the EU average in this respect. For example, the Czech Republic ranks 18th, whereas Poland comes 24th out of the

TABLE 1.1   Changes in key economic indicators in the Visegrád countries between 2019 and 2021

Indicator	Year	CZ	HU	PL	SK	EU27_2020
GDP volume index (constant prices, 2019=100)	2021	97.4	102.3	103.7	98.5	99.1
GDP per capita in PPS (EU27_2020=100)	2021	91.5	76.0	77.4	68.0	100.0
Volume index of exports of goods and services (2019=100)	2021	97.8	103.6	111.8	102.2	101.5
Volume index of imports of goods and services (2019=100)	2021	103.8	104.4	114.6	102.1	100.4
Gross fixed capital formation as a percentage of GDP	2021	25.5	27.1	16.6	19.1	22.0
Volume index of agricultural output (2020=100)	2021	99.0	97.9	99.3	100.3	99.8
Volume index of industrial production, calendar adjusted (2019=100)[a]	2021	98.9	102.3	112.4	100.4	100.1
Research and development expenditures, percentage of GDP	2020	1.99	1.62	1.39	0.92	2.32
Harmonised index of consumer prices (2020=100.0)	2021	103.3	105.2	105.2	102.8	102.9

a   excluding water and waste management.
SOURCE: (HCSO 2022)

27 EU member states. In this league table, Slovakia ranks 22nd and Hungary 23rd (European Commission, 2022). The said ranking thus reveals significant gaps in the level of digital economic development between the Visegrád Group and the 'old' EU member states.

In terms of human development metrics, the Visegrád countries show more variation than the European Union averages (EU 27). The median population age, total fertility rate, employment and unemployment rates are all favourable defining characteristics of the V4 countries. Variables like the number of homes with Internet access, the proportion of people who use the Internet every day, and individual internet purchases are close to the EU average. The average life expectancy at birth in the V4 countries (just under 78), however, is lower than the EU27 average (well over 80). The percentage of people aged 16 to 74 who possess more advanced general digital skills is smaller in the V4 countries. Table 1.2 show changes in the Visegrád countries' basic social indicators between 2019 and 2021.

TABLE 1.2   Changes in basic social indicators in the Visegrád countries between 2019 and 2021

Indicator	Year	CZ	HU	PL	SK	EU27_2020
Average life expectancy at birth, year	2021	77.4	74.5	75.6	74.8	80.1
Median age of population, year	2021	43.3	43.6	41.6	41.4	44.1
Young-age dependency ratio (population 0–14 years to population 15–64 years), %	2021	25.2	22.4	23.5	23.7	23.5
Old-age dependency ratio (population 65 years or over to population 15–64 years), %	2021	31.6	31.2	28.5	25.5	32.5
Total fertility rate, per woman	2020	1.71	1.59	1.39	1.59	1.50
Crude rate of net international migration, per 1000 population	2020	2.5	0.9	0.1	0.8	1.9
Employment rate of population aged 15–64, %	2021	74.4	73.1	70.3	69.4	68.4
Unemployment rate of population aged 15–74, %	2021	2.8	4.1	3.4	6.8	7.0
Labour slack, population aged 20–64, % of extended labour force[a]	2021	3.7	6.9	5.6	8.7	13.4
Early leavers from education and training, in % of population aged 15–29	2021	10.9	11.7	13.4	14.2	13.1
Population aged 15–74 with tertiary educational attainment (ISCED level 5–8), %	2021	21.8	24.6	26.8	23.6	28.0
Households final consumption expenditures, volume index (2019=100)b)	2020	93.2	98.6	97.1	98.7	92.7
Individuals who have above basic overall digital skills, percentage of individuals aged 16–74	2019	26	25	21	27	31
Households with internet connection, % of all households[b]	2021	89	91	92	90	92
Internet purchases by individuals in the last 3 months, percentage of individuals aged 16–74	2021	63	58	48	69	57
Proportion of individuals who use the Internet every day, percentage of individuals aged 16–74	2021	81	82	74	80	80

a   extended labour force includes economically active individuals and economically inactive individuals who intend to work but do not seek work actively or are not available.

b   including non-profit institutions serving households (NPISH).

SOURCE: (HCSO, 2022)

4   Purpose, Subject, Method, and Content of the Book

The aim of this monograph is to present and discuss the Czech Republic, Hungary, Poland, and Slovakia's unique public management and governance responses to the problems posed by 4IR.

Our reflections focus on the changes that are taking place in the V4 countries in the areas of public management and governance that are considered crucial from the perspective of globalisation and technological change, such as responding to social and economic challenges, preventing the peripheralisation of their economies, reconfiguring the state's relations with its stakeholders, developing public e-services, managing data and information flows, open data policies and combating the production of false narratives and disinformation. The concept of globotics, which is understood as the concurrent processes of globalisation and robotisation, identified with technological change in the broadest sense, provides the theoretical framework for the analysis of the changes occurring in the studied areas.

In this book, we have taken a comparative approach. Drawing on an analysis and evaluation of the ways in which the public authorities of the V4 countries have responded to the challenges of 4IR in individual areas of public management and governance, we have identified a range of similarities and differences. Our reflections address the following four research questions regarding the transformations as they occur:

1. What areas of public management and governance have seen the most conspicuous effects of globalisation and technological change?
2. What changes are currently occurring in the field of public management and governance as a result of increasing globalisation and technological change?
3. How do the public authorities in the Czech Republic, Hungary, Poland and Slovakia respond to the effects of globalisation and technological change?
4. Can similar responses to the effects of globalisation and technological change be found in the countries studied, supporting the idea that a specific Visegrád path of public management and governance is emerging to meet the challenges of the Fourth Industrial Revolution?

The V4 countries, being semi-peripheral or dependent economies behind the technological frontier, are in a unique position. On the one hand, they are constrained in their ability to successfully shape the new economic revolution and in the instruments with which to mitigate the social effects of this change independent of EU action. On the other hand, because they are not among the leaders in the use of advanced public management and governance methods and tools, they are able to partly 'leapfrog' the institutional arrangements found in more established democracies to make use of cutting-edge e-government techniques. This poses its own set of challenges, which must be addressed in the absence of an established institutional framework – a novelty in the V4 countries used to importing institutional solutions from abroad.

We assume that the unique features mentioned above (except EU membership) are actually fairly common among the emerging and recently developed countries. In other words, the nations that struggle to develop public management and governance solutions well-tailored to the globalisation challenge may benefit from the experiences of the V4 countries. Moreover, we expect our analyses to contribute to a better understanding of the following:

– new technologies used in various areas of public management and governance,
– opportunities to shape technological change and facilitate the advancement of firms in high-tech value chains.
– methods and tools used to mitigate the negative socio-economic impacts of globotics, especially the widening social and economic inequalities, skills mismatch, and digital exclusion.

The research methodology used to create this monograph comprises literature reviews, source document analysis, and in-depth empirical studies. The latter was carried out in the following stages:

1. Selection of supporting experts from the Czech Republic, Hungary, and Slovakia. The team of experts consisted of: Pavel Horák, Assistant Professor, Department of Social Policy and Social Work, Masaryk University (Czech Republic), Máté Hajba, Director of the Free Market Foundation (Hungary) and Martin Reguli, Senior Analyst at the F. A. Hayek Foundation (Slovakia).

2. Identification of thematic areas of the empirical study by the team of authors and supporting experts and preparation of preliminary reports. The thematic areas selected for investigation are listed in Table 1.3.

3. Preparation of in-depth interview (IDI) scenarios by the team of authors and supporting experts.

4. Selecting and inviting policy experts and practitioners from each V4 country who specialise in the respective topical areas of the study to participate in the research (IDI).

5. In-depth interviews (IDI) with policy experts and practitioners conducted by supporting experts and members of the team of authors.

6. Preparation of reports on the IDIs.

7. Analysis and presentation of findings.

TABLE 1.3 Research areas

Area	Number of research area
Key economic and social challenges resulting from the Fourth Industrial Revolution	1
Technological upgrading and industrial policy in the European globalised semi-peripheral economies	2
Management and regulation of data and information flows	3
Key relationships between the state and its stakeholders during the Fourth Industrial Revolution	4
Communication management – nation state towards narratives and fake news	5
The potential and limits of hierarchical public management in the face of globotics	6

SOURCE: OWN STUDY

A total of 90 interviews were conducted with 81 policy experts and practitioners. Some experts, by virtue of their functions or competences, were invited to participate in interviews on issues covering more than one thematic area. Table 1.4 shows the distribution of interviewees among the surveyed countries.

This approach permitted the authors to supplement the existing literature with insights into the nature of current problems stemming from the impact of the ongoing technological revolution on public management and governance in the V4 countries.

The book consists of ten chapters.

Chapter One argues that the Fourth Industrial Revolution provides a powerful impetus for change in a number of areas of public management and governance. It also outlines the origins and objectives of the Visegrád Group as well as the most recent socio-economic developments in these countries. These characteristics serve as the rationale for the monograph's subject matter, methodology, and content.

Chapter Two, "What model of public management and governance in response to globotics?," is of a general theoretical nature and is based on a literature review. The author, Stanisław Mazur, familiarises readers with major problems associated with the technological revolution and highlights the directions in which the analysed transformation affects the structure and objectives

TABLE 1.4   Number of in-depth interviews (IDI) conducted with policy experts and practitioners from the Visegrád countries

Country	Number of interviews
Czech Republic	23
Hungary	27
Poland	19
Slovakia	21
Total	**90**

SOURCE: OWN STUDY

of the public sector. The discussion is underpinned by Richard Baldwin's (2019) concept of globotics, which involves two mutually reinforcing developments: robotics as a labour-substitutable process of technological advancement, and globalisation, which is primarily concerned with international workforce dispersion. These processes represent a major challenge to dependent economies and governance.

The next seven chapters are empirical in nature. They draw extensively on literature reviews, source documents analyses and findings of empirical research.

In Chapter Three, "The socio-economic consequences and challenges of the Fourth Industrial RevolutionAn empirical study of the Visegrád countries," Maciej Frączek presents the results of his research on the socio-economic consequences of 4IR and the challenges it poses to the V4 countries based on individual in-depth interviews with experts. The current situation and development prospects are presented against the background of the development opportunities of the core countries. According to the report, the Visegrád countries are experiencing significant technological change in a number of sectors, including the labour market, business operations, global competition, systemic stability, quality of life, information security, and state capability. The analysis reveals that the V4 countries studied are not as well prepared as the core countries to handle the socioeconomic issues brought on by 4IR.

The next chapter, "Semi-peripherality, dependency and the institutional foundations of developing a modern industry in the Visegrád countries," is based on the varieties of capitalism approach. Its author, Tomasz Geodecki, examines the institutional foundations of developing a modern industry in the Visegrád countries. Drawing on in-depth interviews with representatives of business and administration, he addresses a variety of questions concerning the role of transnational corporations in building modern industrial processes in the V4 countries and the fields to be targeted by industrial policy in the process. He concludes that in order to combat economic marginalisation, the public sector in the V4 countries should promote technological and digital skills, expand the institutional channels of cooperation between administration and business, and continue to develop e-government.

In Chapter Five, "Models for managing state relationships with stakeholders in the Visegrád countries," Andrzej Kozina focuses on inter-organisational relations taking place between the state and its stakeholders in the Visegrád countries in the context of 4IR. The chapter presents the author's original concept of managing such relations both as a theoretical model and in relation to actual solutions applied in the V4 countries. The significance of the issue at hand is determined by the fact that the efficiency of the process of management of the relations under consideration by the state, their identification, formation, and maintenance, is very important from the standpoint of its effective operation, particularly ensuring effective coordination of the activities of entities (interest groups) functioning within and outside central administration.

Chapter Six, "The development of e-services in the evolution of e-government in V4 countries," offers a comparative analysis of e-services in V4 countries and their impact on e-government. Marcin Kędzierski and Pavel Horák examine this evolution using the seven-stage level model proposed by José Ramón Gil-Garcia and Ignacio Martinez-Moyano (2007), which ranges from the government's initial presence on the Internet to a fully integrated presence that necessitates vertical and horizontal integration of various e-functionalities provided to citizens. Apart from describing specific e-services in the V4, the authors discuss the most recent triggers of integration in e-government. Even though some solutions to that effect have been implemented in recent years, individual countries have not managed to attain the ultimate level of totally integrated presence over the last 20 years, despite the support from the EU structural funds. However, the pandemic and subsequent lockdowns significantly expedited the trend of digitalising public administration.

In Chapter Seven, "The management and regulation of data and information flows in the V4 countries," Bartłomiej Biga analyses the possibilities for cooperation between public administrations between the V4 countries and large technology companies. Given the current challenges faced by semi-peripheral nations, this is a highly sensitive area for collaboration. On the one hand, the authorities are forced to act by public demands for better public services and data protection legislation; on the other, they cannot afford to push the technology giants too far not only because the latter are largely outside their jurisdiction, but also because doing so would be extremely unpopular with the general public. However, the power these corporations wield over public discourse poses a greater danger since it gives them the opportunity to meddle deeply in democratic processes. Semi-peripheral states therefore have a strong incentive to seek the best possible relationship with the tech giants despite the fact that they are currently too weak to negotiate with them as equal partners.

The goal of Chapter Eight, "Open data policy as a response of the V4 countries to the technological shift," written by Marek Oramus, is to compare open data policies among the V4 countries. According to reports such as the European Data Portal's (EDP) yearly Open Data Maturity (ODM 2020, 2021), there are substantial disparities between these countries in this regard. The findings of this study show that Poland is the most advanced V4 country, the Czech Republic is working hard to catch up with the leaders, and Hungary and Slovakia still find themselves below the European average. The comparison is based on Zuiderwijk and Janssen's revised open data policy cycle concept (2014; Charalabidis, Zuiderwijk et al. 2018), which consists of 5 stages: open data policy environment, content, implementation, evaluation, and change or termination. Oramus considers the unique characteristics of the V4, which may have a significant impact on their respective open data policies, as discussed in the previous chapter in the context of semi-peripheral countries. The chapter closes with a comparison of these data policies across the V4.

Chapter Nine, "Communication management – the approach of the Visegrád countries to fake narratives and news," Michał Żabiński and Máté Hajba address the issue of broadly conceived disinformation. Having examined the theoretical aspects of disinformation, they explore the various dangers of modern propaganda for both the state and society at large. In the first part, they discuss the possible negative effects of disinformation on a domestic and international level, as well as institutional responses to misleading information disseminated via the Internet. The second part presents their findings on the institutional response of the V4 countries to the phenomenon at hand. The authors conclude with a review of the potential ramifications of the current situation.

The last chapter focuses on the structure of political power between policies consistently reproduced by global capitalism and analysed in the preceding chapters. It examines to what extent new technological tools perpetuate the current core-periphery distinctions rather than serve to empower the weaker states. It concludes, rather pessimistically, that processes associated inherent in technological disembedding support the first hypothesis, but some observations from the study suggest potential remedial strategies in favour of the semi-periphery. In a performative research act (Piazzoli, 2018), the author set the ChatGPT language model the task of reviewing the benefits of technological re-embedding for the periphery and semi-periphery, emphasising the importance of certain critical processes, such as striving for higher social cohesion and active democracy.

The data and information referred to in Chapters Three to Nine, which were collected during the in-depth interviews (IDI) conducted with policy experts and practitioners, are cited using the following three-part codes: (Cz_2_1), (Hu_1_3), (Pl_4_2), and (Sk_5_1). For example, code (Cz_2_1) denotes that the interview was conducted with a policy expert or practitioner from the Czech Republic (Cz); it dealt with research area 2 (2); and signifies that it was the first interview (1) in the series. Hu, Pl, Sk denote experts from Hungary, Poland, and Slovakia, respectively. A complete anonymised list of experts who participated in the research is provided in the Appendix.

Bibliography

Ambroziak, Ł., Chojna, J., Gniadek, J., Juszczak, A., Miniszewski, M., Strzelecki, J., Szpor, A., Śliwowski, P., Święcicki, I. and Wąsiński, M. (2020). *Grupa Wyszehradzka – 30 lat transformacji, integracji i rozwoju*, Polski Instytut Ekonomiczny.

Baccaro, L., Hadziabdic, S. Operationalizing growth models. *Qual Quant* (2023). https://doi.org/10.1007/s11135-023-01685-w

Baldwin, R. (2019). *The Globotics Upheaval. Globalisation, Robotics, and the Future of Work*, Oxford University Press.

Barber, M., Levy, A. and Mendonca, L. (2007). *Global trends affecting the public sector*, Mc Kinsey & Company.

Bickerton, C. (2016). From Nation-States to Member States: European Integration as State Transformation, In: *The Search for Europe. Contrasting Approaches*, BBVA. Available at: www.bbvaopenmind.com/wp-content/uploads/2017/11/BBVA-Open Mind-ficha-Search_for_Europe-Contrasting-approaches.pdf

Bohle, D., and Greskovits, B. (2012). *Capitalist Diversity on Europe's Periphery*, Cornell University Press.

Charalabidis, Y., Zuiderwijk, A. et al. (2018). *The World of Open Data. Concepts, Methods, Tools and Experiences*. Springer.

European Commission (2022). *The Digital Economy and Society Index* (DESI), European Commission, https://digital-strategy.ec.europa.eu/en/policies/desi

Gil-Garcia, J. and Martinez-Moyano, I. (2007). Understanding the evolution of e-government: The influence of systems of rules on public sector dynamics, *Government Information Quarterly* 24, pp. 266–290.

Grodzicki M, Możdżeń M. (2021) Central and Eastern European economies in a Goldi-locks age: A model of labor market institutional choice, *Economic Modeling*, vol 104, https://doi.org/10.1016/j.econmod.2021.105626

Gupta, A. (2020). *Accelerating Remote Work After COVID-19*, COVID Recovery Symposium 2020.001, Center for Growth and Opportunity at Utah State University.

HCSO (2022). *Main indicators of the Visegrád Group Countries*, Hungarian Central Statistical Office.

Kopyciński, P. (2020). Modes of governance in the Visegrád Countries: towards the hesitant institutional convergence, In: S. Mazur (Ed.), *Public Administration in Central Europe. Ideas and Causes of Reforms* (pp. 106–128). Routledge.

KPMG (2016). *Future State 2030: The global megatrends shaping governments*, KPMG International.

Leonardi, P. M. (2020). COVID-19 and the New Technologies of Organizing: Digital Exhaust, Digital Footprints, and Artificial Intelligence in the Wake of Remote Work. *Journal of Management Studies*, 58, 249–253.

Linthorst, J. and de Waal A. (2020). Megatrends and Disruptors and Their Postulated Impact on Organizations. *Sustainability*, 12, 8740. https://doi.org/10.3390/su12208740

Nölke, A. and Vliegenthart, A. (2009). Enlarging the varieties of capitalism: The emergence of dependent market economies in East Central Europe. *World Politics*, 61, 670–702.

ODM (2020). *Open Data Maturity Report 2020*. Publications Office of the European Union.

ODM (2021). *Open Data Maturity Report 2021*. Publications Office of the European Union.

OECD (2017). *The Next Production Revolution: Implications for Governments and Business*, OECD Publishing, http://dx.doi.org/10.1787/9789264271036-en

Patyk, A. (2022). Forum Ekonomiczne 2022: Jak będzie wyglądać przyszłość Grupy Wyszehradzkiej?, *Obserwator gospodarczy*, https://obserwatorgospodarczy.pl/2022/09/08/forum-ekonomiczne-2022-jak-bedzie-wygladac-przyszlosc-grupy-wyszehradzkiej/

Piazzoli, E. (2018). *Performative Research: Methodology and Methods. In: Embodying Language in Action*. Palgrave Macmillan. https://doi.org/10.1007/978-3-319-77962-1_9

PRB (2021). *2021 World Population Data Sheet*, Population Reference Bureau.

PTPS (2021). *Definicja megatrendu*, Polskie Towarzystwo Studiów nad Przyszłością, https://ptsp.pl/megatrendy, accessed 18 Nov 2021.

Puncreobutr, V. (2017). The policy drive of Thailand 4.0, *Journal of Humanities and Social Sciences*, 3(1).

PwC (2016). *Five Megatrends and Their Implications for Global Defence & Security*, PricewaterhouseCoopers, www.pwc.co.uk/megatrends accessed 18 Nov 2021.

Purchla, J. (2020). The singularity of Central Europe?, In: S. Mazur (Ed), *Public Adminis- tration in Central Europe. Ideas and Causes of Reforms* (pp. 3–24). Routledge.

Rudolph, C. W., Marcus, J., Mah, R. and Zacher, H. (2018). Global Issues in Work, Aging, and Retirement. In: K.S. Shultz, G.A. Adams (Eds.). *Aging and Work in the 21st Cen- tury* (pp. 292–324). Routledge.

Shields S. (2009) CEE *as a New Semi-periphery: Transnational Social Forces and Poland's Transition*, in: O. Worth, P. Moore, (eds) Globalization and the 'New' Semi- Peripheries, Palgrave Macmillan.

Tan, T-B. and Shang-su, W. (2017). *Public Policy Implications of The Fourth Industrial Revolution for Singapore. Policy Report October 2017*, Nanyang Technological Univer- sity.

UNDESA (2015). *World Population Ageing 2015* (ST/ESA/SER.A/390). United Nations, Department of Economic and Social Affairs, Population Division. www.un.org/en/ development/desa/population/publications/pdf/ageing/WPA2015_Report.pdf

UNDESA (2019). *World Population Prospects 2019: Highlights* (ST/ESA/SER.A/423). United Nations, Department of Economic and Social Affairs, Population Division. https://population.un.org/wpp/Publications/Files/WPP2019_Highlights.pdf

Wahba, T., Sameh, N., Wellenstein, A., Das, M., Palmarini, N., D'Aoust, O., Singh, G., Restrepo, C., Goga, S., Terraza, H., Lakovits, C., Baeumler, A. and Gapihan, A. (2021). *Demographic Trends and Urbanization*, World Bank Group, http://documents .worldbank.org/curated/en/260581617988607640/Demographic-Trends-and -Urbanization

Wallerstein I (1976) *Semi-Peripheral Countries and the Contemporary World Crisis*, Theory and Society, vol. 3, no 4, pp. 461–483

Worth O. (2009) *Whatever Happened to the Semi-periphery?*, in: O. Worth, P. Moore, (eds) Globalization and the 'New' Semi-Peripheries, Palgrave Macmillan

Z-Punkt (2021). *Megatrends Update. Understanding the Dynamics of Global Change*, Z_punkt GmbH The Foresight Company, https://z-punkt.de/uploads/files/web1 _zp_megatrends_a5.pdf, accessed 18 Nov 2021.

Zuiderwijk, A. and Janssen, M. (2014). Open data policies, their implementation and impact: A framework for comparison. *Government Information Quarterly, 31*(1), 17–29.

What Model of Public Management and Governance in Response to Globotics?

Stanisław Mazur

1 Introduction

Recent decades have seen significant, exceptionally violent, and highly unpredictable events with profound repercussions that are still incompletely understood. The economy, as represented by the phenomenon known as globotics, is undoubtedly the setting for such events in consequence of structural changes brought on by globalisation and the Fourth Industrial Revolution (4IR). Apart from triggering a dynamic and fundamental reshuffle of the economy and business models, it also invalidates most of the rules and mechanisms of the previously dominant public management paradigms.

Globotics, like any major change, comes with a range of development opportunities as well as numerous economic, social, and political threats. In the face of the latter, the existing governance systems are gradually proving ineffective, which raises a number of questions, including how to redesign public management and governance models so that public decision-makers can create prudent, rational, and effective regulatory frameworks for the development of globotics, allowing them to capitalise on its benefits while limiting its negative consequences. The main aim of this chapter is to attempt to answer this question.

The first section of this chapter defines globotics, analyses the origins of the concept, and highlights its key characteristics with an emphasis on its two major components – globalisation and 4IR. The next section discusses the impact of globalisation on public management and governance frameworks, as well as their various implications. The assumptions underpinning new public management and governance models as a response to the issues coming from the growth of globotics for the democratic-liberal system are then presented and discussed.

2 Globotics

The term *globotics* was first used by Richard Baldwin in his work *The Globotics Upheaval. Globalization, Robotics, and the Future of Work* (2019) to describe the two parallel economic processes of globalisation and robotisation. The author emphasises that their intimate intertwining and exceptional dynamics give them previously unknown relevance as well as the potential for significant socioeconomic and political transformations, including the negative ones. Examples include job losses, falling wages, and lower social security standards for workers.

The effects of globalisation differ from previous economic transitions in two fundamental aspects. The first one is magnitude, particularly visible in services, which is the largest and fastest growing sector of the economy. The other one is time-related. Unlike the transformations of the 19th and 20th centuries, the quickly progressing and mutually reinforcing globalisation and robotisation are not only drastically but also rapidly changing economic patterns.

In terms of magnitude and ramifications, globotics ranks alongside the first and third industrial revolutions. The essence of the first one, known as the Great Transformation brought about by the steam revolution and the growth of technology, which began in the 18th century, was the transition of the economy and society from an agricultural to an industrial economy and urban civilization. The third revolution, which occurred in the 1970s as a result of computer miniaturisation and the advancement of information and communication technologies, was associated with a shift in the centre of economic activity from industry to services. The globotics revolution caused by the development of digital technology leads not only to a rapid growth of services but also to their different configurations and different models of work.

The rapid evolution of 4IR makes it impossible for the existing governance rules and standards to properly control or regulate the processes arising from it or effectively mitigate their unfavourable consequences. This is compounded by an almost global decline in trust in governments and politicians. As a consequence, citizens expect a radical transformation of public management and governance rules, as well as public policy-making models.

A new kind of governance focused on creating synergies between globalisation, technology advancements, social and economic processes is necessary given 4IR's complexity, disruptive potential, and dispersed nature. Its characteristics include:

1. The extraordinary pace of technological development and dynamic proliferation. As a result, unique ecosystems are being created that have a fairly broad range of autonomy and learning capacities due to algorithms and coding rules that are outside human control.

2. Global reach and overwhelming impact on societies. Modern technologies are rapidly expanding with an exponential impact on systems such as investment, organisational strategy, productivity, consumption, and human behaviour. Not only are these technologies difficult to manage, but they also necessitate new policies, approaches, and social protection mechanisms to address issues such as the disruption of labour markets, the environment, and human interactions, as well as ensuring that human labour and creativity are augmented rather than replaced, and that legislation protects democratic and civic participation through the use of technology.

3. The political nature of emerging technologies. The ideas embedded in them, the ideologies of the developers who build them, and the norms and values of the context in which they are designed and applied all impact their uses and consequences.

The pace, scope, scale, and political nature of 4IR and the societal aspirations for its human-focused impact are reasons why we need agile governance. First, the recognition that change and disruption occur much faster and are much more complex than before forces us to rethink and redesign our political processes. Secondly, making explicit the political nature of technology can help us highlight the mandate for agile governance in the area of emerging technologies and their applications. This includes devising the optimal policy framework for integrating value in both domains and specifying where and how value is shaped in the creation and use of technology. Finally, prioritising values that advance societal benefit and well-being in governance can guide the creation and application of developing technologies as well as who they are appropriate for.

In the face of growing inequality and diminishing levels of trust, political leaders and voters are becoming increasingly sceptical of the ability of increased global integration to serve national interests. Meanwhile, private organisations are embracing a variety of new technologies that have no regional or governmental limits. This prompts the following questions: What should responsive and accountable leadership be like in an increasingly fragmented world? What does this imply for the public and private sectors' roles? What new rules, standards, and principles should we establish? In a more divided world, how should these norms be designed and enforced to ensure the best possible outcome for all? These developments present a particular challenge for governments, which, as former US Secretary of State Madeline Albright pointed out, "People are talking to their governments on 21st -century technology. The governments listen to them on 20th-century technology and provide 19th-century responses."

This renders the current public management and governance architecture obsolete, particularly systems that assume the public sector is the primary actor responsible for defining and enforcing appropriate norms. As a result, governments are frequently criticised for their delayed and inept responses (or lack thereof) to the rapid pace of technological progress. In turn, private sector actors, particularly those involved in the development or deployment of new technology, tend to regard governments as short-sighted, ill-prepared, and, more often than not, acting in ways that hinder innovation. As a result, trust between these actors continues to erode, as does collaboration at times and in places where multi-stakeholder action is urgently required. There is much to suggest that new models of public management and governance need to emphasise and recognise that the responsibility for governance does not lie solely with the public sector. It is necessary to harness the knowledge and influence of the private sector, while ensuring that citizens are protected from the negative and disruptive elements of emerging technologies.

The Fourth Industrial Revolution brings both good and bad news for governments. On the one hand, it helps them to foster an open, flexible knowledge- and skills-based economy, promotes trade outside traditional trading blocs, improves the efficiency and effectiveness of health and social care systems, and offers a first-mover advantage in defending and securing sectors for those that make best use of new technologies. But there is also another side to 4IR – governments may become increasingly powerless against megacorporations – described as "exponential organisations" in Salim Ismail, Michael Malone and Yuri van Geest's book of the same title (2014). Regulating the activities of these global giants (and imposing effective taxes on them) may already be beyond the reach of national governments except perhaps those of the United States of America and China.

In the case of the globotics revolution, the novelty is that, as machine learning advances, computers become able to 'think,' acquire new skills, refine their codes and, as a consequence, are increasingly able to do jobs previously done by humans, including those of a specialised and highly skilled nature. Machine learning equips computers and the robots they control with new abilities for enhanced analysis and multi-criteria decision-making in a complex and uncertain environment. As a result, the quality of work completed by robots is gradually outpacing that of human workers in terms of efficiency, speed, and accuracy.

An equally important aspect of the digital revolution epitomised by globotics is the fact that work in the services sector has become aterritorial, which means that it can be performed by people virtually anywhere in the world. As a result, the services sector is rapidly expanding, cutting labour costs and increasing labour efficiency. Yet, from the standpoint of the workforce, it has several detrimental effects, such as a decline in labour standards, particularly pay.

The digital economy, based on electronic platforms enabling direct trade using artificial intelligence and other digital solutions, has opened up hitherto unknown opportunities for companies to operate in a global world. It represents a new era in economic history referred to as the new economy (Fingar and Aronica, 2001; Brynjolfsson and Kahin, 2002). Globotics advances at a rate commensurate with the potential for data processing, transmission, and storage. This extraordinary dynamism, according to Richard Baldwin, puts pressures on the socio-economic system; in particular on the labour market outstripping the latter's ability to adapt. In practice, this means that the system is unable to respond adequately to the decline in the number of jobs and labour standards, including working conditions and pay. This is by no means a new problem: throughout economic history, the disappearance and emergence of occupations has been a common occurrence. However, as long as the economy's primary function was the manufacturing of goods, physical constraints on their transmission limited the dynamics of change. In the age of globalisation, when the information transfer options are disproportionately higher, change, including in the labour market, has acquired extra momentum.

Globotics has a variety of consequences. The positive ones include greater technological sophistication of the economy, acceleration of global economic processes, improved product quality as well as efficiency and growing profitability. The negative ones are job losses, lower labour standards, including wages, and growing social discontent manifested in the rise of anti-globalisation and anti-immigration sentiments, as well as rising populism and a decline in confidence in the liberal rule of law and related public management/governance paradigms. The latter effects of the phenomenon in question are explored below.

Globotics has had a significant impact on salaries and other aspects of labour, including insurance and health care. In developing nations, workers accept lower earnings and more limited social benefit packages (e.g. severance pay, pensions, liberal labour laws, etc.) due to the lower costs of living. Even though phenomenon this has been known for decades, it is currently emerging as a new category of employees known as 'remote workers' or 'telemigrants,' who work from their home country. Furthermore, the robotisation of a range of industries is likely to result in the loss of millions of jobs. As a result, ongoing globalisation and robotisation will undermine the workers' capacity to maintain a stable income in many industrialised economies.

Mounting problems such deindustrialisation, wage stagnation and job losses are causing widespread social discontent. The responses to these threats offered by mainstream politicians have failed to produce satisfactory results, which opened up space for populism to flourish as exemplified by Donald Trump's 2016 election victory or UK's referendum on leaving the EU. These events eloquently illustrate how workers respond when their sources of income and financial situation are jeopardised. Even so, their disempowerment in the developed world is projected to rise as more jobs are taken over by telemigrants and smart robots.

Both Trump voters and Brexit supporters have experienced the impact of robotisation and globalisation. For decades, they, their families and communities have been competing with workers from developing countries and robots, and more often than not, they have lost out. There is much to suggest that, while the negative consequences of these processes used to affect mostly lower-status groups, their ranks may soon be joined by more highly educated workers who have so far voted against populism, due to the negative consequences they will face in terms of reduced wages or outright job losses. They may demand protection from telemigrants and robots. If such a scenario were to materialise, as Baldwin notes, then people who were on opposite sides of the Trump 'fence' in 2016 may find themselves on the same side of a very different fence in the future. Indeed, as Barry Eichengreen (2018) concludes, "populism is activated by the combination of economic insecurity, threats to national identity, and unresponsive political system."

The rise of populism can be illustrated by the concept of a 'hive switch' – a purported social mechanism causing individuals to feel a deeper sense of alignment with a social group as a result of sharing a powerful emotional message. The appeal of Donald Trump's populist ideas provided a good illustration of how this mechanism operates. A sizeable proportion of Americans responded as members of a vulnerable community rather than as individuals in economic distress. They saw the moral order crumble, the country lose coherence and diversify, and blamed politicians for failure to respond. In doing so, they instinctively reached out for autocratic solutions. "It is as though a button is pushed on their forehead that says 'in case of moral threat, lock down the borders, kick out those who are different, and punish those who are morally deviant'" (Haidt, 2013).

Employees in numerous European countries have expressed outrage over the practice of hiring lower-paid foreign workers. The term 'social dumping' has become synonymous with unfair competition. Although the actual extent of this phenomenon was insignificant at first, the emotions it triggered it were considerable.

The situation radically changed as a result of growing wage and tax disparities in Europe and the economic downturn after 2008, which led to increasing numbers of delegated workers and a political backlash. As Jean-Claude Juncker stated in 2014, "In a Union of equals, workers should earn the same pay for the same work in the same place." A similar reaction was sparked by the rise of telemigration. Local workers will certainly perceive telemigration as social dumping – a breach of the unwritten social contract between employers and employees.

Rapid technological breakthroughs in ICT have resulted in unparalleled worldwide solutions to make people's and businesses' lives easier. But, as the digital economy has grown, the issue of digital inequality has emerged. As previously stated, variations in access to information technology, empowerment, general (communication, analytical) and technical (IT) capabilities, which translate into the way and purposes for which people use internet technology, are at the foundation of digital inequality (DiMaggio and Hargittai, 2001).

Along with social stratification, digital inequality is intimately tied to economic development. Access to the Internet is determined by the condition of infrastructure and social potential as a critical component in the successful use of the information to be delivered and processed. When characterising digital disparities, it is critical to emphasise the relevance of ownership and the resulting control associated with Internet access. The development of digital platforms, the aggregation of information in various databases, and large-scale data processing lead to the emergence of new social, political, sociological, and psychological problems. These require an interdisciplinary approach to analyse the consequences of information flows on a global scale, the asymmetry of information, and the resulting inequality between the network manager and the users. In order to build tools to help eliminate such inequalities, given the differences due to economic status, gender, age, and education, digital inequalities must be viewed in their socio-political and sociological context.

In general, the advancement of globalisation and robotisation should be regarded as the best way ahead. Finding viable solutions to undesirable phenomena, namely the incredibly fast pace of change and the social injustice associated with unfair competition, job loss, and lower labour standards, are undoubtedly critical. Governments must stimulate the creation of new employment, assist employees in adapting to job changes, and, if job losses are outpacing job creation, minimise the former. To this end, they must:

1. Strengthen policies that make it easier for people to adapt, especially those that have proved to be successful in Europe, such as retraining programmes, income support, and relocation assistance.

2. Develop strategies to make rapid job relocation politically acceptable to the majority of voters. Governments that want to avoid violent protests must find ways to gain political support for the coming changes.

3. Develop a flexible workforce while proving economic security for employees by adopting a strategy similar to that in place in Denmark, where the government allows firms to hire and fire freely, but puts the onus on them to find jobs for redundant workers.

Globotics was enabled by the neoliberal project, often referred to as the Washington Consensus, characterised by:

- trade liberalisation,
- liberalisation of financial markets,
- free movement of capital,
- privatisation,
- deregulation,
- reduction in public spending (fiscal discipline),
- tax reform (broadening the tax base, lowering tax rates, progressive taxation),
- making the labour market more flexible.

Globalisation, which can be seen as an economic, ideological, political, and institutional project underpinned by technological revolution, ideological, and political change, is at the heart of these reforms, with the goal of strengthening the role of international financial institutions and reconfiguring the geopolitical landscape (Giddens, 1999; Held and McGrew, 2007; Kennett, 2008). A significant part of the negative image of globalisation arises from the public perception of transnational corporations in many nations as proponents of technological change that threatens employment and income stability.

The neoliberal project is supported by multinational corporations. To understand the power of corporations under globalisation, it makes sense to start by outlining the different ways in which business exercises power. To facilitate this, a conceptual distinction is made between structural and agency power.

Structural power can be defined simply as the ability to influence policy without exerting agency, and it stems not from what corporate actors do, but from the monopolisation of capital: financial assets, industrial plants, and machinery. According to structural power theories, multiple forces limit policymakers' and labour's options and actions to those that promote investment, competitiveness, and profitability. Tax revenues and a stable political environment are dependent on company investment and profitability, and a breakdown in either of these can result in spending cuts and a loss of power (Block, 1990, pp. 300–305; Lindblom, 1977; Offe and Ronge, 1982).

Employee–employer relations are similar, and they drive workers and states to align their interests and goals with the desires of capital owners (Przeworski and Wallerstein, 1988, p. 12; Lindblom, 1977; Offe and Wiesenthal, 1980, p. 180), thus further strengthening the power and position of capital. In effect, business becomes an ideological hegemon, because its interests can be legitimised as akin to "national interest" (Farnsworth, 2008).

The second form of capital's power lies in agency – the political activism of business and its allies. According to Miliband (1969) and Domhoff (1967), entrepreneurs and those in key positions of power belong to the same social class. As a result, business has open access to a variety of public power resources ranging from capital to public funds (Farnsworth, 2008).

A number of factors affect power and influence, making them variable. First, power, especially structural one, is clearly dependent on the extent to which business has a real, rather than imagined, ability to move investment to other countries. Second, the power of business, especially causality, depends on the homogeneity of the corporate world's ideologies and interests. Finally, national governments and supranational organisations play a significant role in determining commercial power. The location of decision-making, the nature of democratic processes, the historical dominance of specific groups or interests, the political make-up of major parties, and the openness of governmental institutions are all crucial here. The following section discusses how these factors affect various manifestations of power and the effect of businesses on socioeconomic life (Farnsworth, 2008).

States characterised by a high level of cooperation and coordination between firms and other stakeholders, referred to as coordinated market economies by Hall and Soskice (2001), tend to be less exposed to the risks of capital reallocation. Their firms are more firmly embedded in national economies and attach greater importance to the social compact negotiated with workers. They are also more reliant on the skills and competencies of the workforce, which are developed through publicly funded programmes (Farnsworth, 2008). Conversely, liberal market economies in Hall and Soskice's terminology (2001), lack such coordinating structures. For this reason, governments face much greater challenges from global firms seeking investment locations with higher rates of return and greater degrees of liberalisation in terms of labour resources and capital flows (Farnsworth, 2008).

3   The Context of Governance in the Globotics Era

In this new landscape, governance scholars are particularly preoccupied with the relationships among the key actors in the governance system. Kooiman, for one, analyses these relationships using the concept of socio-political governance or interactive governance between various social and political actors. The concepts of diversity, dynamism and complexity are central features of governance itself. The socio-political system is increasingly diverse and has multiple centres in which "actors are continuously shaped by (and in) the interactions in which they relate to each other" (Kooiman, 2003, p. 2). The role of government is to enable interactions, to encourage a wide variety of policy coping arrangements, and to ensure the equitable distribution of services between actors through self- and co-regulation and public-private partnerships, or what Kooiman calls *types of social interaction, actions*, and *modes and orders of governance*. For Kooiman, no single governing agency can deliver legitimate and effective governance: "No single actor, public or private, has all knowledge and information required to solve complex dynamic and diversified problems; no actor has sufficient overview to make the application of needed instruments effective; no single actor has sufficient action potential to dominate unilaterally [...]" (Kooiman, 1993, p. 4).

Although globalisation is not the only factor affecting the nature of governance, it is clearly the key context in which the political process must be understood (Hudson and Lowe, 2004). According to Cerny (1999), structural economic change is at the heart of globalisation because it "critically challenges deeply entrenched socio-cultural and political structures, provoking dynamic responses of advancement, adaptation and resistance" (p. 199), both within and outside the state. It is the nature of competition in this changing environment that has had the greatest impact on governance structures, as the marketised competitive state seeks efficiency in an increasingly economically penetrated world (Cerny, 1999, p. 199).

The political and ideological context in which globalisation was allowed to flourish was characterised by a major reorientation of the economy and policy-making and a fundamental "breakdown in the economic policy consensus that had guaranteed more than two decades of almost uninterrupted economic growth and prosperity for the North" (Weiss, 1991, p. 144). The Bretton Woods system of closed capital accounts and fixed exchange rates and the gradual shift from the General Agreement on Tariffs and Trade (GATT) to trade liberalisation came to an end in the 1970s. Over the next decade, the ensuing international policy environment facilitated economic integration and increased capital mobility by deregulating financial markets and removing most restrictions on capital flows. The establishment of the World Trade Organisation (1995) after eight years of difficult negotiations heralded a change in the multilateral trade regime. The WTO, made up of 184 member governments, has a much broader remit than its predecessor, going beyond tariffs and trade in goods to include agriculture, standard-setting, intellectual property and services. Moreover, the "single undertaking" binds member governments to all WTO agreements as does its dispute settlement system (Sinclair, 2003). Increasing competition in global markets, pressure from international institutions, decisions by national governments to reduce barriers to international economic transactions, combined with the impact of new technologies, "created the conditions for the advent of globalisation" (Biersteker, 1998, p. 24).

More recently, in the context of a well-established but still evolving globalisation and governance architecture, new forms of governance have emerged, encompassing what Rosenau (1990) described as the growing importance of private "actors without sovereignty," multinational corporations, transnational societies as well as international governmental and non-governmental organisations. The dominance of market-driven approaches to stimulate growth and competitiveness has, according to Wilkinson, transformed transnational corporations into capital mobilisers, technology generators and legitimate international actors with a role to play in the emerging system of global governance (2005, p. 37).

Concerns about the social and environmental impacts of globalisation, corporate irresponsibility, unsustainable growth, and the nature of emerging governance structures became particularly evident in the 1990s. Democracy deficit and the lack of transparency in powerful international institutions were and continue to be major concerns, as is the rising awareness of the harmful impact of the neoliberal policies espoused and implemented by these institutions in the 1980s, particularly across Global South (Kennett, 2008, pp. 3–4)

Rhodes argued that governance reform is a global trend, whereas "good governance is the World Bank's latest mantra, shaping its lending policies towards Third World countries" (1996, p. 656). This stands in contrast to the 1980s, when the Washington Consensus, which included the common neoliberal themes of deregulation, privatisation, and trade liberalisation, was regarded as the most desirable form of economic and political governance. This reflected the emerging new economic orthodoxy as advocated by the most powerful state actors, subsequently conveyed to developing-country communities through influential international financial institutions such as the World Bank and the International Monetary Fund.

4 Governance in Times of Globotics

The ramifications of globalisation and governance for the state have been a prominent subject in the debate since the turn of the century. According to Pierre (2000), the main question is whether the liberal-democratic concept of the state as the unchallenged centre of political power and monopolist in the articulation of public interest is still relevant in an era of economic globalisation, the declining legitimacy of the state, and its marketisation. Is the nation-state in decline, or are we experiencing its transformation aimed at developing the capacity to face civilisation's problems?

As Rose and Miller argue, "shifting certain aspects of governance to the private sector or the NGO sector does not necessarily make them less governable" (1992, p. 200). It is not a question of reducing government, but rather of diffusing its power through new strategies and technologies. Global processes can be linked to the changing nature of the constraints faced by the state and the patterns of interaction between states and their environment. This does not imply that national governments have become irrelevant, only that their ability to initiate change has diminished. Jessop (2004) characterises the contemporary policy arena as an area of "unstructured complexity" (p. 17), in which national governments, international organisations, firms, international governmental organisations (IGOs), non-governmental organisations (NGOs), and civil society may collaborate or compete in carrying out tasks and delivering public services (McGinnis, 2000).

Nation-states remain key players in regulating the processes inherent in economic and political globalisation – they are not passive observers, but its main architects. What we are witnessing is thus state adaptation rather than state withdrawal (Weiss, 1988). Weiss referred to the process of "state augmentation," in which globalisation strengthens the role of national institutions. He stated that there is considerable evidence that the rise of contemporary governments parallels the development of global companies and transnational organisations, and that these current global networks remain inextricably linked to nation-states and national frameworks. In other words, transnational networks emerge alongside national networks. This is a story of structural and political intertwining, mutual reinforcement rather than power shifts.

Swyngedouw discusses three dimensions of governance, which contribute to a "rearrangement of the relationship between state, civil society, and market" (2005, p. 1998). They involve the externalisation of some state functions through privatisation, deregulation and decentralisation; the reduction of governance to include local practices; and the extension of regulatory functions and other roles to supranational levels of governance exercised by structures such as the EU, IMF, and WTO. These governance structures are accompanied by polycentric environments and horizontal networks between private, civic and state actors (Swyngedouw, 2005) operating within what Hajer (2003) calls an "institutional void." According to Swyngedouw (2005), "the rescaling of policy transforms existing power geometries, resulting in a new constellation of governance articulated via an expanding labyrinth of opaque networks, fuzzy institutional arrangements, poorly defined responsibilities and ambiguous political goals and priorities. Despite this, the state is central to these arrangements, as it plays a key role in defining the contours and content of this new form of networked governance."

Jessop further argues that states have never existed "in majestic isolation, overseeing the rest of their respective societies, but are embedded in a wider political system (or systems), other institutional orders and lifeworlds." The state, and its relationship with other institutional forms, is "historically mutable and socially constructed" (2004, p. 12). Jessop refers to a number of opposing trends evident in the ongoing processes of reorganisation of the nation-state. The dispersion of state power among actors, networks and institutions at different spatial scales represents the denationalisation of statehood. It has also created spaces for the emergence of new state authorities, albeit at different territorial scales – and this represents the reterritorialisation of nationhood, as the state seeks to play a central role in this "unstructured complexity" (2004 p. 17). Thus, according to Jessop, the shift from management to governance has not weakened the role of the state. On the contrary, it is because of the blurring of the boundaries between public and private and the changing relationship between organisations that new responsibilities have emerged at different spatial scales.

The governmentality approach also reinforces the view that the neoliberal state "not only retains its traditional functions, but also takes on new tasks and functions" (Lemke, 2001, p. 201). Central to the notion of governmentality are the concepts of political rationality and the technology of government (Foucault, 1996). Political rationality, according to Lemke (2001), refers to the discursive field in which the exercise of power and forms of action are rationalised. This rationalisation occurs through the emergence of concepts, arguments and justifications and the production of objects. Lemke argues that political rationality "constitutes an intellectual transformation of reality, which political technologies can then deal with." This results in the construction of a kind of reality for which specific political technologies are then deemed acceptable and started by a variety of organisations, agencies, and legal forms (Barry et al. 1996; Burchell et al. 1991). For Foucault (1982), government is also a "conduct of conduct," or the capacity to affect the actions of oneself and others.

According to Lemke (2001), it specifies how the modern state and autonomous subjects jointly determine each other's appearance. The state is itself a tactic of government, "because it is the tactics of government that make it possible to constantly define and redefine what is within the remit of the state and what is not, public versus private and so on" (Lemke, 2002, p. 58). Thus, the transition from government to governance can be understood as a consolidation of new technologies of governance with the dominance of neoliberal government rationality and a transformation of technologies of governance, from formal to informal techniques and the inclusion of new actors in the process, rather than as a weakening or reduction of state sovereignty and reductions in the state's planning capacity (Lemke, 2002).

Globalisation and governance are clearly interrelated processes, each with the potential to affect the other. The former should be understood not as a dynamic, unavoidable phenomenon "attributed a kind of pervasive causal force" (Tickell and Peck, 2003, p. 163) that affects states and governance structures, but as a process that unevenly and incessantly shapes the field of action of governance structures. National governments continue to play a key role in guiding and supporting, to varying degrees, the pace, scope and impact of global interactions. However, as power has become more diffuse within an "increasingly complex structure of socio-economic forces and levels of governance" (Cerny, 1999, p. 190), the ability of states to influence and participate in global governance has become more diverse. States have very different capacities to exercise power internally and internationally (Jessop, 2004). In the global era, states with the ability to exercise power both economically and politically should not be seen as the "undisputed masters of the global economy;" nor should we think that we are experiencing the "end of territoriality." What is most relevant to an understanding of contemporary politics and policy-making is that they involve dynamic, dialectical, and diverse processes.

An important voice in the globalisation debate is the claim that there are now a number of non-negotiable external economic constraints that make certain policy choices necessary for governments and workers to survive in the globalisation era. The argument behind it typically emphasises that globalisation exceeds the geographic remit of national government regulation; at the same time, the institutions of global governance are too weak to control the process; thus, global markets can effectively escape political regulation. Moreover, the demands of global competition impose on national governments a certain set of economic governance structures. If they are ignored, a country runs the risk of having some of its economic activities promptly relocate to other economic spaces with more favourable governance structures.

There is no doubt that, even in the face of increasing pressure from capital and global corporations, nation-state governance is still of vital importance (Skocpol, 1985, p. 28). For institutionalists such as Skocpol (ibid.), the state is potentially autonomous and capable of acting independently of the interests and pressures of the world of capital. It is not only states that are capable, at least in theory, of controlling investment flows, but, according to Skocpol (ibid.), also state officials who create economic and social policies (Martin, 1989, p. 194).

Despite the fact that national governments still retain a great deal of power, influence and autonomy under globalisation, national governance institutions are less flexible than is often believed. The way they are organised and operate is strongly influenced by historical legacies. For this reason, many countries are forced to tailor their domestic policies, especially in the social and fiscal spheres, to the expectations of business by reducing taxation, lowering labour standards, and scaling back social benefits. Diverging from these trends or even attempting to do so may put present and future investments in danger. The extent of this risk will be determined by how a country has been 'sold' to investors in the past and how rapidly its economy is able to adapt to new means of ensuring future investment; thus, the importance of the institutional and economic environment must be emphasised once more.

The political room for manoeuvre of states and intergovernmental organisations also depends on the access of key players to decision-making bodies. Because of the importance of business to governments' economic and even political fortunes, its voice is unlikely to be ignored in key policy forums. Contrary to popular belief that business and lobbyists invade policy makers gain access to decision-making processes, governments and intergovernmental organisations often strive to include corporate players into decision-making bodies. In some instances, access is formalised, as is the case in corporate states; in others, attempts have been made to strengthen the voice of business. This is especially true of the newly emerging international governance structures. For example, one key forum that brings together business and political elites – the Transatlantic Business Dialogue (TABD) – was founded not by business, but by the European Commission and the US Department of Commerce (Balanya et al., 2000, p. 103). Business-sponsored political forums, most notably the World Economic Forum in Davos, have also evolved into international celebrity events attended by the world's corporate and political elite, including top executives of major corporations, prime ministers and presidents of both small and large countries. Via such channels, international business obtains vital access to the international political arena and gains the potential to impact the debate and choices made by these bodies (Kennett, 2008).

5   Final Remarks on the Evolution of Public Governance

5.1   *Agile Governance*

The World Economic Forum defines the concept of agile governance as "adaptive, human-centred, inclusive and sustainable policymaking, which acknowledges that policy development is no longer limited to governments, but rather is an increasingly multi-stakeholder effort."

Traditionally, governing in the public sense has been the domain of governments and is usually effected by those in power in the form of legislative or executive measures based on their policy contexts. Governance, on the other hand, is an activity that also occurs on a daily basis in private organisations, formal and informal civil society organisations, and in social contexts among family and friends. The traditional concept of governance is shifting as new technologies transfer power away from governments and towards companies and non-state players. The dynamics of 4IR, as well as the fact that humanity's numerous concerns cannot be solved by a single actor, suggest that governance must become a multi-stakeholder endeavour. This shift in governance is also occurring because governments and policymakers are increasingly forced to respond to changes resulting from rapidly evolving technological innovation. This offers new roles for the corporate sector and academia to collaborate with government officials to give expertise in developing modern technologies, applying them, and analysing their ramifications.

From artificial intelligence to autonomous vehicles to the confluence of systems underlying the global economy, the private sector keeps developing and disseminating new technologies which have a profound impact on social and economic structures. These technologies and systems affect social behaviour and generate new norms for human interaction. Notwithstanding the lack of a political mandate, technology pioneers are increasingly developing private rules, certification schemes, standards, social norms, or policies that indirectly regulate how societies live, work, and interact, often without the involvement of public authorities.

Agility comprises innovativeness, flexibility, and adaptability. In the software industry, the term has been used since the 1990s. The Agile Manifesto was written by 17 software developers in 2001 and expanded for the policy-making sphere by the Global Agenda Council's report on the Future of Software Development and Society. Its authors encouraged broader participation in control and supported the self-organisation of the technology community by emphasising its superiority over centralised government. These guidelines are still widely applied in technology development today.

The concept of agile governance aims to change the way policies are made, developed, introduced, and enforced during 4IR. Taken together, they embody the assumption that governance can – and, some would argue, should – be more agile in order to keep up with rapid societal change largely driven by the rapid development and deployment of new technologies. Decision-makers need to become more proactive in shaping these changes. The distinction between plan-based policymaking and the concept of agile governance reflects a shift in the importance placed on time.

In fact, agility can facilitate rational policy-making by involving more stakeholders in the process and being able to iterate quickly to meet citizens' needs. Agile governance can also ensure long-term sustainability by establishing systems for regularly monitoring and updating public policies through the use of new technologies, as well as optimising collaboration between business and civil society.

A precise definition of good governance necessitates clarifying what it is not. The popularity of the term in recent years, first in new technology, then in academia, and now in public management, has led to its application in a variety of contexts. This has occasionally caused confusion, especially when used side by side in different contexts. Most commonly, the term is associated with the Agile Manifesto ideals in the field of public service delivery, but has recently been more widely applied to advanced technologies used in day-to-day government operations (e.g. e-government). The desire of public authorities to accomplish more with fewer resources drives the use of modern technologies in the public sector.

Building an agile government requires:

a   the presence of practical difficulties in applying traditional regulatory approaches (e.g. the size of transactions or their technological sophistication),

b   areas of common interest between the public and private sectors where collaboration is mutually beneficial,

c   the ability of the technology sector to proactively find solutions to address regulatory and social issues.

The key areas of agile governance include industry self-regulation and setting ethical standards.

Industry self-regulation is an important illustration of how the private sector manages emerging technologies. This takes numerous forms, ranging from the establishment of market conditions such as pricing controls, market entrance constraints, product standards, and customary contractual terms to societal obligations, including environmental controls, safety laws, as well as advertising and labelling rules. Several aspects of self-regulation make it more adaptable than official legislation. The former allows for faster rulemaking, monitoring, enforcement, and remediation, which implies that consumers can be protected better and sooner. Self-regulation fosters a flexible regulatory framework in which guidelines evolve over time, paving the way for innovation. Since these concepts are founded on societal norms rather than top-down directives, they can also help organisations internalise behaviour and ethical principles, strengthening the impact of regulation.

The concept of *overarching regulator* is a crucial component of self-regulation that advocates for rules and regulations developed by competing private regulators, which are then reviewed by public regulators as needed. Non-public regulators, such as standards bodies, consortia, and alliances working on AI algorithm protocols and the Internet of Things, increasingly believe that standards and interoperability are critical for capturing the economic and social impact of new technologies. Despite the fact that the technology community is interested in implementing standards that support technological development and interoperability, many corporations keep developing their own rules, recognising the economic benefits of establishing their own systems based on autonomous standards and protocols. Moreover, since new technologies blur the boundaries between industries, they enable new business models and societal impacts on a larger scale. The capacity to set standards in the 4IR era goes beyond the remit of current technology bodies or industry standard setters.

The other critical aspect of agile governance involves ethical norms. The goal of issue-specific stakeholder networks is to build practical protocols and reach consensus on ethical standards that govern research and industry activities. These may include actual solutions such as informal frameworks or standards that fill a specific governance gap, including detailed specifications, operational processes, implementation guidelines, verification instruments, maintenance procedures, and/or dispute resolution systems.

In the absence of an organisation that has sufficient credibility to set new technology standards, industry leaders are advocating for the adoption of new ethical principles to guide research and industry activities. Examples of initiatives pursued by the AI industry, which currently has 3,800 leaders, include the development of the Asilomar AI principles. As a result, agile standard-setting and interoperability pilots are emerging, where solutions are designed with specific social uses in mind.

5.2   *Areas of Common Interest*
Promoting transparency and trust in technological innovation in an environment where the secrecy of algorithms and data is an important source

of competitive advantage, open IT infrastructure and protocols are the key tools for developing governance principles seen as open, vendor-independent IT standards and certifications. The Open Group, a global consortium that enables business goals through IT standards, brings together over 500 member organisations to identify, understand and resolve current and emerging issues as well as establish principles and share best practices, facilitate interoperability, develop consensus, and integrate open source specifications and technologies. As an open platform, it enables members to contribute to standards in a flexible, fluid and collaborative way. Both the private and public sectors have an incentive to prioritise consumer needs and build long-term strategies. These common interests should contribute to increased trust and provide opportunities for collaboration and partnerships.

5.3   *What Can Be Done?*

If governments are to exploit the full potential of 4IR, they must address its four critical areas:

1. They need to try to understand the future as much as possible, especially the opportunities and threats that lie ahead. Only then will they be able to devise appropriate public policies.

2. To reap the benefits of technological change, they must provide the appropriate technical infrastructure, while at the same time countering cybersecurity threats, whether criminally or politically motivated. Governments must be catalysts for change, while resisting the temptation to pick winners or manage the market itself.

3. They must develop an understanding of the potential impact of technological change on the role of government, the relationship between citizens and businesses, and other organizations. It is of the utmost importance that this includes the possibility of increasing public revenue by taxing the technology sector.

4. They must preserve social cohesion in the face of potentially catastrophic shocks such as labour market volatility and considerable shifts in income distribution. For example, according to computer simulations, 47% of jobs in the UK will be at risk, which will pose a significant challenge to society. Even the OECD's more conservative estimate of roughly 10% jobs in jeopardy, although it did not yet materialize, poses a serious problem for national and local governments . What role should governments play in dealing with the unavoidable turbulences brought on by 4IR? What about job security, technology regulation, taxation, and guaranteed basic income for all?

5.4 *Four Scenarios for Governments*

Governments could implement a variety of measures to address the challenges posed by the Fourth Industrial Revolution. Four of them are listed below:

1. *Market governance.* The European Union has begun to devise a strategy for a digital single market based on the collaboration of the Member States and set a regulatory framework in which it expects technological change to take place. The aim is to ensure stability and equitability. However, the EU may be unable to control the exponential organisations that are the vanguard of technology, moreover, it may be viewed as too conservative in implementing change and thus become less attractive as a place for investment in technology.

2. *Taking control.* Powerful countries without a well-established democratic-liberal tradition may strive to seize control of new technologies and exploit them to their own ends whether economic or political, as is the case in China. In this case, the risk is that democratic countries will create space for the rapid development of technology as well as new business and social models, while other countries will try to take advantage of them.

3. *Openness to business.* Governments, particularly those of smaller countries, may not be able to control the consequences of 4IR, but they can do their best to attract investment, for example, by creating attractive tax regimes, lighter regulation, infrastructure investment (e.g. 5G), and open up to trade with other parts of the world. Singapore is a prime example. Ireland, despite being a member of the EU, follows a strikingly similar path.

4. *Withdrawal.* Governments may decide that the logical solution to integrating new technology that will empower both large corporations and local communities (through blockchain currencies and local energy production) is to radically downsize by devolving more functions to regional and local levels, retaining only a few key ones, including defence, security, and foreign policy. The implementation of this scenario would be a kind of revolution in itself as it entails the dispersion of central government power, since "no one has done it yet" (WEF 2018).

Bibliography

Balanya, B., Doherty, A., Hoedeman, O., Ma'anit, A. and Wesselius E. (2000). *Europe Inc.: Regional and Global Restructuring and the Rise of Corporate Power.* Pluto Press.

Baldwin, R. (2019). *The Globotics Upheaval. Globalization, Robotics, and the Future of Work*, Oxford University Press.

Barry, A., Osborne, T. and Rose, N. (Eds.) (1996). *Foucault and Political Reason: Liberalism, Neo-Liberalism and Rationalities of Government*. UCL Press.

Biersteker, T. J. (1998). Globalization and the modes of operation of major institutional actors, *Oxford Development Studies, 26*(1), 15–32.

Block, F. (1990). Political choice and the multiple 'logics' of capital, In: S. Zukin and P. DiMaggio (Eds.), *Structure of Capital* (pp. 293–310). Cambridge University Press.

Brynjolfsson, E. and Kahin, B. J. D. (eds.) (2002). *Understanding the Digital Economy: Data, Tools, and Research*. The MIT Press.

Burchell, G., Gordon, C. and Miller P. (Eds.) (1991). *The Foucault Effect: Studies in Governmentality*. University of Chicago Press.

Cerny, P. G. (1999). Globalization, governance, and complexity, In: A. Prakash and J. A. Hart (Eds.), *Globalization and Governance* (pp. 188–212). Routledge.

DiMaggio, P. and Hargittai, E. (2001). From the 'Digital Divide' to 'Digital Inequality': Studying Internet Use as Penetration Increases. *Working Papers 47*, Princeton University, School of Public and International Affairs, Center for Arts and Cultural Policy Studies.

Domhoff, W. G. (1967). *Who Rules America?*. Prentice Hall.

Eichengreen, B. (2018). *The Populist Temptation: Economic Grievance and Political Reaction in the Modern Era*, Oxford University Press.

Farnsworth, K. (2008). Governance, business and social policy: international and national dimensions In: P. Kennett (Ed.), *Governance, Globalization and Public Policy*. Edward Elgar.

Fingar, P., Aronica, R. (2001). *Death of "e" and the Birth of the Real New Economy: Business Models, Technologies and Strategies for the 21st Century*. Meghan-Kiffer Press.

Foucault, M. (1982) Afterword: the subject and power, In: H. L. Dreyfus and P. Rabinow (Eds.) *MichelFoucault: beyond structuralism and hermeneutics*, pp. 208–225. Chicago: University of Chicago Press).

Foucault, M. (1996). Governmentality, In: G. Burchell, C. Gordon and P. Miller (Eds.), *The Foucault Effect: Studies in Governmentality* (pp. 87–104). University of Chicago Press.

Frey, C. B., and Osborne, M. A. (2017). The future of employment: How susceptible are jobs to computerisation? *Technological Forecasting and Social Change, 114*, 254–280. doi:10.1016/j.techfore.2016.08.019

Georgieff, A. and A. Milanez (2021), What happened to jobs at high risk of automation?, *OECD Social, Employment and Migration Working Papers, No. 255*, OECD Publishing, Paris, https://doi.org/10.1787/10bc97f4-en.

Giddens, A. (1999). Risk and Responsibility. *Modern Law Review, 62*, 1–10. https://doi.org/10.1111/1468-2230.00188

Hajer, M. (2003). Policy without polity? Policy analysis and the institutional void, *Policy Sciences*, *36*, 175–95.

Hall, P. A. and Soskice, D. (2001). Introduction, In: P.A. Hall and D. Soskice (Eds.), *Varieties of Capitalism: The Institutional Foundations of Comparative Advantage*. Oxford University Press.

Held, D. and McGrew, A. (2007). *Globalization / Anti-Globalization: Beyond the Great Divide*, 2nd Edition. Wiley.

Hudson, J. and Lowe, S. (2004). *Understanding the Policy Process: Analysing Welfare Policy and Practice*. Policy Press

Haidt, J. (2013). *The Righteous Mind: Why Good People Are Divided by Politics and Religion*. Penguin Books Ltd

Ismail, S., Malone, M. S. and van Geest, Y. (2014). *Exponential Organizations: Why New Organizations are Ten Times Better, Faster, and Cheaper Than Yours (and what to Do about It)*, Diversion Books.

Jessop, B. (2004). Hollowing out the 'nation-state' and multi-level governance, In: P. Kennett (Ed.), *A Handbook of Comparative Social Policy*. Edward Elgar.

Kennett, P. (2008). *Governance, Globalization and Public Policy*. Edward Elgar.

Kooiman, J. (2003). *Governing as Governance*. Sage Publications.

Kooiman, J. (1993). Social-political governance, In: J. Kooiman (Ed.), *Modern Governance* (pp. 1–6). Sage.

Lemke, T. (2001). 'The birth of bio-politics': Michel Foucaults's lecture at the College de France on neo-liberal governmentality, *Economy and Society*, *3*(2), 190–207.

Lemke, T. (2002) Foucault, Governmentality, and Critique, *Rethinking Marxism*, 14(3), pp. 49 –64.

Lindblom, C. (1977). *Politics and Markets: The World's Political Economic Systems*. Basic.

Martin, C. J. (1989). Business influence and state power: the case of US corporate tax policy, *Politics and Society*, *17*(2), 189–223.

McGinnis, M. D. (2000). Rent-seeking, redistribution, and reform in the governance of global markets, In: A. Prakash and J. A. Hart (Eds.), *Globalization and Governance* (pp. 54–76). Routledge.

Miliband, R. (1969). *The State in Capitalist Society*. Quartet Books.

Offe, C. and Ronge, V. (1982). Theses on the theory of the state, In: A. Giddens and D. Held (Eds.), *Classes, Power and Conflict*. Macmillan.

Offe, C. and Wiesenthal, H. (1980). Two logics of collective action: theoretical notes on social class and organisational form, In: M. Zeitlin (Ed.), *Political Power and Social Theory*, vol. 1 (pp. 67–115). JAI Press.

Pierre, J. (Ed.) (2000). *Debating Governance: Authority, Steering, and Democracy*. Oxford University Press.

Przeworski, A. and Wallerstein, M. (1988). Structural Dependence of the State on Capital. *The American Political Science Review*, *82*(1), pp. 11–29.

Rhodes, R. A. W. (1996). The new governance: governing without government, *Political Studies*, 44, 652–67.

Rose, N. and Miller, P. (1992). Political power beyond the state: problematics of government, *British Journal of Sociology*, 43, 173–205.

Rosenau, J. N. (1990). *Turbulence in World Politics: A Theory of Change and Continuity*. Princeton University Press.

Sinclair, S. (2003). The WTO and its GATS, In: J. Michie (Ed.), *The Handbook of Globalisation* (pp. 347–57). Edward Elgar Publishing.

Skocpol, T. (1985). Bringing the state back in: current research, In: P. B. Evans, D. Reuschemeyer and T. Skocpol (Eds.), *Bringing the State Back In* (pp. 3–43). Cambridge University Press.

Swyngedouw, E. (2005). Governance innovation and the citizen: the Janus Face of governance-beyond-the-state, *Urban Studies*, 42(11), 1991–2006.

Tickell, A. and Peck, J. (2003). Making global rules: globalization or neoliberalization?, In: J. Peck and H. Wai-chung Yeung (Eds.), *Remaking the Global Economy* (pp. 163–82). Sage.

WEF (2018). *Agile Governance Reimagining Policy-making in the Fourth Industrial Revolution*. White Paper. World Economic Forum.

Weiss, L. (1988). *Industry in Developing Countries: Theory, Policy and Evidence*. Croom Helm.

Wilkinson, R. (2005). The Commission on Global Governance: a new world, In: R. Wilkinson (Ed.), *The Global Governance Reader* (pp. 26–44). Routledge.

CHAPTER 3

The Socio-Economic Consequences and Challenges of the Fourth Industrial Revolution: an Empirical Study of the Visegrád Countries

Maciej Frączek

1 Introduction

The primary aim of this chapter is to identify and compare the major social and economic challenges brought on by the Fourth Industrial Revolution (4IR) for the Visegrád countries, referred to as semi-peripheral ones, and the core or dominant countries.[1] A subsidiary aim is to compile an inventory of the main impacts of 4IR on the Visegrád countries (V4) in terms of both actual and perceived emerging processes.

The following research questions are addressed in the study:

1. What are the major socio-economic consequences of 4IR for the V4 countries?
2. What are the major socio-economic challenges of 4IR faced by the V4 countries?
3. What are the similarities and differences between the impacts of these challenges across the studied groups of countries?
4. To what extent does the nature and intensity of these impacts differ between these groups of countries?

This analysis of semi-peripheral countries will focus on the Czech Republic, Hungary, Poland, and Slovakia. The study is based on the findings of 19 individual in-depth interviews conducted with experts from the V4 countries (5 from the Czech Republic, 7 from Hungary, 4 from Poland, and 3 from Slovakia). The group included officials from central and municipal government units, scholars and specialists in public policy, economic and social policy, public management, and representatives of business, employers' organisations as well as trade unions. The chapter also briefly reviews the literature on the socioeconomic consequences and problems of 4IR in the V4.

1　Later in this chapter, the author will also discuss the perspectives of Industry 4.0 (4IR), also known as Economy 4.0, particularly in regard to economic processes.

Knowing how difficult it is in practice to draw a clear distinction between social and economic issues, the author opted to follow the respondents' perspectives; as a result, several topics covered in this chapter may have both social and economic implications, which are reflected in the narrative. The selected dimensions were combined to reflect their proximity, impacts on specific public policies and values attached to them by individual respondents.

2   Literature Review

This brief literature review covers only studies devoted to the socioeconomic consequences of 4IR and related issues for the V4. Since the discussion of individual study findings is the major objective here, it is not intended to be exhaustive. For the same reason, it only includes publications that deal with the V4 as a whole and excludes those that focus on specific countries.[2]

To begin with, the digitisation processes taking place in the V4 countries (from the vantage point of the public policy perspective relevant to this monograph), including privacy and data protection, cyber security, e-participation, social media, smart city, and e-government are discussed by Hemker et al. (2020).

The most pertinent economic texts are those that describe the progress of 4IR in the V4 countries and include Kim and Seo (2018), Naudé et al. (2019), Lazanyi and Lambovska (2020), Szabó (2020), Nurzynska (2021), Éltető (2021), and Gyimesi (2021). In these publications, the V4 countries are contrasted with one another or with other countries based on various metrics (mainly quantitative) that reflect a number of functional parameters of 4IR (mostly developed by the EU). These analyses are supplemented with a number of strands concerning the latter's impact on socioeconomic processes in the above-mentioned group of countries.

A number of scholars also address the perceptions of 4IR throughout the V4 countries (Götz, Sass and Éltető, 2021) and the relationships between 4IR and more specific issues such as:
- human resources (Csath, 2018);
- migration and education (Svobodová et al., 2020);
- future of work (Keese, 2020);
- innovation capacity (Ministry of Economy and Finance, 2020);

---

2 There are too many publications in this area to mention even some of them in this brief review. For similar reasons, studies available only in V4 national languages have also been excluded.

- structural change (Compagnucci, 2020);
- FDI (Götz et al., 2020);
- robotisation (Cséfalvay, 2020);
- prospects for the automotive industry (Szalavetz, 2020);
- reshoring (Éltető, 2020);
- artificial intelligence (Bencsik, 2022).

Important insights are also provided by assessments completed for every EU member state, allowing comparisons to be made between the socioeconomic conditions in the V4 nations and the more developed EU27. The European Commission's reports on the Member States' digital performance and progress released since 2014 are especially relevant to the topics raised in this chapter (DESI – Digital Economy and Society Index, cf. e.g. European Commission, 2021). They take into account a number of socio-economic indicators organised into four dimensions: 1. human capital, 2. connectivity, 3. integration of digital technology, and 4. digital public services.[3]

It is also worth mentioning one of the previous 4IR studies, which contains an *RB Industry 4.0 Readiness Index*[4] (Roland Berger, 2014) – a special edition of the Eurobarometer on attitudes to the impact of digitisation and automation on daily life (European Commission, 2017a), national review of 4IR policy initiatives in EU (European Commission, 2017b), digital transformation scoreboard of 2018 (European Commission, 2019), another study proposing an index to measure 4IR performance[5] (Atik and Ünlü, 2019), and a report on readiness for digital lifelong learning (Beblavý et al., 2019).

To summarise this overview, it should be noted that while studies are available describing the degree of progress of 4IR (as the main strand of analysis) and its impact on social and economic processes taking place in the V4 (as a complementary strand), there is still a significant research gap in the literature. This includes a lack of a cross-sectional description of the socioeconomic impacts and problems of 4IR in this group of countries, particularly their socially embedded aspects. The author hopes that his study findings discussed below will at least partially fill it.

---

3 In the 2021 league table, the Czech Republic ranked 18th, Slovakia 22nd, Hungary 23rd, and Poland 24th (out of 27 EU Member States).

4 In the 4 identified groups, namely frontrunners, potentialists, traditionalists, and hesitators, the Czech Republic, Slovakia, and Hungary were assigned to the 3rd group, whereas Poland to the 4th one.

5 The methodology used to create the Industry 4.0 Index was developed by the World Economic Forum. Among the 33 European countries studied, the Czech Republic was ranked 16th, Slovakia 22nd, Poland 25th, and Hungary 30th.

3   The Socio-Economic Consequences of 4IR in the V4 Countries

Our experts' perspectives on the primary social and economic ramifications of
4IR for the V4 countries fall into the following categories: labour market, business processes, competitiveness and globalisation, systemic stability, quality of
life and inequalities, information, security, state capacity, and others.

3.1   *Revolution on the Labour Market*
The respondents believe that the labour market is the primary area where the
most significant effects of 4IR are to be felt. They classified most processes
as economic repercussions. The growing flexibility of the labour market and
working conditions are unquestionably significant when examining the labour
market as a whole (Cz_1_1), which may lead to increasing job insecurity manifested as precarisation (Pl_1_2). In contrast to a number of scholars who deal
with the topic, our respondents do not anticipate a rise in unemployment
(Pl_1_3; Cz_1_2) or a decline in the number of jobs (Cz_1_4). The V4 countries
have not yet experienced the anticipated uncertainty caused by robotics, especially among low-skilled workers, or fear of losing one's job (reflected in personal feelings and political ideas) (Cz_1_2). This is due to the fact that, even
though some jobs are being lost to automation and other technology, new ones
keep emerging (Cz_1_5).

Changes in the form and content of current jobs (Cz_1_3) and in the employment structure (Pl_1_1) are also expected. In the former case, the respondents'
opinion that some jobs will disappear to be replaced by new ones (Pl_1_2;
Cz_1_3; Cz_1_5; Hu_1_5) is not surprising. A range of completely new professions and skills (Pl_1_1; Hu_1_1) have emerged, e.g. new IT subspecialties, product designers, and traders (Cz_1_4). The changing nature of employment may
give rise to new types and forms of work (Cz_1_3), which tends to be associated with increasing individualisation, e.g. the gig economy, platformisation
of work, the impact of AI, and the perennial question: *Who actually is the
employee?* (Pl_1_2; Pl_1_4). The following phenomena have also been mentioned: increasing detachment from the workplace (Pl_1_1), increasing preva-
lence of remote work (Pl_1_4; Cz_1_3) and hybrid work (Pl_1_1).

As regards structural changes, the workforce has an opportunity to move
from menial jobs to high-performance and high-paying ones (Sk_1_2). More
and more workers leave industry for services (low-skilled workers tend to
migrate to the service industry, where digital technology and robotics are less
likely to replace them) (Cz_1_2).

A major area in which the consequences of 4IR are felt or are about to be felt
is employee qualifications. The demand for IT skills is growing (favouring the

younger generation of workers) as is, paradoxically, the emphasis on general skills (despite the fact that people with broader skill sets are considered more adaptable and more willing to change jobs) (Cz_1_2). This is accompanied by skills obsolescence (which represents a challenge for the older generation to keep pace with developments in the contemporary labour market) (Cz_1_2) and risk of high unemployment and low employability among those who fail to acquire the requisite digital skills (Hu_1_6; Sk_1_2). It is worth mentioning, however, that in the v4 countries, skilled labour shortage (Hu_1_6) is already evident, as stated by one of the Slovak respondents. In his view, Slovakia is under increasing pressure from employers due to a dearth of suitable workers to fill open positions in rapidly digitalising industries (ICT and car manufacturers). This trend leads to both wage pressures and the automation of operations where increasing wage pressures render the use of labour unprofitable (Sk_1_3).

However, respondents see encouraging demand-side changes: higher labour productivity (e.g. via automation) (Cz_1_4; Hu_1_5; Sk_1_1; Sk_1_2; Hu_1_4) and reduction of labour cost due to remote work (Pl_1_4).

From the supply side perspective, the expected positive changes involve improved working conditions: dirty, hard, physically strenuous work and shift work are declining (Cz_1_2), wages are increasing (Pl_1_3; Cz_1_4), and less time is spent at work (Cz_1_4).

Respondents have also noted several other significant changes, such as foreign nationals being employed as machine operators, since the Czech workforce tends to be more interested in higher-level jobs, often exploiting the opportunities offered by 4IR (Cz_1_3). This trend may intensify (especially in Poland) once the situation in Ukraine has stabilised after Russia's invasion, the mutually reinforcing processes of exodus of skilled labour and low-tech local businesses leading to higher prices of services and products (and their declining quality) (Hu_1_6), as well as the brain drain from the v4 countries (Hu_1_1; Sk_1_1; Pl_1_3).

A variety of social effects of 4IR on the labour market were also cited by respondents, but they were undoubtedly less numerous than the economic ones. As far as remote work is concerned, it appears that the bargaining power of gig workers or remote employees is somewhat constrained, but at the same time, the rise in remote work has already demonstrated that it is feasible to reintegrate many people into the labour market (Pl_1_2). The risk of unemployment in individual industry branches (e.g. car manufacturing) and people with substandard skill sets being made redundant has been noted, leading to increased pressures on unemployment benefits and the potential for social unrest (Sk_1_2). The immigration system also finds itself under increasing pressure due to the growing demand for both low and highly skilled occupations. In terms of low-skilled employment, both illegal and legal labour from the Balkans is frequently exploited. Conversely, ICT-oriented enterprises are under pressure to take advantage of the potential of available and eager ICT experts or students from countries such as Ukraine or Belarus, which has been maximised by Slovakia's neighbours (Sk_1_3). From the societal standpoint, it is also crucial to note that the transition of low-skilled individuals from industry to services may have a negative effect on their sense of identity and self-esteem (as compared with highly qualified workers) (Cz_1_2).

One of the Polish respondents noted that "there is also a drive to establish what Jeremy Rifkin has defined as a zero marginal cost society, which will also have an impact on the world of work,"[6] an apt summary of this part of study (Pl_1_2).

3.2   *Changing Business Processes*

In general, respondents are optimistic about the impact of 4IR on business processes. They expect business operations to accelerate (Cz_1_1) as a result of both incrementally introduced new technologies based on 4IR principles (Cz_1_2) and improved contacts with state administration (Cz_1_1).

The effects of 4IR are perceived mostly in broadly defined production, although jobs may also be lost in management due, among other things, to a more widespread use of AI (Pl_1_2). Respondents mainly mention automation and robotisation of production and service processes (manual and mental work) (Pl_1_1; Pl_1_2; Pl_1_3; Pl_1_4) in the largest companies (Pl_1_1). Others, however, claim that what we are witnessing now are instances of cost optimisation rather than implementing new technologies or innovation (Pl_1_3). Other consequences of 4IR in the V4 countries also include the emergence of new business models (Pl_1_1) and new products (Cz_1_1), production of goods and services based on data processing (Pl_1_3), and reduced transportation costs (Pl_1_1).

An important outcome of 4IR is the enhanced capacity of labour market actors in the industrial sector to respond adequately to customer demand: rapid production change, adaptation to consumer requirements, delivery of tailor-made products (Cz_1_4; Pl_1_1), which could potentially become a market niche for the V4 countries. Interestingly, two different trends appear to be emerging in this context. On the one hand, new digital solutions provide businesses with new potential to expand their operations and reach out to more

---

6   See Rifkin (2014).

distant customers throughout the country or even across borders. This has become one of the important ways for businesses to minimise their operating costs and mitigate the negative effects of the pandemic (Sk_1_3). On the other hand, fairly independent units explore prospects for collaboration at a local level, which leads to increased food production and consumption, reduced transportation needs, and more leisure time (Cz_1_4).

This part of the study findings can be summarised as follows: 4IR refers to, among other things, the expansion of the start-up ecosystem, which has produced new technological solutions developed by small but rapidly grow-ing businesses (Sk_1_1) and the development of new business models using the opportunities that have improved connectivity between customers and providers, particularly during the pandemic, when both sides were forced to rely on better access (Sk_1_1). Nevertheless, we should be aware of the fact that enterprises are under greater pressure to digitalise their business models, which many find difficult due to insufficient financial reserves. The stock mar-ket or angel finance options available to SMEs, start-ups, and scale-ups is still underdeveloped and hence untapped (Sk_1_3). However, respondents are gen-erally enthusiastic about their development prospects, anticipating increasing profits (better labour productivity, higher added value), particularly thanks to more efficient management and new technical solutions (Cz_1_4; Hu_1_5; Sk_1_1; Sk_1_2).

3.3   *Increasing Competition and Globalisation*

From the perspective of national economies and enterprises located in the V4 countries, it is important to measure their competitive potential in the increasingly globalised world market. The respondents emphasise the dual nature of these processes, which are supported by 4IR: global and national competition will intensify as access to overseas markets and the number of competitors entering domestic markets both expand (Pl_1_1; Hu_1_4; Hu_1_5). Even as the distinction between what is local and what is global/international become blurred (Hu_1_4), interconnectivity with global supply and technology networks increases. For the V4 countries, the removal of borders proved to be critical for businesses which are no longer limited or hampered by traditional obstacles. Their representatives advocate for streamlined business regulations across Europe, which has a favourable impact on the drive to harmonise EU policies (Sk_1_1).

Undoubtedly, 4IR will likely redefine winners and losers while setting new directions for international trade and new supply chains across Europe as well as other parts of the world (Sk_1_2). In this context, respondents tend to expect negative consequences for the V4 countries: surplus products and profits due to automation are unlikely to remain in the V4 (Hu_1_1); companies will increasingly turn into monopolies, especially in the US and to some extent in Europe due to the development of user-friendly IT platforms (Cz_1_2); as the gap between digital leaders (China, USA, Japan, and South Korea) and regions such as the CEE continues to increase (Sk_1_2). Still, one Slovak respondent mentioned a potentially favourable development scenario, which involves strengthening the economic potential in specific sectors of the economy that take advantage of digitalisation: Slovakia depends on exports and is extremely sensitive to international competition which invests faster in the digital infrastructure (Sk_1_3).

3.4   *Systemic Stability at Risk*
The increasing pace of change and the reluctance of various social groups to respond to it are currently being observed (Pl_1_1). As a result of automation and robotisation, the middle part of the income ladder will gradually disappear, which will likely undermine the socio-economic system as a whole, since the middle class tends to guarantee the stability of the entire system (Pl_1_2). An increasing lack of trust in the system by many different social groups is also expected (Sk_1_1). Furthermore, one respondent mentioned widespread outrage towards employers, firms, and capitalism as a whole (Hu_1_4), whereas another noted the absence of neo-Luddism in Poland (Pl_1_4).

3.5   *Changing Quality of Life and Increasing Inequalities*
Moving on to the social ramifications of 4IR, it is worth noting that technological advancement offers greater personal freedom of choice (e.g. shopping, ideas, opinions) (Hu_1_4). Respondents anticipate better quality of life for urban populations, which now have more access to new technology and digital solutions. The rural population has also benefited in these respects, but to a lesser extent (Sk_1_3). The main dividing line in terms of quality of life will now be the availability of infrastructure that attracts high-value-added jobs. This will intensify the regional disparity between the so-called forgotten regions and cities and major industrialised areas (Sk_1_3).

Many respondents emphasise the consequences of increasing inequality. In a technology-dominated society, the divide between rich and poor areas and socioeconomic groups, as well as disparities in infrastructure, resources, and access to technology, poses a significant risk to social equity (Hu_1_1). Groups particularly at risk include the least qualified employees (Pl_1_1; Cz_1_3), residents of less developed regions (Sk_1_2; Sk_1_3), and the digitally excluded (Pl_1_4; Sk_1_2; Cz_1_1; Hu_1_1). The third group is characterised by, among other things, low digital competence (Hu_1_6) and increasing digital illiteracy (Hu_1_4; Hu_1_7). Due to the extreme inequality in access to technology, those who have no opportunity to become tech literate will lag behind even further, widening the gap between social classes and groups. As a result, access to online civil services and, consequently, to democracy, may be compromised (Hu_1_1).

3.6 Information or Knowledge?

Access to general knowledge and sources of international information has been improved thanks to 4IR (Hu_1_4), however, respondents much more frequently mentioned a host of negative social effects of changes in the information and communication environment, which include: fake news, misinformation, overabundance of information, and the populist contents reaching a significant proportion of people, especially if they are confused and are unable to verify the contents themselves (Pl_1_3); unbearable information noise (Hu_1_4); living in information bubbles (Pl_1_1); increased susceptibility to hoaxes and information warfare (Sk_1_3); the spread of political propaganda and disinformation through "alternative media" (Sk_1_2), and changing public communication – "no facts, only emotions" (Pl_1_1). All of these phenomena contribute to the emergence of movements that contest scientific knowledge (Pl_1_1), the societal drift, and the propensity of the populace to accept false information uncritically (Sk_1_1).

3.7 Digital (in)Security

The transfer of numerous economic and social activities to the digital sphere comes with a number of risks, including cyberattacks on both public institutions and private individuals (Pl_1_1), increased incidence of privacy violations and the theft of sensitive or personal data (Sk_1_3), the takeover of personal data by corporations (Pl_1_4), surveillance in all spheres of life (especially in education), low resistance to digital crime, digital misinformation (Hu_1_6), and online anonymity (Pl_1_1).

Expanding automation and implementing new technological solutions without the necessary expertise results in flawed systems and security problems, such as exam results being hacked, political polls being rigged, digital identity theft, and more. Without the necessary digital literacy, using the aforementioned tools may leave users vulnerable to all manner of crime. Furthermore, the ethics of technology have not been thoroughly established and agreed upon, which necessitates the creation of a new social compact (Hu_1_1).

3.8   *Fragile State Capacity*

The interviewees also mentioned numerous major ramifications of 4IR in terms of their countries' current and future ability to respond to quickly changing conditions, including technology-related ones. The first one concerns the digitalisation of public administration and institutions, as well as access to and use of large databases, which may be both advantageous and troublesome for public institutions (Pl_1_1); the latter mainly due to reliance on foreign technologies not just in government monitoring systems but also in the provision of public services (Hu_1_6). Another risk is that by adopting 4IR technology, transnational corporations may actually become market regulators (Pl_1_4).

Despite their varying opinions, respondents generally agreed that public institutions in their home countries are committed to preparation for 4IR. For instance, Slovakia's government has modified its economic policy by identifying the key digital transformation areas in which it needed to improve (Sk_1_1). In contrast, the transition to 4IR in Hungary is a top-down process, which is not really conducive to success. The state administration's initiatives fall short and frequently underestimate major obstacles (Hu_1_7). The Czech Republic, on the other hand, has seen a shift in thinking about the involvement of state and non-state actors in the fields of energy, housing, healthcare, and education, with a greater emphasis on the role of regions (regional government and state and non-state labour market actors), whose task it is to manage regional production and consumption of goods and services (Cz_1_4).

Respondents also noted a major impact of 4IR on the sustainability of public finances, namely the need for substantial investment in physical and digital infrastructure (Sk_1_2; Sk_1_3), which will create pressures on spending in all areas where the government has a monopoly or near monopoly (Sk_1_3); and possible decline in revenues due to reduction in the number of workers. Taxing robots may be an appropriate way to address this particular problem (Pl_1_2).

In the case of public services, respondents mentioned the possibility of improved access to key services (Sk_1_2), as well as the emergence of new products and technologies in the fields of culture and sports (Cz_1_1). Robotisation (new technologies that are more expensive, safer, and less confrontational for patients), co-production (replacement of traditional ways of providing services by online services), and special demands placed on health professionals are all perceived to have a significant impact on the healthcare sector (Cz_1_1). In the case of education, respondents frequently bring up the perennial inability of education systems to adapt to changes in the labour market (Cz_1_3), functional illiteracy (Hu_1_7), too much red tape (Hu_1_7), and the fact that online teaching cannot replace face-to-face contact (Cz_1_1). Furthermore, public services are subject to increased pressure, in other words, people have higher expectations of what the government and public sector should provide in terms of job security or compensation for lost industries as a result of digitalisation (Sk_1_3).

One of the respondents from Slovakia mentioned interesting development opportunities resulting from 4IR. As part of smart city projects, new models of social development of space in urban development have been initiated, and a stronger push for more non-economic development is taking place – from cultural to social and educational projects, with municipalities and regional governors taking on new roles (Sk_1_1).

3.9   *Other Important Consequences*

When discussing the other economic effects of 4IR, respondents frequently brought up the topic of consumption. Production cycles, in their view, shorten product life cycles and alter consumption patterns (Pl_1_1). Consumption in modern society is becoming more and more internet-based, which leads to a prosumer system (Pl_1_4). Finally, more providers of goods and services are vying for clients who previously had fewer available options – now, due to digitalisation they have more providers to choose from (Sk_1_3).

As regards the economic structure of the V4 countries (where the level of employment in industry is relatively high), more attention should be paid to the presence of industry in the economy, which has far-reaching consequences, since industrial investment tends to be long term – much longer than in other sectors (Hu_1_2). One of the respondents from Slovakia had this to say about the establishment of IT hubs in his country: "The early stages of digitalisation in Slovakia resulted in the emergence of new IT communities and IT collaborations primarily between the country's key ICT-oriented faculties and universities and the research and business community" (Sk_1_1). His remark indicates that digitalisation has positive impacts on corporate efficiency, resource savings, energy efficiency, and the environment, all of which are becoming more important among employees and customers (Sk_1_3).

The social impacts less frequently mentioned by respondents include increasing social and political radicalism, which involves the emergence of extremist political movements (Pl_1_1), the rise in handout populism, as well as defiantly nationalist populism demanding self-sufficiency (Hu_1_6). They all helped to raise the profile of anti-democratic groups, who have gained public support as a result of misinformation and dissatisfaction in the forgotten regions (Sk_1_3).

As regards the effects of 4IR on social relations, contacts between individuals have significantly changed – young people tend to spend most of their time in front of screens, trading real-world interactions for virtual space (Cz_1_1). On a more limited scale, new partnerships between various actors and stakeholders have materialised (Sk_1_1). Another respondent cites a favourable effect on the environment, which can help remedy the situation in cities where industry and/ or transportation have had a negative impact on the quality of life of their residents (Sk_1_2). In terms of demographics, the COVID-19 crisis-induced acceleration of digitalisation and the ensuing ability of many people to work from home have resulted in a certain degree of decentralisation in Slovakia, along with new smart city solutions adopted by smaller metropolitan areas (Sk_1_1).

4   Socio-Economic Challenges of 4IR in the V4 Countries

Respondents were then asked to consider socioeconomic concerns largely through the prism of a modern state's ability to meaningfully influence important processes via the public policy channel.

4.1   Readiness of Public Administration to Assist in the Implementation of 4IR

In the eyes of the respondents, one of the unresolved issues is the approach of their respective governments to 4IR. Their remarks unmistakably demonstrate that there is no coherent long-term vision for deploying 4IR (or simply digitisation) for socioeconomic growth in the V4 countries (Pl_1_2; Pl_1_3; Cz_1_5). The government has no interest in implementing 4IR, the main reasons being the lack of political will to push for improvements (Cz_1_5) and the absence of necessary knowledge among decision-makers (Hu_1_3). 4IR is evolving on its own as a result of the government's lax approach, since business can independently secure funding, handle investment, and resolve issues as they arise (Cz_1_4).

4.2   Public Resources Needed for Change

To break out of the inactivity trap outlined above, authorities need to mobilise a variety of resources: mechanisms, equipment, and people. Introducing digitalisation (critical digital infrastructure and services and their accessibility, digital governance, education) (Cz_1_1; Cz_1_2; Sk_1_2), achieving this on the national and regional levels (Cz_1_2), and in the businesses sphere (Sk_1_1; Sk_1_3) will undoubtedly pose a considerable challenge since it requires appropriately skilled public administration (Hu_1_7). Where it lacks expertise in the area of new forms of development, the civil service needs to depoliticise and create a new professional force that can produce predictable and sustainable change (Sk_1_1). Smart data management is also becoming an important feature of an efficient state. Better-informed decisions based on expanding resources are needed, as well as providing public institutions with access to data on individuals (while maintaining their security) as well as educating them in how to process such data (Pl_1_1).

Moreover, respondents consider it necessary to minimise unduly centralised and controlled governance (Hu_1_3; Hu_1_6) and implement the value for money principle in public investment (Sk_1_1; Sk_1_2). The current public administration should implement a clear division of competencies and responsibilities, be more proactive, prepare clear plans, and a regularly evaluate their outcomes (Cz_1_5). It should also be capable of making more accurate predictions about how the economy and labour market are likely to develop (Cz_1_5). Finally, it needs to be more transparent (Cz_1_1).

In terms of public resources, the approach of authorities to public finance management is critical. Respondents emphasised the importance of public finance stabilisation and tax reform as this will enable rewarding economic production (Sk_1_1), help curb inflation (Sk_1_2), provide for crucial groups in the future (pensioners, the disabled), and support the entire welfare system (Sk_1_3), while ensuring adequate public investment (Sk_1_2; Sk_1_3).

Another considerable challenge for the v4 countries is to develop and implement appropriate and effective regulations for the digital economy, including: AI technologies (Hu_1_5; Pl_1_4); remote and platform work (Pl_1_4); digital taxation at the national level, because it has a global scope and requires international cooperation (Cz_1_2); responsibility (legal, financial) for the decisions taken by machines/robots/AI (Pl_1_4); legal issues at the consumer-producer or software producer-user interfaces; and curbing the market dominance of digital giants (Hu_1_4). In the latter instance, a major revamp of the public administration and regulatory structure is required to protect against both the noncompliance of many digital enterprises and the establishment of a Europewide regulatory framework to combat irregularities (Sk_1_2).

The tools required for change should include a range of development models. In this context, respondents were mostly concerned about ensuring that technological advancements and developments benefit all members of society as equally and fairly as possible (Hu_1_4); devising new ways of collaboration among the government, the key stakeholders, and actors in the area of public and private development (Sk_1_1); finding the right middle ground between dealing with matters pertinent to subsidiarity (Hu_1_4); and attempting to translate global/national trends into the specifics of regional/local markets/communities. In the last instance, large gaps constrain the activities of public institutions. Building development models in local systems (Pl_1_1), increasing municipal participation in the development of smart city solutions will improve welfare and public services in economically disadvantaged areas

(Sk_1_3) as well as provide citizens with the tools to successfully launch bottom-up initiatives (Hu_1_4).

4.3   Strengthening Social Foundations

Building social capital is undoubtedly one of the most important challenges in the era of rapid technological change. This requires first of all an appropriate amount of social trust (Pl_1_2); however, government strategies tend to be mistrusted by society at large, which is a decidedly negative development (Sk_1_1). To make change possible, it is necessary to muster support for social capital by promoting direct dialogue between capital and labour such as joint initiatives of unions and employers, and bilateral dialogue (Pl_1_2).

Another significant problem in this area is democratisation, which will necessitate maintaining variety of viewpoints and beliefs without encroaching upon personal liberties (e.g. freedom of speech) and respecting people's choices in terms of fundamental freedoms and human rights (Hu_1_4).

It is also vital to promote trustworthy social communication. The critical question is how to demonstrate the importance of change to society (e.g. in the area of education) (Pl_1_1). Nowadays, a large proportion of society is dissatisfied with the direction of transformation, the lack of effective government communication strategy to foster trust and take into account the shifting preferences of citizens and businesses (Sk_1_1). For this reason, it is crucial to stimulate public debate (Pl_1_1), and offer the general public balanced and objective information (Hu_1_4).

The last major challenge in this area is to reduce social inequality. Efforts in this area should address the increasing income inequality and the widening gap between winners and losers of digital transformation and post-socialist transformation (Sk_1_1); regional differences in quality of life and opportunities to reap the benefits on new areas of digital and shared economy (Sk_1_3); as well as the widening gap between high-skilled, high-paying jobs that will benefit from greater digitalisation and low-wage positions left for those unable to acquire the requisite skills and thus find a place in the new labour market (Sk_1_3).

4.4   Key Directions and Areas of Change – a Policy-Mix for 4IR

For the authorities of the V4 countries, an important challenge is to encourage individual sectors of the economy to respond to the challenges of 4IR (Pl_1_2).[7]

---

7   Czech respondents note that their country already has well-developed sectoral 4IR strategies, but they are not implemented (Cz_1_3; Cz_1_5). Another important problem is the coordination of activities between individual ministries, which would facilitate dealing with issues that fall within the remit of more than one department (Cz_1_5).

Therefore, sectoral strategies are required to determine which industries are most vulnerable to technological labour substitution and to prepare new plans for these industries (Sk_1_2). It is also necessary to deploy a long-term strategic approach that would encompass a number of distinct yet interrelated sectors of public policy, including education (R&D), physical and digital infrastructure, labour market policy, and others (Sk_1_2). Respondents mentioned the following areas of intervention: industrial policy (Pl_1_4); programs for SMEs (Hu_1_5); social policy – the problem of social security (Pl_1_4); compensation packages for people made redundant due to automation (Pl_1_4); integration of minorities into the digital transformation and the labour market (Sk_1_3); health policy – addressing new psychosocial risks in the work environment; occupational health and safety (Pl_1_2; Cz_1_5), and labour market policy – retraining and training support for current employees in order to maximize the participation of the aging workforce (Cz_1_5; Sk_1_1; Sk_1_3).

Many respondents focus on the challenges associated with education and training. In the former area, respondents mentioned the need to: implement meaningful reforms (Hu_1_3; Sk_1_1; Sk_1_2), develop new methods and techniques (Cz_1_2), and keep up with rapidly changing technologies (Hu_1_1) to prepare graduates for careers in the digital economy (Sk_1_3). More specifically, the following actions will be required: shifting the focus of primary education to future competencies, self-organisation, the ability to build cooperative relationships, cognitive flexibility; critical thinking, having at least basic digital skills, as well as developing core knowledge (Pl_1_1); changing the role of the teacher and trainer in the educational/training process (Pl_1_1); a stronger focus on critical thinking in schools to help well-educated young people identify and combat fake news and disinformation in alternative media (Sk_1_2). In the modern educational system, this should be done by prioritising the transmission of broad interdisciplinary knowledge over current general and specific skills (Cz_1_2).

The lack of a strategy focused on the development of human capital and life-long learning needs to be addressed proactively by encouraging both employers and employees (Pl_1_2). In terms of qualifications, we should stop talking about professions and instead focus on specific qualification and competence packages; improve qualifications not only via short training courses or lifelong learning but also at university level (Pl_1_1); retrain existing employees in companies rather than hire new ones (Cz_1_3); and encourage the recognition of multiple viewpoints in personal and professional attitudes (Pl_1_1).

A properly designed energy policy will also be a major challenge for the state authorities. 4IR requires a significant amount of energy, and the rising costs of CO_2 emissions will likely increase the already high electricity prices in the V4

countries (Pl_1_3). To avoid the risk of running out of power in the v4 countries in the near future national energy mixes must be modified with the aid
of digital technolog ies (Pl_1_2; Cz_1_4). However, as one Czech expert pointed
out, large energy firms are unwilling to invest in the Energy Internet (Cz_1_4).

The last point is very closely related to sustainable development. From this
perspective, the most important challenges for public authorities include
the following: changing the economic development model (Pl_1_1); ensuring
that technological advancements and developments benefit all of society as
equally and fairly as possible (Hu_1_4); and finding the fine line between economic development and environmental protection (Hu_1_4) by promoting
investment in the green economy (Pl_1_3).

4.5   Old Economic Challenges in a New Digital Environment

One of the persistent economic challenges facing the v4 economies is how to
improve their international competitiveness in the face of rapid technological change. From the perspective the EU as a whole, it is necessary to identify
the critical factors to enable it to catch up with the digital leaders such as the
United States, Japan, and China (Sk_1_2). Strengthening regional ties within the
v4 (plus Austria) is also needed to emulate the leading countries (Sk_1_3). It is
thus critical for individual countries to strike the right balance vis-à-vis other
ones depending on their importance and articulate their interests accordingly
(Hu_1_4). The challenge will undoubtedly involve far stronger international
competition since geographical distance matters considerably less and the v4
countries compete against those from outside the EU as well (Sk_1_3). However, the desire to replicate successful municipal and national economic and
development policies in order to enhance their economies (Sk_1_1) may present an opportunity for these countries.

Another group of challenges posed by international economic resource
flows is the capacity to attract investors thanks to a well-developed industry.
Given the latter's importance for national economies and the scale of investment so far, the respondents' opinions can be considered representative of the
entire v4. They are still concerned about economic volatility caused by regulatory issues, which may have a negative effect on investment, both domestic
and foreign (Pl_1_3). As a result, the challenge will be to improve the stability,
dependability, and predictability of enterprises expanding to or starting their
activity in the v4 countries (Sk_1_1). Unfortunately, there is a high risk of leak-
age of foreign investment; for example in Poland, the price of labour is so low[8]

---

8   The situation is similar in other v4 countries.

that robots remain uncompetitive. When people rather than machines are the main cost, it is easier to discontinue investment. This may result in Poland's loss of its major competitive advantage (Pl_1_3). It is also worth noting that in Poland, investment decisions associated with the deployment of new technologies (which require very high expenditure) are delayed due to the high level of human capital (Pl_1_3). The impact of the middle-income trap is also considerable, for example, in the automotive industry in the v4, where there is a high risk of investment withdrawal due to less developed technology ecosystems (Pl_1_1). Respondents also mentioned the negative impact of low levels of innovation, low levels of public investment in this field, and administrative barriers put in the way of private enterprises (Hu_1_6).

4.6   Other Important Challenges

Eliminating obstacles that would make the adoption of new business models faster and more profitable is a notable economic challenge in the v4 (Sk_1_1). One of the respondents had an interesting development suggestion, stating that new business models are required in non-traditional economic segments, such as the cultural and other sectors that can make use of other types of social and human capital (Sk_1_3). Moreover, as public services are being moved to online platforms, the latter should become simpler to use in order to advance a healthier society and democratic values (Hu_1_1).

As regards other challenges, respondents emphasised the changing production profiles of enterprises (Pl_1_1), the outflow of highly skilled employees (both native and migrant) from the v4 countries (Pl_1_3; Sk_1_1), and comprehensive efforts of industries and companies aimed to bring about a paradigm shift (Hu_1_3).

While addressing the topic of social challenges, it is also important to consider the issue of work-life-balance, since we are dealing with increasing interpenetration of private life, professional activity, and remote work (Pl_1_4).

5   Similarities and Differences Between the v4 Countries and the Core Countries in Terms of the Challenges Posed by 4IR

The respondents initially stated that in general, the challenges faced by semi-peripheral countries are very similar to those that affect the dominant ones (Cz_1_1; Pl_1_4). However, the more detailed their answers, the more pronounced were the perceived differences between these two groups of countries.

When considering the very general development conditions associated with 4IR, it is clear that historical contexts and intergenerational transmission affect the perceptions of the same social phenomena in individual countries (Pl_1_1). Furthermore, their readiness to adopt new technologies are often conditioned by cultural differences (Hu_1_3). Respondents also indicate that demographic considerations have a substantial impact on the paths taken by 4IR processes. The social consequences of robotisation in the v4 countries may be less severe than in other ones that are not confronted with a similar demographic challenge. In fact, the most pressing current problem appears to be how to ensure an adequate number of workers to fill the existing vacancies (Pl_1_2; Pl_1_1; Sk_1_1).

From the social perspective, it is interesting to note that both groups of countries experience similar negative effects of technological change in relation to contesting social movements, such as anti-vaxxers (Pl_1_1), however, the v4 countries are more exposed to fake news due to the very low level of social trust (Pl_1_2).

The economic analysis began by evaluating the status of 4IR implementation. Automation is more difficult to implement in the v4 countries due to their technological backwardness (Pl_1_1). Another respondent notes significant investment delays (associated with 4IR) in relation to the dominant countries (Pl_1_3). Even though local capital is fairly concentrated, the broader institutional setting is not conducive to its engagement with 4IR. The most common approach used by investors appears to be rent-seeking rather than profit-seeking through innovation (Hu_1_1). One statement by a Hungarian respondent is symptomatic: "Hungary is mostly a technology follower and user. New technologies are introduced mostly at the discretion of the top management of parent companies with adequate resources at their disposal. These businesses are the most technologically advanced, whereas smaller ones will face greater disadvantages if they lack access to these technologies. Hungary, being simply a technology user, may only realise a small percentage of these advantages, but will suffer the downsides more acutely. Economically dominant players can see the effects of 4IR in their parent firms, such as redundancies due to automation" (Hu_1_5).

It is important to note, however, that according to some respondents, the situation in the Czech Republic is comparable to that of developed European nations, such as Germany (Cz_1_4). Owing to its long-standing industrial traditions, especially in the automotive sector (Pl_1_1), the Czech economy is significantly more robotised. According to one respondent, "In industry, the Czech Republic, like Germany and other European countries, is ready for 4IR. At present, the principles of 4IR are being implemented by about 10% of companies. The nature of industry in the Czech Republic is the same as in Germany, suppliers, especially small and medium-sized enterprises, are pushed

to implement the principles of 4IR, because they must adapt production technologies to the requirements of developed countries, otherwise they will not
be competitive" (Cz_1_4).

When assessing the degree of digitalisation, one of the respondents noted
the ever-increasing pressure to digitalise state administration and society in
both groups of countries, but he emphasized the reluctance to tap the considerable potential of IT staff in public administration (Cz_1_1).

The V4 countries face numerous problems as a result of their international
standing. According to one interviewee, thanks to the launch of 4IR, the Czech
Republic has the potential to manufacture final goods and offer them to multiple customers at once on the global market (Cz_1_4). Nevertheless another
one sees the Czech Republic as a rigid industrial economy that lags behind
the US, Europe, and Germany (Cz_1_3). On the other hand, Poland boasts a
large market and, somewhat paradoxically, an untapped political and economic potential. Its representatives often patronise partners from other V4
countries (Pl_1_2). As regards Hungary, according to one of the respondents,
"the similarities arise simply from the difference in size, and therefore, in influence between Hungary and the core countries. I think the latter are facing the
same challenges, but on such a different level, since they are considered global
pacesetters when it comes to topics like climate change, technological development or international cooperation, and countries like Hungary can only
adapt to them" (Hu_1_4). Slovakia is economically dependent on FDI which
has brought in crucial technologies and businesses; it also depends on the supply chains where it plays a subordinate role to the trendsetters in the economic
core (Sk_1_3).

When considering global resource flows, it is worth bearing in mind the
considerable brain drain from the semi-periphery to the core due to insufficient opportunities and a broader dissatisfaction with the former's economic,
social, and political environment (Hu_1_1; Sk_1_3). At the same time, however, according to one of the Czech respondents, there is a tendency to export
medium-skilled labour from the USA and Western countries to Eastern European ones where the demand for such skills levels is growing (Cz_1_2). Finally,
the V4 economies are heavily dependent on technology and FDI (Cz_1_3;
Hu_1_1; Sk_1_3).

Significant differences can also be observed between the V4 and core countries in terms of the state potential (including its authorities and public administration) to deal with the challenges of 4IR. The first one is the lack of drive
and urgency among political elites to embrace improvements brought about by
4IR (Sk_1_3), associated with the fact that public administration is not always
willing to accept technological progress. As one of the respondents points out,

"While in the US and in the UK public administration is an open system, in Hungary, it is very firmly closed. As a result, market innovations, and new processes are becoming integrated at a much slower pace. Labour force mobility is also very slow and limited. The administrative culture doesn't support this and closes ranks when faced by large-scale innovations as a smart solution may result in redundancies. The embeddedness of the aspiration for innovation is higher in the English speaking world, as the tradition of taking risks is part of their identity" (Hu_1_7). According to another expert, in the post-EU accession environment, CEE governments have turned to populism and politicised the civil service, which proved to be an extremely turbulent process and frequently resulted in a lack of qualifications to prepare legislation and the government's infrastructure for 4IR (Sk_1_1).

Respondents noted that core countries are much smarter in dealing with certain phenomena (e.g. fake news) that impact policies, which tend to be more populist and less proactive in the V4 countries. Some even observed that the latter do not really implement policies because they concern themselves with politics, which are short-term by definition (Pl_1_3). This may be due to the fact that Europe is divided into the core and semi-periphery primarily along the lines of coordination mode. It implies that the former show a much more serious attitude towards social partners in the process of pioneering various kinds of change. In the V4 countries, the government's attitude can be described as irresponsible (Pl_1_4). Bilateral dialogue in core countries, unlike in the V4, focuses on the main challenges (e.g. climate change, demographics, technological challenges) (Pl_1_2). In terms of the quality of social dialogue between business and employee representations, the V4 countries compare very unfavourably. The West boasts a long-standing tradition of direct relations, negotiation, and dialogue between employers and trade unions (Pl_1_2). So the West and the North of Europe are institutionally better prepared to take advantage of the multi-stakeholder approach where employers and trade union members see each another as partners (Pl_1_4).

Another weakness of the V4 countries is the smaller economic clout of their governments: differences arise from the limited amounts of money spent on public administration and individual public policies, which results in the purchase of mostly inexpensive and inferior technologies (Cz_1_1), state involvement in R&D is relatively low, and there are fewer incentives for private actors to engage in R&D. As a result, local universities and other research institutions tend to rank lower than their counterparts in core countries (Hu_1_1). The differences in starting points and flexibility have been exacerbated by a similar factor in both core and semi-peripheral countries, namely the rapidly growing public debt to GDP ratios which accumulated especially in the late 2010s. As a result, the last 10 years have seen insufficient innovation and public invest-ment in infrastructure on the governments' agendas. This, along with a gener-ally populist nature of the governments has had a strong negative impact on openness to new technology and the opportunities to implement the neces-sary changes in the economy (Sk_1_3).

The challenge faced by semi-peripheral countries in the CEE is far greater in terms of the efforts that need to be put in to make the government a predict-able and responsible partner for businesses. Furthermore, the lack of reforms in education has been detrimental to the capacity of more independent actors that could become the drivers of the change outside of the political spectrum (Sk_1_1). Moreover, Hungary is often cited as a country lacking transparency and as an example of a closed system with no meaningful organisations or entities independent of the state (Hu_1_3).

Last but not least, a number of respondents commented on institutions. The observed differences result from the fact that core countries have had much more time to achieve closer convergence with institutional norms and practices than semi-peripheral ones (Sk_1_1; Pl_1_4; Hu_1_1). The importance of the institutional factor is evident in the remarks of a Slovak expert, who noted that "The core countries, mainly in Europe, have proved capable of getting way ahead of the semi-periphery in terms of key social and economic investments and preparation of the institutional capacity to withstand pressures from the ideologically charged and often populist governments in CEE. The institutions and their resilience are critical and offer a better foundation for the develop-ment of sound economic and institutional policies mainly in the areas of digital infrastructure, R&D, and development of the partnerships between the public and private sector. Thanks to this head start, Western European countries have managed to attract talented people from the CEE countries and are now better prepared for the implementation of the changes in their public systems and regulatory environment. Likewise, the post-2004 environment in the CEE led to a rebirth of reactionary and nationalist rhetoric that has partially undone the positive changes of the EU accession procedures and post-2008 crisis also undermined the trust of the political populists in the EU leaders" (Sk_1_2). The statement by one of the Hungarian respondents adds a tragic punch line to this line of thought: "The disproportionate influence of one man's personal world view on politics and thus the state and the country means that his wil-ful and proud ignorance of and disregard for anything digital will always put digital priorities on the back burner, unless they can serve as a magnet for EU funds" (Hu_1_6).

To summarise, according to the respondents, the Visegrád countries are generally less prepared than core ones for the socioeconomic challenges presented by 4IR. However, some interviewees notice greater progress in the execution of specific technological processes in the Czech Republic owing to its economic structure and cooperation links with Germany.

6   Conclusion

The views discussed in this chapter demonstrate the broad array of effects of 4IR on the social and economic processes unfolding in the Visegrád countries. Current social-economic trends and data imply that these effects may not be as significant as was initially thought. According to respondents, their main social and economic repercussions include:
- multidimensional changes affecting the labour market (both on the demand and supply side) and business processes;
- increasing competition and globalisation;
- substantial erosion of systemic stability and the social contract;
- spread of social inequalities;
- threats arising from the information space;
- security threats to individuals and the community;
- declining capacity of nation states to respond to rapid technological change.

The list of socio-economic challenges facing these countries is almost equally extensive:
- readiness of public administration to create conditions conducive to the implementation of 4IR;
- committing sufficient public resources necessary to change the development paradigm;
- strengthening social foundations by building social capital, democratisation, social communication, and reducing social inequalities;
- implementing appropriate sectoral and cross-cutting policies;
- ensuring the necessary level of competitiveness and innovation of domestic economies.

According to the respondents, the challenges faced by their respective countries are essentially the same as those faced by the core countries; however, their impacts differ depending on the key socioeconomic processes. The most notable difference is in the quality of state institutions: political authorities, public administration, public management, and public policy are all rated lower in the V4 countries.

Interestingly, despite the purposeful selection of participants for the survey (experts in 4IR), many of them viewed the implications and challenges of

4IR through the lens of current and 'traditional' phenomena. This most likely reveals that following the initial fascination with the revolutionary importance of technological change in the V4 countries, socioeconomic realities (including various disruptions) slowed down the 4IR development processes, which affected the experts' perceptions of the phenomenon itself. This lends credence to the hypothesis that continued development of the 4IR concept and practice will follow an evolutionary and adaptive path. One of our respondents summarised it vividly and accurately: "The introduction of technology into our lives is a gradual process that we have learnt to accept, not a shock therapy. However, it may come as a surprise when it suddenly becomes clear that in times of crisis, like the pandemic, for instance, it may help us carry on with our daily lives. Technological control, quite possibly associated with the Fourth Industrial Revolution, enters our daily lives in such a peaceful, steady, and gradual manner" (Pl_1_4).

It should be mentioned that the development of technology is just one of the megatrends that have a significant impact on the communities and economies of the V4 countries. Many experts consider today's climate and energy crises as well as the demographic situation to be equally critical. This viewpoint is shared by the author of this chapter, who believes that the framework of public policies implemented in the V4 countries must include joint multidirectional efforts in the social and economic spheres in order to lay a solid foundation for sustainable development and significantly reduce the development gap. Without taking into account the possible outcomes of the above-mentioned megatrends, the rapid modernisation of these countries' economies may have detrimental economic and social consequences.

Bibliography

Atik, H., and Ünlü, F. (2019). The measurement of industry 4.0 performance through Industry 4.0 Index: an empirical investigation for Turkey and European Countries. *Procedia Computer Science, 158*, 852–869. https://doi.org/10.1016/j.procs.2019.09.123

Beblavý, M., Baiocco, S., Kilhoffer, Z., Akgüç, M., and Jacquot, M. (2019). *Index of Readiness for Digital Lifelong Learning Changing How Europeans Upgrade Their Skills. Final Report.* CEPS – Centre for European Policy Studies in partnership with Grow with Google.

Bencsik, A. (2022). Artificial Intelligence in the Middle East European Countries. In: J. Munoz and A. Maurya (Eds.), *International Perspectives on Artificial Intelligence* (pp. 52–62). Anthem Press.

Csath, M. (2018). The key to increasing competitiveness is investing into human resources. *Annals of Marketing Management and Economics, 4*(2), 31–46. https://doi.org/10.22630/AMME.2018.4.2.15

Compagnucci, F., Gentili, A., Valentini, E., and Gallegati, M. (2020). Technical Progress, Structural Change, and Robotisation: Insights from the Growth Patterns of the "Visegrád" Countries. *Economia and lavoro, Rivista di politica sindacale, sociologia e relazioni industriali, 1*, 13–29. DOI: 10.7384/97663

Cséfalvay, Z. (2020). Robotisation in Central and Eastern Europe: catching up or dependence?, *European Planning Studies, 28*(8), 1534–1553. DOI: 10.1080/09654313.2019.1694647

Éltető, A. (2020). Industry 4.0 and reshoring investments – consequences for the Visegrád countries. In: Z. Gál, S.Z. Kovács, and B. Páger (Eds.), *Flows of Resources in the Regional Economy in the Age of Digitalisation. Proceedings of the 7th CERS Conference* (pp. 156–172). Hungarian Regional Science Association, Pécs, Hungary.

Éltető, A. (2021). Challenges of Industry 4.0 in the Visegrád Group. *Hungarian Journal of Industry and Chemistry, 49*(2), 23–27. https://doi.org/10.33927/hjic-2021-17

European Commission (2017a). *Attitudes towards the impact of digitisation and automation on daily life: report.* European Commission, Directorate-General for Communications Networks, Content and Technology. https://data.europa.eu/doi/10.2759/835661

European Commission (2017b). Key Lessons from National Industry 4.0 Policy Initiatives in Europe. *Digital Transformation Monitor.* May.

European Commission (2019). *Digital transformation scoreboard 2018: EU businesses go digital: opportunities, outcomes and uptake.* European Commission. https://op.europa.eu/en/publication-detail/-/publication/683fe365-408b-11e9-8d04-01aa75ed71a1

European Commission (2021). *Digital Economy and Society Index (DESI) 2021: thematic chapters.* European Commission. https://ec.europa.eu/newsroom/dae/redirection/document/80563

Götz, M., Éltető, A., Sass, M., Vlčková, J., Zacharová, A., Ferenciková, S., Bic, J., and Kaczkowska-Serafinska, M. (2020). *Effects of Industry4.0 on FDI in the Visegrád countries. Final report.* Vistula University, supported by the International Visegrád Fund. https://industry4ofdi.files.wordpress.com/2020/11/final-report.pdf

Götz, M., Sass, M., and Éltető, A. (2021). Perceptions of Industry 4.0 in Visegrád Firms. *DANUBE, 12*(4) 239–241. https://doi.org/10.2478/danb-2021-0016

Gyimesi, Á. (2021). National Industry 4.0 Platforms in the Visegrád 4 Countries – A Comparison with the Frontrunner Digital Economies in Europe. *Studia Universitatis Babes-Bolyai Oeconomica, 66*(3), 21–39. https://doi.org/10.2478/subboec-2021-0012

Hemker, T., Müller-Török, R., Prosser, A., Scola, D., Szádeczky, T., and Urs, N. (Eds.). (2020). *Central and Eastern European e|Dem and e|Gov Days 2020.* Conference

Proceedings. Facultas Verlags- und Buchhandels and Austrian Computer Society. https://ocgitservice.com/demo/ceeegov2020/files/ceeegov2020.pdf

Keese, M. (2020). The Future of Work in the Visegrád Group of Countries. *Society and Economy, 42*(2), 124–145. https://doi.org/10.1556/204.2020.00011

Kim, D. H., and Seo, D.-S. (2018). Analysis Research on Preparation of 4th Wave (AI) of the Visegrád Group. *The Journal of Asian Finance, Economics and Business, 5*(4), 201–211. https://doi.org/10.13106/JAFEB.2018.VOL5.NO4.201

Lazanyi, K. and Lambovska, M. (2020). Readiness for industry 4.0 related changes: A case study of the Visegrád four, *Ekonomicko-manazerske spektrum, 14*(2), 100–113. dx.doi.org/10.26552/ems.2020.2.100-113

Ministry of Economy and Finance (2020). *Strengthening the Innovation Capacity toward the Era of Industry 4.0 for the Visegrád Group Countries.* 2019/20 KSP Policy Consultation Report. Ministry of Economy and Finance, Republic of Korea and Korea Development Institute.

Naudé, W., Surdej, A., and Cameron, M. (2019). The Past and Future of Manufacturing in Central and Eastern Europe: Ready for Industry 4.0? *IZA Discussion Papers*, No. 12141, Institute of Labor Economics (IZA), Bonn. www.econstor.eu/handle/10419/196639

Nurzyńska, D. (2021). Adaptation to Industry 4.0 in the Visegrád Group. *Catallaxy, 6*(2), 35–48. https://doi.org/10.24136/cxy.2021.003

Rifkin, J. (2014). *The Zero Marginal Cost Society: The Internet of Things, The Collaborative Commons, And the Eclipse of Capitalism.* Palgrave Macmillan.

Roland Berger (2014). *Industry 4.0: The New Industrial Revolution: How Europe Will Succeed.* www.rolandberger.com/publications/publication_pdf/roland_berger_tab_industry_4_0_20140403.pdf

Svobodová, L., Hedvicakova, M., and Kuznetsova, A. (2020). Education Needs in Context of Migration and Industry 4.0 in Selected EU Countries. In: E. Popescu, T. Hao, TC. Hsu, H. Xie, M. Temperini, and W. Chen (Eds.), *Emerging Technologies for Education. SETE 2019. Lecture Notes in Computer Science*, vol. 11984. Springer. https://doi.org/10.1007/978-3-030-38778-5_12

Szabó, S. (2020). Transition to Industry 4.0 in the Visegrád Countries. *European Economy Economic Brief 052*, European Commission.

Szalavetz, A. (2020). Digital transformation and local manufacturing subsidiaries in central and eastern Europe: Changing prospects for upgrading? In: J. Drahokoupil (Ed.), *The challenge of digital transformation in the automotive industry: Jobs, upgrading and the prospects for development* (pp. 47–64). ETUI.

CHAPTER 4

Semi-peripherality, Dependency and the Institutional Foundations of Developing a Modern Industry in the Visegrád Countries

Tomasz Geodecki

1 Introduction

The core-periphery relations manifest themselves as a distinction between developed and developing countries, although what they actually reflect is the fact that actors located in a given territory engage in operations characterised by high or low added value (Wallerstein, 2004). In Latin American development theories, industrialisation was expected to aid development efforts, since the manufacturing industry was historically viewed as a source of stable foreign trade earnings and indigenous technological knowledge (Prebisch, 1950; Cardoso and Faletto, 1979). In the 1990s, mutually reinforcing improvements in long-distance communication techniques and the removal of successive barriers to the movement of goods and capital markedly increased the involvement of the global South in international industrial production (Jones and Kierzkowski, 2005; Baldwin, 2012; Baldwin and Lopez-Gonzalez, 2015). The primary motive for relocating certain stages of the manufacturing process to less developed countries is wage differentials. As a result, nations categorised as global periphery experience extraordinary industrialisation, whereas central countries undergo deindustrialisation defined as a declining scale of industrial production (Baldwin and Lopez-Gonzalez, 2015).

Some scholars hypothesise that it is not so much the acquisition of older technologies from developed countries as the development of high-tech sectors in developing countries that may counterintuitively offer more favourable prospects. This is a matter of as yet unoccupied market niches, a large gap between high or rising productivity and relatively low wages, as well as the ability to exploit economies of scale through an export strategy instead of the import-substituting industrialisation previously pursued in Latin America (Stehrer and Wörz, 2001; Amsden, 2001; Kaldor, 1966; Kubielas, 2009; Veloso, 2006; Low and Tijaja, 2014).

Globalisation tendencies in Central and Eastern European countries mirror these trends. The Visegrád countries (Czech Republic, Hungary, Poland, and Slovakia) managed to avoid deindustrialisation by becoming integrated in Western companies' production networks (Augustyniak et al., 2013; Stehrer and Stöllinger, 2015). In view of the increasing subordination of local industry to decisions made in the headquarter economies of transnational corporations in the 2000s, the effectiveness of this development model became a matter of intense debate. Adopting different perspectives, researchers attempt to answer the questions of whether, thanks to their fairly innovative industry, the Visegrád countries will succeed in "moving up in the world economic league" (Hausner, 2013) and "take back control" (Naczyk, 2021), or whether they will remain "integrated peripheries" (Pavlinek, 2017; Krpec and Hodulak, 2019) "condemned to be left behind" (Drahokoupil and Galgóczi, 2017). On the one hand, learning from co-operators in global value chains (GVCs) offers prospects for accelerated industrial advance (Mudambi 2008; Collier and Venables 2007); but on the other, in view of the desire of multinational corporations (MNCs) to maintain their dominant position vis-à-vis their competitors, suppliers and employees, the process of industrial learning is subject to numerous constraints and does not imply that involvement in GVCs automatically translates into a corresponding increase in the share of value added (Milberg and Winkler, 2013), thus helping to overcome peripherality. For industrial upgrading of local actors in GVCs understood in this way, factors such as complexity, ability to codify transactions and capabilities originating in the quality of human capital, remain crucial (Gereffi et al., 2005).

Building on the varieties of capitalism framework, we contend that corporatist state institutions present in continental Europe, such as chambers of industry and commerce, have a significant impact on the ability to develop contemporary industries employing Industry 4.0 solutions. In charting the shared objectives of business and the government, they guarantee institutionalised channels for developing human capital and representing the interests of regional entrepreneurs. Moreover, they provide a framework for competent regulatory design that results in the interests of all the parties concerned, not just the strongest ones, being taken into consideration.

The aim of this chapter is to answer the question to what extent the presence of multinational corporations (MNCs) supports modern industrial processes in the Visegrád countries and to identify areas where the public sector could attract high value-added stages of modern value chains. Challenges in this respect, in our opinion, are mostly due to the Visegrád countries' dependency and semi-peripherality, as evidenced by entrepreneurs affiliated with business interest organisations and public administration representatives.

The analysis therefore focuses on the deficits of local socio-institutional systems in the following areas:
- relationships between indigenous companies and foreign investors from headquarter economies;
- the institutional set-up to promote proprietary standards on the one hand, and on the other, to develop competencies and shape industrial relations in a way that ensures a stable supply of appropriately skilled labour;
- the public sector's ability to effectively implement development policy and assist the development of digital and human capital.

The study was based on 17 semi-structured interviews – a research methodology recommended when dealing with a complex set of topics (Jennings, 2005) such as exploring the respondents' perceptions of the component factors of dependency and peripherality. Standardised interviews may lead to biased findings when initial assumptions about the studied subject prove to be incorrect. Furthermore, if people with fairly different experiences in interest representation institutions and the public sector in the v4 countries were reached, their different perspectives might not be captured in a structured interview. Conversely, in a survey that covers motivations and perceptions, open-ended questions permit respondents to express their opinions and raise issues that are relevant to the topic at hand (Selltiz et al., 1967).

The survey consisted of the following questions:

1. Is the presence of foreign investors among the business entities in the national economy conducive to the latter's (including local entrepreneurs and local affiliates of MNCs) involvement in increasingly more technologically advanced stages of production or are the high-tech and high value added stages of corporate value chains reserved for headquarter economies?

2. Is the institutional model of your national economy conducive to representing the interests of domestic entities in both national and EU's decision-making processes?

3. To what extent did public administration in the v4 countries (i.e. in your country) in 2008–2020 change its approach to promoting high value added processes in home economies and to supporting local entities in technological upgrading?

4. To what extent Industry 4.0 solutions:
   - favour the technological upgrading of business activities of firms in your home country?
   - once introduced, are accompanied by the technological substitution of labour?
   - support the administration in development policy-making?

Respondents were selected from among those active in business organisations and from representatives of public administration of whom the vast majority have experience in business. Their list is included in the Appendix.

The remainder of the chapter is organised as follows: Section 2 reviews the literature on the conditions for industrial upgrading in global value chains, the institutional foundations of comparative advantages manufacturing industries in the Visegrád countries, and the consequences of the lack of business interest representation institutions. Section 3 discusses the research findings based on in-depth interviews with representatives of entrepreneurs and business organisations, and public administration. Section 4 discusses the results and offers a handful of conclusions for the public sector.

2   Industrial Upgrading in Global Value Chains and the Role of the Public Sector in Dependent Market Economies

2.1   *Upgrading in Value Chains and the Attendant Difficulties*

According to Porter (1985), a value chain represents "firms' activities from the conception of a product to its end use and beyond." It increasingly involves actors in different locations around the world, as reflected in the term *global value chains* (GVCs) (OECD, 2013). Participation in GVCs has become a path to industrialisation for many developing countries. Local actors learn from the lead firms and through them gain access to wealthy and demanding buyers (cf. Hobday, 1995; Pietrobelli and Rabellotti, 2011; Baldwin, 2012). In this way, countries that have not managed to build a complete industrial infrastructure or a wide range of capabilities may join the global economy (Baldwin, 2006; Collier and Venables, 2007). It turns out that workers in developing countries not only perform simple production activities, but also engage in R&D and design as noted by Markusen (2005) who identified a third factor of production apart from skilled and unskilled labour, namely knowledge-based capital whose owners have rights to technology, know-how, and access to rich markets. By engaging skilled labour in the global South at a fraction of the wages offered in the North, an MNC may contribute to the development of advanced manufacturing competencies in one or more links along its value chain. Before the globalisation era, these competences were only built if an economy managed to specialise in all stages of production of a given good.

One strand of GVC analysis (see Bair, 2005), represented by the Gereffi school, focuses on industrial upgrading and demonstrates how entrepreneurs from developing countries advance in GVCs. Ernst (1998) defines industrial upgrading as "significant changes in national specialisation and knowledge base that enhance the ability to create value." Gereffi (1999) and Amsden (2001) identify this capacity with occupying technologically sophisticated capital and skill-intensive economic niches. The traditional two mechanisms of industrial upgrading included product and process innovation. Research on GVC s has identified two more, namely chain upgrading or the ability to participate in new chains based on existing production experience, and functional upgrading which involves improving a firm's position in an existing chain (OECD 2013; Geodecki and Grodzicki 2015). The latter has a special place in the discussion of developing countries' advancement prospects thanks to empirical studies showing that relatively little value is created in the offshored production stages of global lead firms (Dedrick et al., 2010; OECD, 2013; Stöllinger, 2021). The first and last links of the value chain – namely management, R&D, and design at one end, and marketing and customer service at the other – have much more potential in this respect.

For this reason, an earlier strand of GVC s research based on Wallerstein's world systems theory (1974, 2004) is less optimistic about the development prospects for countries in the global South, emphasising that the international core-periphery division of labour reproduces itself via the mechanisms of the capitalist economy (Wallerstein and Hopkins, 1977). Ways of maintaining an advantage over developing country actors include all the instruments provided by mono- and/or oligopolistic structures at the top of value chain hierarchies as well as competition among workers and suppliers. They include mergers and acquisitions, blocking technology transfer, drastic cost control on the supplier side by stimulating competition among them or imposing production standards by the lead firms (Milberg and Winkler, 2013; Geodecki and Grodzicki, 2015). The initial advantage in terms of access to rich markets or intellectual property rights is controlled by countries where multinational corporations are based. Therefore, the core-periphery division, although referring to high and low value-added processes, leads to a stratification of the world's countries that is obvious to everyone (Wallerstein, 2004).

GVC analysts (Gereffi et al., 2005; Dicken, 2015) identify three variables that determine which model of coordination of activities will be used in a given value chain – more hierarchical and asymmetric or one that permits a more equitable distribution of benefits. These include 1. the complexity of transactions between suppliers and the lead firm; 2. the ability to codify these transactions; and 3. skills and capabilities in the supply base. For example, the relatively high ability to codify transactions in the IT sector permits Indian IT providers to leverage the knowledge they have acquired by serving their global core buyers and start providing worldwide IT services under their own brand

(Fernadez-Stark et al., 2011; Dicken, 2015). In this way, they managed to reduce the asymmetry of power vis-à-vis the lead firms and acquired the ability to capture a larger share of value added in the market.

Since all sustainable value chains that do not rely on purely market-based relationships between buyers and sellers are characterised by a fairly high degree of complexity (variable 1), the distribution of value added between suppliers and buyers is determined by the ability to codify transactions (variable 2), and the knowledge base of local suppliers (variable 3). Therefore, developing countries with a strategically oriented and successful industrial policy are characterised by very high investments in building capabilities and human capital (Fagerberg and Godinho, 2004), while striving to set or at least influence international standards. As Wuebbeke et al. (2016) note when discussing China's industrial strategy, raising the profile of domestic standards facilitates exporting indigenous technologies and reduces royalties for international patents, consequently increasing the capacity to capture value-added. It seems that when describing industrial upgrading in the Visegrád countries, the asymmetry of power should be not so much an explanatory variable as the fourth variable determining the capacity for creating value added on a local basis. Unlike liberal market economies (LMEs), coordinated market economies (CMEs), and newly industrialised East Asian economies, the hierarchical subordination of local industrial establishments in the Visegrád countries to MNCs in headquarter economies (Baldwin, 1995; Baldwin and Lopez-Gonzalez, 2015) was a deliberate step taken in the hope of encouraging foreign technology transfers and sustaining employment.

2.2 Challenges to Building Capabilities in Dependent Market Economies

Manufacturers from the Visegrád countries cannot boast comparable success stories to Indian or Chinese firms, although the v4 economies are considered as developed in most international classifications.[1] The main reason for this is the comparatively small number of large domestic industrial companies. In fact, most industry is owned by multinational corporations (Nölke and Vliegenthart, 2009). However, applying the traditional categories of dependency after Cardoso and Faletto (1979), Bruszt and Greskovits (2009) note that today, this characteristic is no longer at odds with even advanced forms of industrialisation. Admittedly, the v4 countries still depend on technological and managerial knowledge from core countries; nevertheless, investors have a vested

---

1 All of them have Human Development Index values above 0.800; are OECD members and 'high income' economies, according to the World Bank; and their per capita income (purchasing power parity) exceeds $22,000, according to the IMF. Exception: in another IMF classification, Hungary and Poland are not yet ranked as 'advanced' economies.

interest in maintaining high levels of human capital and social cohesion as these are prerequisites for high productivity. Both of these qualities must be guaranteed by an efficient state, which is why the EU supports institution building in its new Member States. Furthermore, the Visegrád countries have an advantage over most dependent countries in that they previously experienced a relatively high level of industrialisation and built up high technical competence under socialism (see Berend, 1996; Klazar et al., 2020). This enables them to produce high-technology goods for export and sometimes to use their high competences in R&D (cf. Munich et al., 2014), which is why Bruszt and Greskovits call them semi-core countries as opposed to the semi-peripheries represented by the Eastern Balkans, the Baltic states, and Latin American countries.

Nölke and Vliegenthart come to a different conclusion, emphasising that the dependent nature of the Visegrád economies is manifested by the absence of institutions, whether characteristic of LMEs or CMEs typical of developed countries. The competitive advantage in this model combines a relatively cheap labour force and an educated population, which makes it possible to master at least intermediate production technologies. The peculiarities of capitalism in the V4 countries are associated with the dominant ownership of industry by multinational corporations, especially in sectors producing tradable goods, which are key to preserving comparative advantages in international trade (see Table 4.1). This ownership structure is the aftermath of post-socialist privatisation in the absence of a local bourgeoisie. The hierarchy typical of these corporations' relations with their foreign subsidiaries reflects the central coordinating mechanism in this kind of capitalism, which is why Nölke and Vliegenthart call these countries dependent market economies (DMEs) and perceive the fact as a threat to local innovation and competitiveness.

Nölke and Vliegenthart's 2009 analysis draws on the theoretical approach of varieties of capitalism, developed from Hall and Soskice's 2001 book subtitled *The Institutional Foundations of Comparative Advantage*. This perspective combines the achievements of the new institutional economics with the idea that comparative advantage in international exchange manifests itself as high productivity thanks to the capacity to deliver technologically advanced products. Thus, the most important resources in this race are not inherited – the engineering and scientific base has to be constantly recreated (Porter, 1990). The idea of "systemic competitiveness" (Altenburg et al., 1998), in which, apart from micro- and macroeconomic factors, the authors distinguish between meso and meta levels, is part of this trend. The analysis conducted at the meso-economic level is based on the observation that it is no longer individual firms that compete against each other, but rather industrial clusters or networks of

TABLE 4.1   Share of foreign ownership in three strategic sectors in the Visegrád countries (percentage of turnover)

	Manufacturing		Automotive[a]		Electronics[b]	
	2004	2018	2004	2018	2004	2018
CZE	52.6	69.4	93.1	95.6	74.8	91.4
HUN	60.3	70.8	93.2	97.5	92.2	96.6
POL	45.2	49.7	90.8	91.9	70.3	80.2
SVK	68.5	80.0	97.3	99.2	79.0	93.6

a   For 2018: NACE Rev. 2: C29 Manufacture of motor vehicles, trailers and semi-trailers.
b   For 2018: NACE Rev. 2: C26 Manufacture of computer, electronic and optical products.
SOURCES: 2004: NÖLKE AND VLIEGENTHART (2009, P. 683); 2018: EUROSTAT (FATS)

firms. They derive their advantages from the technological infrastructure and institutions supporting competence development, hence the growing importance of the national or local environments. The quality of regulation and development funding as well as the production of collective goods in the fields of R&D, training, and infrastructure,[2] can all be improved thanks to its effective organisation. In such as heterarchical structure, the state continues to be a crucial actor due to its coordination, moderation, and communication functions. It cannot, however, replace businesses and their organisations in the creation and implementation of collective strategies. By transferring some of its responsibilities to an advanced networked form of coordination of collective action, creativity is unleashed and the knowledge spread across the system can be economically exploited, supporting the government's legitimacy (Mayntz, 1991; Altenburg et al., 1998).

2.3   *The Role of Public Management in Overcoming Dependency*
2.3.1   The Capacity to Conduct Industrial Policy and Administrative Competencies
If enabling value-added growth by assisting businesses to fill lucrative niches in value chains is the state's primary duty and source of legitimacy, then it must

---

2   The metalevel refers to development-oriented cultural values, consensus on the necessity of industrial and international trade development, and cooperation of social actors in formulating strategies.

establish the necessary institutions to that end. States with such capabilities are developmental states as opposed to predatory ones, which allow incumbents to push their own goals at the expense of the common good (Evans, 1995; Rodrik, 2016). The meritocracy that arises from a bureaucrat's career based on a long-term professional perspective is a feature of public administration in a developing state. Weberian-style bureaucrats have a strong sense of autonomy and are anchored in social networks, which they use to institutionalise the channels for continual renegotiation of policies and their goals (embeddedness). This seemingly contradictory combination of institutional allegiance and social connectedness – what Evans refers to as "embedded autonomy" – has served as the foundation for state intervention in industrial change among others in East Asian countries. In order to find its institutional origins, Evans and Rauch (1999) explored the relationship between the way the administrative apparatus is organised and growth rates in developing countries between 1970 and 1990. They found a clear positive correlation between growth rates and the presence of a Weberian type of bureaucracy, i.e. one that actively formulates economic policy goals and maintains an appropriate distance from interest groups. This is ensured by institutional solutions such as professional recruitment, employment stability, degree of intertwining of state and corporate operations, and the desirability of jobs in administration.

Weberian professionalism in administration results not only from a well-designed civil service but also from institutions that provide a bridge between business and administration. In the formative era of modern states, it became an important exception to the rule of impartiality and administrative supremacy to include social partners in setting the key economic policy parameters. They have a knowledge advantage, and without it, implemented solutions would be less effective (Weber, 2019). In this way, not only entrepreneurs (see Hausmann and Rodrik, 2002), but also the officials involved in negotiations acquire knowledge about the conditions needed to enable firms to deliver more added value. This makes it possible to "link to some extent the authority of notables and expertise in the domain of the private economy with the expertise of professional civil servants" (Weber, 2019).

2.3.2   Negotiating with Institutions Representing Business Interests

Business associations became an important part of European coordinated market economies already in the 19th century. With this type of coordination of economic activities (cf. Streeck and Schmitter, 1985), after the Spring of Nations in Austria and Germany, entrepreneurs gained the status of a self-governing community as a subject of decentralised state administration, which set them apart from the Napoleonic governmental chambers. The essence of business self-government lies in the fact that, apart from the public-law corporation system and compulsory membership, they have administrative authority (Wykrętowicz, 2013). Being at the same time a subject of state administration and a representative of entrepreneurs, the chambers of industry and commerce gained the status of a partner rather than a petitioner in their relations with government administration. This is why S. Wykrętowicz calls Germany the home of business self-government.

According to Nölke and Vliegenthart, the root causes of the V4 countries' dependency are more complex than foreign investors' dominance in industry. Multinational corporations became the natural source of capital and business competence in this region following the destruction of native capitalists under communism (Nölke and Vliegenthart, 2009; Bohle and Greskovits, 2012). This translated into a lack of ability to articulate interests by local entrepreneurs and an ensuing inability of local societies to enforce reciprocity with the companies that benefit most from local resources. Indeed, the system of interest representation in DMEs differs from both the continental corporate model and the Anglo-Saxon pluralist model. In the corporate system, the business self-government has administrative authority and firms are obliged to participate in the activities of its institutions (Abramowicz, 2009; Wykrętowicz, 2013). The pluralist model, on the other hand, assumes that economic interests are articulated by groups with voluntary membership that strive to persuade decision-makers of the legitimacy of taking their demands into consideration through lobbying.[3] The Visegrád countries, unlike the Anglo-Saxon ones, lack big national enterprises with global reach, and, unlike those of continental Europe, lack substantial business self-government. The latter has not been revived in its pre-war form imitating the German and Austrian chambers of commerce. True, in Slovakia and Hungary (as well as Slovenia[4]), chambers of commerce with compulsory membership were temporarily re-established in the 1990s, but they did not survive into the 21st century.[5] The Polish model is also a pluralistic one. The absence of universal chambers of commerce

---

3   As European integration progresses, however, it seems that LMEs such as the UK and Ireland are less represented in decision-making bodies in Brussels (Kohler-Koch et al., 2013), especially in the first stages of legislation.

4   In 2006, Slovenia abolished compulsory membership in chambers of commerce. All of these countries attempted to restore the institutions that had existed during the Austro-Hungarian empire, of which they were a part.

5   Entrepreneurs were dissatisfied with compulsory membership and the inability of chambers to articulate their needs or adequately protect their vested interests. The chambers' failure to identify needs and represent small and medium-sized businesses as well as emerging industries was considered the main factor in their demise (Duvanova, 2013, p. 184).

resulting in (and partly due to) the dominance of foreign investors in industry can be perceived as a central feature of the institutional landscape of the business environment in the V4 countries.

2.3.3 Support for Bargaining in Industrial Relations and Human Capital Reproduction

The risks associated with this particular model of capitalism in the DME s reveal themselves in areas crucial to the development of advanced forms of industry. The investors' desire to keep the benefits reaped from the V4 countries, i.e. productive and cheap labour, neither induces workers to cooperate in the long term nor encourages investment in skills, which eventually leads to their disappearance (Nölke and Vliegenthart, 2009). The needs of local business, from which society and employees could expect reciprocity in return for supporting expansion, are not taken into account. Unlike in LME s and CME s, local business is poorly represented and is not recognised as a partner by public administration (Ost, 2010; Duvanova, 2013). In the sphere of industrial relations, the industry-dominant large foreign employers are reluctant to accept organised labour into the bargaining system or collective sectoral agreements. However, businesses are keen to sustain staff satisfaction in terms of hiring, firing, and compensation due to their more immediate concern over losing human resources (Nölke and Vliegenthart, 2009). The negotiating position of labour in these countries is becoming steadily weaker due to a decline in trade union density; consequently, cost competitiveness in the V4 is maintained through wage growth that is consistently lower than productivity growth (see Astrov et al., 2019, Schröder, 2020). However, this led to an increasing scarcity of trained labour, mostly due to emigration and a lack of investment in training (Polska S.I., 2019; Atoyan et al., 2016), which necessitated wage growth in the late 2010s.

The relative abundance of technical competences to date is the result of the relatively early industrialisation of the Visegrád countries – some of their regions were well-known industrial centres before World War I (cf. e.g. Klazar, 2020; Davies, 2014). After the World War II, Soviet-style industrialisation focused on heavy industry and traditional engineering sectors. The fairly high level of primary education was accompanied by a quantitatively and qualitatively limited higher education dominated by specialised vocational training (Berend, 1996). From the 1970s onwards, this model was becoming anachronistic, with labour- and resource-intensive and low-quality products further reducing its competitiveness. The collapse of global communism found these countries with an outdated industrial infrastructure, while the post-transformation recession reduced the propensity to invest in technical skills (Nölke and Vliegenthart, 2009). The lack of universal business self-government only exacerbated the problem, since, apart from interest representation, professional skills formation has traditionally been the most important area of support for traditional guilds and modern chambers, (de Tocqueville 1866; Estevez-Abe et al., 2001). The provision of industry- and firm-specific skills is thus served not only by adequate employment protection reducing individual risk of investment in knowledge (Estevez-Abe et al., 2001). Analyses of CMEs demonstrate that it is principally supported by a system of individual negotiations of qualifications by employer and employee organisations, which public administration would be unable to replace even if it wanted to (Culpepper, 2001).

Nowadays, in a period of re-industrialisation associated with the emergence of the Central European manufacturing core (Augustyniak et al., 2013; Stehrer and Stöllinger, 2015; Grodzicki and Geodecki, 2016), technical competencies are becoming scarce in the Visegrád countries. Neither weak employment protection nor a disorganised system of vocational training has fostered investment in knowledge comparable to that during the socialist industrialisation. For example, the lack of engineers equipped with adequate technical knowledge was reported in Poland as a far greater obstacle to the development of Industry 4.0 than the lack of digital skills (Poland S.I., 2019, pp. 25–33). Automation and robotisation are thus not only a challenge of the future but also a response to the growing labour shortage and record low unemployment rates compared with the rest of the EU (Bykova et al., 2021). A shortage of workers also implies a shortage of digital skills. Approximately 6% of companies in Hungary and the Czech Republic reported problems with recruiting employees with specialised ICT-skills, and the EU average in the share of ICT specialists in employment in 2019 was only achieved by the Czech Republic (ibid., pp. 50–51).

Apart from promoting human capital investment, a significant new administrative function has evolved, namely the provision of public services when face-to-face contacts become impossible due to a pandemic. It also encourages investment in digital skills, while e-government services promote and support the deployment and use of digital technologies (Schwab, 2016). In this way, they facilitate the emergence of new forms of human collaboration and can significantly contribute to socio-technical changes (Meijer and Bolivar, 2016).

3   Perspectives and Barriers to the Development of Industry 4.0 as Perceived by Economic Actors in the Visegrád Countries

3.1   *The Current Situation*

On the one hand, progressive European integration leads to the liberalisation of more market areas (Cz_2_4, Sk_6_3), in which previously large players are losing their dominant position and smaller ones are already being eliminated by better-equipped foreign competitors (Cz_2_1, Cz_2_2). The technological change associated with the COVID-induced spread of the Internet of Services opens up the market to new players in many areas (including telecommunications and postal services), which in the eyes of local economic actors intensifies competitive pressure. On the other hand, the manufacturing sector in the Visegrád countries currently reports a stronger demand for its products (Cz_2_3, Hu_2_1, Pl_2_1, Pl_2_4). This is mainly due to two factors: first, a shift in the sourcing practices of European firms which started to consider the risks inherent in pursuing cheap labour and to appreciate geographic proximity after the pandemic interrupted their supply chains (Pl_2_1); and second, the diminishing importance of China as a supplier of intermediates in global supply chains associated with rising wages in the Middle Kingdom and the recognition of China as a strategic economic adversary by the USA (Pl_2_1). Although it had already been documented that proximity matters, the epidemic strongly reinforced this perception (Pl_2_1).

The result was a rapid increase especially in export-oriented production in the Visegrád countries (Pl_2_4), which resulted in widespread inability to meet the demand for labour. Unemployment is practically non-existent (Cz_2_2, Sk_2_1), labour is becoming more expensive and more difficult to access (Sk_2_3). This is associated with a reduction in the availability of skills across the V4 countries (Pl_2_4), although previously high quality human capital used to be their asset (Cz_2_2, Hu_2_4). This problem is exacerbated by emigration and demographic decline (Hu_2_1) and means that human capital has to be imported from other countries in the region (Sk_2_4, Cz_2_2, Cz_2_3).

3.2   Industrial Upgrading in the Context of Dominance of Foreign Capital

Respondents agreed that foreign investors play a significant role in their economies. Those with extensive experience in corporate management well remember a neoliberal quirk, which consisted in the acceptance of unfair competition between international businesses and ill-equipped domestic firms, as well as popular support for the former, which characterised the 1990s reforms (Cz_2_3). On the one hand, this resulted in the displacement of indigenous enterprises from the market (Cz_2_1, Cz_2_2), but on the other, it led to a rapid productivity growth in all open markets (Cz_2_1, Pl_2_4, Sk_2_1, Sk_2_3, Sk_2_4,). This occurred due to the influx of new "technologies, software solutions and managerial capabilities" (Sk_2_4).

New technology solutions, including in Industry 4.0, "trickle down" from MNCs to local SMEs (Hu_2_2, Pl_2_4) through employee and contractor learning (Pl_2_3). Many Industry 4.0 technology solutions are demonstrated, promoted and supported by international trading partners (Pl_2_3). Technical change is being driven by competition and the pursuit of productivity gains.

Positive aspects of this situation include:

- The avoidance of deindustrialisation – industry is located where relatively cost-competitive labour is available – which opens up possibilities to develop Industry 4.0 with further prospects for cost reductions and productivity enhancements (Pl_2_1);
- Sustaining R&D processes, as in the long run product development is only possible where production takes place (Hu_2_1, Pl_2_1); lower labour costs in the v4 also apply to R&D divisions (Hu_2_1, Pl_2_2).

The interviewees mostly mentioned investors taking advantage of the R&D competences of engineers in the southern part of the Czech Republic, the automotive industry and business services in Slovakia, German companies representing the automotive and engineering industries (Audi, Bosch) in Hungary (Gyor and Budapest), or engineering centres of global companies located in Krakow, such as Motorola Solutions (communication technology USA), Ericsson (IT centre, SWE), Aptiv (automation in automotive, DEU), and ABB (automation and robotics SWE-CHE). The common perception is that MNCs from certain parts of the world, notably Asia, are less likely to transfer technology to their subsidiaries located in this part of Europe. Respondents from Slovakia also commented on a niche occupied by its economy, which serves as a testing ground for digital services in IT and banking due to its comparatively small size (Sk_2_2, Sk_2_4).

Some respondents identified weaknesses in CEE's reliance on the FDI-based development model. In their view, local semi-peripheral economies tend to attract specialties which, according to the empirical concept of the smiling curve, are less likely to generate high value added (Hu_2_1, Hu_2_2, Hu_2_3, Pl_2_1). This is perceived to be a consequence of the low manufacturing costs, and leads to further specialisation in manufacturing activities (Pl_2_1, Hu_2_4).

The problems faced by CEE countries in their development efforts and inability to turn investor relations into benefits are due to:

- the lack of ownership advantages, i.e. technology ownership (Pl_2_4);
- the use of solutions based on standards developed by market leaders, mostly from developed countries, resulting in a weaker position vis-à-vis them, and higher costs (Pl_2_1, Pl_2_2);
- the lack of sustainable reproduction of human capital at the level of intermediate technical competences (Pl_2_1, Pl_2_4), digital competences (Pl_2_1), managerial competences (Pl_2_1, Hu_2_4), as well as the public sector ones (Pl_2_1, Hu_2_2, Hu_2_4).

3.3　*Relations with the Environment in the Absence of Universal Interest Representation Institutions*

In the absence of universal business self-government in the V4 countries based on the Austrian or German models, the institutional representation of business interests depends on the individual approach of those responsible for social dialogue (Sk_2_1, Sk_2_4). This leads to instability of legislation which affects entrepreneurs, most notably unconsulted changes enacted during the fiscal year. From this perspective, the representation of business interests at EU level is perceived to be better than at national level (Sk_2_4). In the absence of interest representation institutions, business chamber membership is relatively small (Hungary 8–10% [Hu_2_4], Poland 2% [Ministry of Development 2018]). Paradoxically, the COVID-19 pandemic prompted SMEs to self-organise against some lockdown restrictions (Pl_2_2). Limited representation contributes to inequality in reaching decision-makers, whereas governments have the opportunity to co-opt chamber members for increased influence on the economy (Hu_2_4). MNC s have their own contact channels with central government regardless of the benefits they bring to the local economy (Hu_2_4). German companies in particular (Hu_2_1) or large companies in general, especially in the automotive sector (Hu_2_3) play a big role. Favouritism for foreign firms is most obvious in Hungary, but it was also common in the Czech Republic (Cz_2_3). In Slovakia, on the other hand, one respondent (Sk_6_3) emphasised the long-standing shielding of domestic entrepreneurs from the liberalisation of certain markets. Despite the existence of representation structures, they are not widespread, and MNC s are more active (Hu_2_1, Hu_2_3) not only because of their importance, but also because they take for granted their expectations of the government and support systems, which they know from their home countries (Pl_2_2).

Respondents from the Czech Republic and Slovakia appeared to have stronger faith in the ability of market mechanisms to control the commercial environment and, consequently, business performance. Respondents from Poland and Hungary, however, focus on a greater impact of business on governmental institutions, even though domestic entrepreneurs do not always take advantage of the available opportunities (Hu_2_2, Pl_2_2).

3.3.1　Industrial Relations

Labour shortage and its high cost for employers was the problem most frequently mentioned by respondents regardless of country (Cz_2_2, Hu_2_2, Pl_2_1, Pl_2_2, Sk_2_1, Sk_2_2, Sk_2_3, Sk_2_4), notably by almost all the respondents from the relatively small Slovak economy. It was in this context that the importance of representing entrepreneurs' interests in discussions with labour unions was emphasised (Sk_2_4, Sk_2_2). The cited reasons for wage growth included the influx of orders during the pandemic and shorter supply chains (Pl_2_1), rapid economic growth (Hu_2_1, Pl_2_1), demographic processes (Hu_2_1, Sk_2_2, Sk_2_4), and emigration (Hu_2_1, Sk_2_2). Working conditions are improving for employees in both the public and private sectors (Hu_2_1), including education, healthcare and other sectors not subject to marketisation (Sk_6_3), whereas manufacturing is forced to compete with services for labour (Cz_2_2). More often than Polish or Hungarian respondents, Czech and Slovak experts take the employers' perspective, which may be due to their status as entrepreneurs. They note that political links between the government and trade unions (Sk_2_1, Sk_6_3) gives the latter a stronger position compared with the 1990s and the early 2000s. Hungarian and Slovak respondents also mentioned links between the government and business organisations (Hu_2_1, Hu_2_4, Sk_2_2).

The hallmarks of Industry 4.0 – including intensive use of robots and automation, the digitalisation and automation of production and customer service processes in CEE countries – are primarily intended to address shortages in the labour market (Pl_2_1, Sk_2_2, Sk_2_3).

As a result, the situation of employees is palpably better than at the beginning of the transition period, whereas that of the employers has become more difficult. Firstly, employees are needed to implement processes in which machines cannot replace humans (Cz_2_4, Hu_2_2, Hu_2_3, Hu_2_4, Pl_2_3, Pl_2_4, Sk_2_1). Business organisations supporting the introduction of Industry 4.0 solutions even recommend carrying out any in-house changes with the participation of respected employees and without causing undue fear of job losses (Pl_2_3). Secondly, in view of the historically low unemployment rates, entrepreneurs are lowering their requirements, which together with the natural waning of technical competences (Pl_2_1, Pl_2_3, Sk_2_4) exacerbate the already present deficits. Thirdly, immigrants who come from non-EU countries of the former Yugoslavia and the former USSR, sometimes even from Western Europe, are highly sought after (Cz_2_2, Cz_2_3, Pl_2_3, Sk_2_4).

3.3.2 Human Capital Building

The overall decline in the availability of technical skills is perceived not only in terms of their shortage in a "red-hot economy" (Pl_2_4), but also as a result of years of neglect. Respondents note the lack of skills amongst younger technical workers (Sk_2_4), as the older ones, mostly educated in the 1960s and 1970s, are now retiring (Pl_2_1, Sk_2_2). The need to combine the digital skills of the younger generation with the technical abilities represented by the now-disappearing older generation exacerbates this issue. Older workers who lack digital competences may fear losing their position and block change (Pl_2_1, Pl_2_3). Naturally, therefore, the technical change associated with the implementation of Industry 4.0 solutions will continue over the next several decades, possibly facilitated by public support for the integration of digital and technical competences. However, the rising labour costs and the need to substitute it with technology is already increasing the value of the often underappreciated vocational training courses and a growing recognition of the preferences of young job seekers (Hu_2_4, Sk_2_2, Sk_2_3).

In view of the above-mentioned skills deficits, the semi-peripheral nature of the v4 economies may be aggravated by their inability to overcome their dependence on suppliers (Pl_2_1).

Problems also affect the institutional sphere, the most serious of which are deficits in public education, the lack of support for educational functions on the part of industry, and an absent business self-government. As regards education, it was emphasised that local administration does not perform as well as higher levels of government in identifying educational needs and business conditions (Cz_2_2, Pl_2_1). In terms of specific business solutions, certain kinds of knowledge are simply unattainable without industrial practice (Pl_2_1).

On the business side, the most important deficits include the lack of funds for the reproduction of human capital (Cz_2_2, Hu_2_1, Hu_2_2, Pl_2_4) and the lack of managerial skills (Hu_2_2, Pl_2_1). A generational change is only just taking place in this area, which, along with a lack of manpower and contractor requirements, will be the most important factor in the spread of Industry 4.0 solutions (Hu_2_2, Pl_2_1, Sk_2_3).

3.4   *Areas of Influence of the Public Sector on the Development of Industry 4.0*

Based on the respondents' statements, four areas of public sector influence on the development of Industry 4.0 can be identified:

1. Industrial policy with a stronger support for business at national and European levels both during the pandemic and previous industrial revival efforts is becoming increasingly accepted (Pl_2_2, Sk_2_4);
2. The digitalisation of public services disseminating digital standards, especially in health (Cz_2_2, Hu_2_2, Pl_2_1, Pl_2_2), social security (Pl_2_2), taxation (Hu_2_2), utilities (Hu_2_2, Pl_2_3, Sk_2_2, Sk_2_3), running a business (Pl_2_1, Pl_2_2), and in the context of deficits in this area, mainly in commercial courts (Pl_2_2), civic affairs (Hu_2_2, Pl_2_1) and conducting economic policy in general (Hu_2_4). Despite progress, the pace of digitalisation in some areas of public service delivery is still unsatisfactory;

3. Support for lifelong learning, including the development of competencies of young people, employees, managers, and business owners as a response to the deficits identified in the workforce (Hu_2_4, Pl_2_1), the vanishing technical competencies (Pl_2_1, Cz_2_2), the shortage of digital competencies for the development of I4.0 (Hu_2_2, Pl_2_1, Sk_6_3), and the lack of awareness of entrepreneurs (Hu_2_2, Hu_2_4, Pl_2_1, Pl_2_3).

The internal organisation of the public sector and government administration (Pl_2_1) was identified as the fourth deficit area, cutting across the three above-mentioned areas of public sector activity, which is partly due to the lack of intermediary institutions dedicated to knowledge exchange between public administration and business, affecting the competence deficits of public sector employees (Cz_2_2, Hu_2_2, Pl_2_1).

- Industrial policy: limited exchange of knowledge between policy-makers and businesses is due to the lack of institutions ensuring a fair representation of domestic entrepreneurs (Hu_2_1, Hu_2_3, Pl_2_2), hence its design can be more easily influenced by large actors, including MNC s. Negotiating the scale and scope of restrictions during the pandemic underscored the need for SMEs to contact central administration representatives (Pl_2_2). The difficulties in defining one of the instruments in the process of establishing a tax credit to be used across industry was noted as an example of the lack of transmission of expertise from business to government. (Pl_2_1).
- E-government and digitalisation of public services: limited knowledge of technical conditions by procurement departments and their excessive decentralisation were also underscored (Pl_2_1, Pl_2_2). Thousands of individual units (Pl_2_1) are unable to implement administrative change processes as efficiently and competently as large centralised organisations.
- Professional competence formation and human capital reproduction: the deficits are again due to the limited potential of public administration to recognise the needs of entrepreneurs, insufficient resources dedicated to needs analysis (Pl_2_1) as well as excessive decentralisation of educational tasks in administration. From the perspective of business self-government, effective cooperation occurs at least at the regional level (Cz_2_3). Likewise, the devolution of vocational education in Poland to the local level is viewed as a negative development (Pl_2_1).

4 Conclusions for the Public Sector

By adopting an institutional perspective modelled on the enhanced varieties of capitalism framework (Nölke and Vliegenthart 2009), it is possible to combine the analysis of the institutional factors of competitive advantage in the development of modern industries (Porter 1990; Hall and Soskice 2001) with dependency theory (Cardoso and Faletto 1979), which gave rise to one of the approaches to analysing global value chains (Wallerstein 1974; Bair 2005). Based on the answers to the survey questions, we were able to draw a number of conclusions about the role of the public sector in industrial transformation, which allowed us to test the our initial hypotheses concerning the ability of the Visegrád countries dominated by foreign firms to develop modern industries.

First, there is no evidence to support the claim made by Nölke and Vliegenthart (2009) that foreign investors from headquarter economies do not fund the development of Industry 4.0 or the acquisition of skills necessary for the high-tech manufacturing segments in the Visegrád countries. Respondents believe that foreign investors do actually invest in local education systems, albeit to a lesser extent than in their home countries. They help their local partners to acquire the skills required to use Industry 4.0 instruments in performing complex industrial processes both directly and indirectly through demonstration, dissemination of standards, and direct assistance, as well as through the secondment of trained staff. Empirical studies of FDI in the V4 reveal that investors are increasingly looking for skilled workers rather than inexpensive labour (Stephan, 2013), and invest in local R&D centres (Münich et al., 2014). Dunning's framework for analysing MNC investment decisions shows that FDIS are made to maximise profit rather than to support the economic strategies of headquarter economies. The pursuit of comparative advantages, such as cheap labour, instead of focusing on modern industry development (Lin and Chang, 2009), appears to be due to flaws in the host countries' economic strategies rather than deliberate efforts by investors to lock their contractors into activities based on simple labour.

Second, according to the survey participants, the institutional framework of the Visegrád countries' economies, which is distinct from both liberal and coordinated market economies (Nölke and Vliegenthart, 2009), does not favour the representation of interests of domestic companies. MNCs with their strong negotiating leverage and experience dealing with government agencies are at an advantage in this regard. The disadvantages of this situation for domestic enterprises are visible in a number of critical areas for the development of Industry 4.0. Employers are unable to negotiate employment terms with organised labour in the V4 countries due to the lack of universal chambers of industry (cf. Ost, 2010; Thorkaltson and Kattel, 2013), which affects labour supply and makes it more difficult to plan investment in production automation. The non-existent business self-government may be the missing link in human capital formation, as the formal education system does not have a sufficient potential to combine theoretical knowledge with skills acquired on the job. Moreover, attempts to induce employers to co-invest in workers' skills in the absence of CME institutions have generally failed (see Culpepper, 2001; Layard et al., 1994).

The problem of technology standards is a crucial area where the drawbacks of the DME model become even more evident, especially with the emergence of Industry 4.0 standards. While in CMEs (e.g. Germany) corporate strategies see standards as an infrastructure that leads to improved cooperation, LMEs treat them as proprietary goods or services to be exchanged (Tate, 2001). The public sector in the Visegrád countries has failed to create specified interoperability standards, which encourages technology providers to create mono- and oligopolistic structures and raises prices for local industry. In contrast, developing Asian nations aggressively employ national standards as a barrier to imports and a means of promoting indigenous goods (Tate, 2001; Wübbeke et al., 2016).

Third, our research findings do not support the hypothesis of a distinct paradigm shift in the industrial policy pursued in the Visegrád countries in the second decade of the 21st century. The evolution of economic policy in the wake of the 2008/2009 crisis tends to be noted by government representatives rather than economic actors[6] who regard pandemic-induced changes in the operation of the public sector as far more significant. Instead, the common denominator for all the changes that occurred in the Visegrád countries in the 2010s is the demographic shift, which, in conjunction with previous emigration and the current good economic situation, has had a strong impact on labour shortage, as emphasised by almost all respondents. This is what actually necessitated the automation of production, the digitalisation of service provision, and communication implemented by business. If the upward pressure on wages is not matched by increased productivity (e.g. in the face of the dwindling skills base), the region may lose its cost competitiveness (cf. Bykova et al., 2021).

One of the respondents attempted to identify the key factors in the impending reorganisation of industrial production in accordance with the 4.0 formula, which are consistent with our findings. These include the following:
– the pressures of the labour market, including skills deficits and a declining labour supply;
– a generational shift in private firms established in the 1990s during the transition period, accompanied by a more strategic approach to doing business;

---

6 Except for Poland, where improvements in innovation funding and support for Industry 4.0 competence creation were recognised.

– cooperation with large foreign customers who require new technological solutions, reinforced by the inflow of greenfield investment made in accordance with Industry 4.0 standards (Pl_2_1).

The response of the public sector should take into account the above-mentioned conditions in policy design, its institutional self-organisation, and human resources policy.

The first challenge is to pursue an industrial policy aimed to promote business activities that are knowledge-based and generate high added value. Such a strategy must be inherently long-term, since the current comparative advantages held by the v4 countries are exactly the opposite and involve competing with relatively low labour costs.

Second, the high quality of human capital, which necessitates the replacement of vanishing technical skills and the development of new digital competencies, will remain a crucial factor in maintaining the competitiveness of the v4 countries in the face of rising labour costs. Without the assistance of the business community, public administration is unlikely to be able to complete this task.

Third, given the need to disseminate digital solutions from both the supplier side and the standpoint of consumer demand reflected online, maintaining a reasonably high level of e-government in the v4 countries (IMD, 2021) will remain a challenge.

Fourth, public administration must address the anachronistic decentralisation of some of its functions, including the identification of competences needed by business on a local basis, and the aspects of public procurement that require highly qualified human resources. On the other hand, these skills can be improved in cooperation not so much with individual entrepreneurs as with the common representation of local business interests.

When looking for a common denominator among the deficits and challenges discussed in the spirit of varieties of capitalism, one may mention the need to create a knowledge-transmission level or institutional intermediaries between entrepreneurs and public administration. This knowledge includes the challenges faced by businesses, skills gaps that exist in the labour market, and potential remedies. In CME s, this is done by chambers of commerce and industry, which facilitate the planning of investment in new technical solutions by entering into long-term agreements with employees on behalf of firms.

The relevance of institutional analysis to the study of semi-peripheral countries may be a significant finding for the public sector. By emphasising it, the varieties of capitalism approach pioneered by Hall and Soskice and later expanded to include dependent market economies (Nölke and Vliegenthart,

2009) appears to convincingly explain the disparity in economic performance achieved by the Visegrád countries vs. the so-called Old Europe. Despite their considerable involvement in manufacturing activity and refusal to succumb to de-industrialisation, industrial salaries in the former are significantly smaller (cf. Astrov et al., 2019). Regardless of their considerable exports of high-tech goods, industrial value added remains much lower, which M. Srholec (2007) with reference to the Philippines calls the "statistical illusion" of dealing with a developed country. The focus on institutional disparities also implies that the quality of the public sector and state institutions may actually be the secret to technological catch-up, which so few countries have managed to unravel (cf. Hirschman, 1984; Amsden, 2001; Wade, 2012).

Bibliography

Abramowicz, B. (2009). *Dialog społeczny w Polsce – instytucjonalizacja i praktyka.* 0035–9629.

Altenburg, T., Hillebrand, W., and Meyer-Stamer, J. (1998). *Building systemic competitiveness: Concept and case studies from Mexico, Brazil, Paraguay, Korea and Thailand.* German Development Institute.

Amsden, A. H. (2001). *The rise of "the rest": Challenges to the west from late-industrialising economies.* Oxford University Press.

Astrov, V., Holzner, M., Leitner, S., Mara, I., Podkaminer, L., and Rezai, A. (2019). *Wage developments in the Central and Eastern European EU member states.* wiiw Research Report.

Atoyan, R. V., Christiansen, L. E., Dizioli, A., Ebeke, C. H., Ilahi, N., Ilyina, M. A., ... Rhee, M. A. P. (2016). *Emigration and its economic impact on Eastern Europe.* International Monetary Fund.

Augustyniak, B., Ebeke, C., Klein, N., and Zhao, H. (2013). German-Central European Supply Chain—Cluster Report—First Background Note—Trade Linkages. *IMF Multi-Country Report, 13,* 263.

Bair, J. (2005). Global capitalism and commodity chains: Looking back, going forward. *Competition and Change, 9*(2), 153–180. https://doi.org/10.1179/102452905X45382

Baldwin, R. (2012). Global supply chains: Why they emerged, why they matter, and where they are going CEPR Discussion Papers 9103. *Discussion Papers: CEPR.*

Baldwin, R. E. (1995). The eastern enlargement of the European Union. *European Economic Review, 39*(3–4), 474–481.

Baldwin, R. E. (2006). Globalisation: The great unbundling (s). *Economic Council of Finland.*

Baldwin, R., and Lopez-Gonzalez, J. (2015). Supply-chain trade: A portrait of global patterns and several testable hypotheses. *The World Economy, 38*(11), 1682–1721. http://dx.doi.org/10.1111/twec.12189

Berend, I., and Berend, T. I. (1996). *Central and Eastern Europe, 1944–1993: Detour from the periphery to the periphery* (Vol. 1). Cambridge University Press.

Bohle, D., and Greskovits, B. (2012). *Capitalist Diversity on Europe's Periphery.* Cornell University Press.

Bruszt, L., and Greskovits, B. (2009). Transnationalization, social integration, and capitalist diversity in the East and the South. *Studies in Comparative International Development, 44*(4), 411–434.

Bykova, A., Grieveson, R., Hanzl-Weiss, D., Hunya, G., Korpar, N., Podkaminer, L., ... Stöllinger, R. (2021). *Avoiding a Trap and Embracing the Megatrends: Proposals for a New Growth Model in EU-CEE.* wiiw.

Cardoso, F. H., and Faletto, E. (1979). Dependency and development in Latin America, trans. Marjory Mattingly Urquidi, *University of California Press,* 60.

Collier, P., and Venables, A. J. (2007). Rethinking trade preferences: How Africa can diversify its exports. *World Economy, 30*(8), 1326–1345.

Culpepper, P. (2001). Employers, public policy and the politics of decentralised co-operation in France and Germany. *Varieties of Capitalism: The Institutional Foundations of Comparative Advantage,* Edited by Peter Hall and David Soskice, 275–306.

Davies, N. (2014). *Europe: A history.* Random House.

de Tocqueville, A. (1866). *L'ancien régime et la révolution.* Michel Lévy.

Dedrick, J., Kraemer, K. L., and Linden, G. (2010). Who profits from innovation in global value chains?: A study of the iPod and notebook PCs. *Industrial and Corporate Change, 19*(1), 81–116.

Dicken, P. (2015). *Global shift.* Guilford Press.

Duvanova, D. (2013). *Building business in post-communist Russia, Eastern Europe, and Eurasia: Collective goods, selective incentives, and predatory states.* Cambridge University Press.

Ernst, D. (1998). Catching-up crisis and industrial upgrading: Evolutionary aspects of technological learning in Korea's electronics industry. *Asia Pacific Journal of Management, 15*(2), 247–283.

Estevez-Abe, M., Iversen, T., and Soskice, D. (2001). Social protection and the formation of skills: A reinterpretation of the welfare state. *Varieties of Capitalism: The Institutional Foundations of Comparative Advantage,* 145–183.

Evans, P. (1995). *Embedded Autonomy: States and Industrial Transformation.* Princeton University Press.

Evans, P., and Rauch, J. E. (1999). Bureaucracy and growth: A cross-national analysis of the effects of "Weberian" state structures on economic growth. *American Sociological Review,* 748–765.

Fagerberg, J., and Godinho, M. M. (2004). *Innovation and catching-up.* Georgia Institute of Technology, in: J. Fagerberg, D. C. Mowery, and R. R. Nelson (2004). *The Oxford handbook of innovation.* Oxford University Press, 514–543.

Fernandez-Stark, K., Bamber, P., and Gereffi, G. (2011). The offshore services value chain: Upgrading trajectories in developing countries. *International Journal of Technological Learning, Innovation and Development, 4*(1–3), 206–234.

Galgóczi, B., and Drahokoupil, J. (2017). *Condemned to be Left Behind?: Can Central and Eastern Europe Emerge from Its Low-wage Model?* ETUI aisbl.

Geodecki, T., and Grodzicki, M. J. (2015). Jak awansować w światowej lidze gospodarczej? Kraje Europy Środkowo-Wschodniej w globalnych łańcuchach wartości. *Public Governance/Zarządzanie Publiczne, 33*(3), 16–40. https://doi.org/10.15678/ZP.2015.33.3.02

Gereffi, G. (1999). International trade and industrial upgrading in the apparel commodity chain. *Journal of International Economics, 48*(1), 37–70.

Gereffi, G., Humphrey, J., and Sturgeon, T. (2005). The governance of global value chains. *Review of International Political Economy, 12*(1), 78–104. https://doi.org/10.1080/09692290500049805

Grodzicki, M. J., and Geodecki, T. (2016). New dimensions of core-periphery relations in an economically integrated Europe: The role of global value chains. *Eastern European Economics, 54*(5), 377–404.

Hall, P. A., and Soskice, D. (2001). *Varieties of Capitalism: The Institutional Foundations of Comparative Advantage.* Oxford University Press.

Hausner, J., Geodecki, T., Majchrowska, A., Marczewski, K., Piątkowski, M., Tchorek, G., Tomkiewicz, J. and Weresa, M. (2013). *Towards a Competitive Poland: How Can Poland Climb the World Economic League Table?* Economy and Public Administration Foundation.

Hirschman, A. O. (1984). A dissenter's confession: The strategy of economic development revisited. *Pioneers in Development, 1*(1), 85–111.

Hobday, M. (1995). East Asian latecomer firms: Learning the technology of electronics. *World Development, 23*(7), 1171–1193.

Hopkins, T. K. and Wallerstein, I. (1977). Patterns of development of the modern world-system. *Review (Fernand Braudel Center)*, 111–145.

IMD (2021), *IMD World Competitiveness Yearbook*, Institute for Management Development.

Jennings, G. R. (2005). 9 Interviewing: Techniques. *Tourism Research Methods*, 99.

Jones, R. W. and Kierzkowski, H. (2005). International fragmentation and the new economic geography. *The North American Journal of Economics and Finance, 16*(1), 1–10. https://doi.org/10.1016/j.najef.2004.11.005

Kaldor, N. (1966). *Causes of the slow rate of economic growth of the United Kingdom: An inaugural lecture.* Cambridge UP.

Klazar, S., Ochrana, F., Plaček, M. and Vacekova, G. (2020). The development and specific features of outsourcing, offshoring, and knowledge intensive business services in the Czech Republic: the case of Prague and Brno, In: Ł. Mamica (Ed.). *Outsourcing in European emerging economies: Territorial embeddedness and global business services* (pp. 114–128). Routledge.

Kohler-Koch, B., Quittkat, C. and Kurczewska, U. (2013). *Interest intermediation in the European Union revisited: Report on a survey study.* Working Paper 151. Mannheimer Zentrum für Europäische Sozialforschung (MZES).

Krpec, O. and Hodulák, V. (2019). The Czech economy as an integrated periphery: The case of dependency on Germany. *Journal of Post Keynesian Economics, 42*(1), 59–89.

Kubielas, S. (2009). *Innovation and technological gap in the global knowledge-based economy. Structural and macroeconomic conditions.* Uniwersytet Warszawski, Wydział Nauk Ekonomicznych.

Layard, R., Mayhew, K. and Owen, G. (Eds.) (1994). *Britain's Training Deficit*, Ashgate Publishing Limited.

Lin, J. and Chang, H. J. (2009). Should Industrial Policy in developing countries conform to comparative advantage or defy it? A debate between Justin Lin and Ha-Joon Chang. *Development policy review, 27*(5), 483–502.

Low, P. and Tijaja, J. (2014). Effective industrial policies and global value chains. In: *A World Trade Organization for the 21st Century*. Edward Elgar Publishing.

Markusen, J. R. (2005). *Modeling the offshoring of white-collar services: From comparative advantage to the new theories of trade and FDI.* National Bureau of Economic Research Cambridge.

Mayntz, R. (1991). *Modernization and the Logic of Interorganizational Networks*, Max-Planck-Institut für Gesellschaftsforschung.

Meijer, A. and Bolívar, M. P. R. (2016). Governing the smart city: A review of the literature on smart urban governance. *Revue Internationale Des Sciences Administratives, 82*(2), 417–435.

Milberg, W. and Winkler, D. (2013). *Outsourcing economics: Global value chains in capitalist development.* Cambridge University Press.

Mudambi, R. (2008). Location, control and innovation in knowledge-intensive industries. *Journal of Economic Geography, 8*(5), 699–725.

Münich D., Srholec M., Moritz M. and Schäffler J. (2014). Mothers and Daughters: Heterogeneity of German Direct Investments in the Czech Republic. *Prague Economic Papers, 1*, 42–62.

Naczyk, M. (2021). Taking back control: Comprador bankers and managerial developmentalism in Poland. *Review of International Political Economy*, 1–25.

Nölke, A. and Vliegenthart, A. (2009). Enlarging the varieties of capitalism: The emergence of dependent market economies in East Central Europe. *World Politics, 61*, 670–702.

OECD. (2013). *Interconnected economies: Benefiting from global value chains*. OECD Publishing.

Ost, D. (2000). Illusory Tripartism in Eastern Europe: Neoliberal Tripartism and Post-communist Class Identities. *Politics and Society, 28*(4) reprinted in 2010 by Szkoła Główna Handlowa, *Warsaw Forum of Economic Sociology, 1*(2), 91–122.

Pavlínek, P. (2017). *Dependent growth: Foreign investment and the development of the automotive industry in East-Central Europe*. Springer.

Pietrobelli, C. and Rabellotti, R. (2011). Global value chains meet innovation systems: Are there learning opportunities for developing countries? *World Development, 39*(7), 1261–1269.

Polska, S. I. (2019). *Smart Industry Polska Raport z badań*. Ministry of Development/Siemens Sp. z o.o.

Porter, M. E. (1985). *The Competitive advantage: Creating and Sustaining Superior Performance*. Free Press.

Porter, M.E. (1990). *The Competitive Advantage of Nations*, Free Press.

Prebisch, R. (1950). *The Economic Development of Latin America and Its Principal Problems*. United Nations Department of Economic Affairs, Economic Commission for Latin America (ECLA). Retrieved from http://archivo.cepal.org/pdfs/cdPrebisch/002.pdf

Rodrik, D. (2016). Premature deindustrialisation. *Journal of Economic Growth, 21*(1), 1–33.

Schröder, J. (2020). *Decoupling of labour productivity growth from median wage growth in Central and Eastern Europe* (No. 448). wiiw Research Report.

Schwab, K. (2016). *The fourth industrial revolution*. Currency.

Selltiz, C., Jahoda, M., Deutsch, M., and Cook, S. W. (1967). Research Methods in Social Relations (Revised). Holt, Rinehart and Winston.

Srholec, M. (2007). High-tech exports from developing countries: A symptom of technology spurts or statistical illusion? *Review of World Economics, 143*(2), 227–255.

Stehrer, R. and Wörz, J. (2001). *Technological Convergence and Trade Patterns*, The Vienna Institute for International Economic Studies (WIIW). WIIW Working Papers.

Stehrer, R. and Stöllinger, R. (2015). *The Central European Manufacturing Core: What is Driving Regional Production Sharing?* FIW Research Reports.

Stephan, J. (2013). *The technological role of inward foreign direct investment in Central East Europe*. Springer.

Stöllinger, R. (2021). Testing the smile curve: Functional specialisation and value creation in GVCs. *Structural Change and Economic Dynamics, 56*, 93–116.

Streeck, W., and Schmitter, P. C. (1985). Community, market, state-and associations? The prospective contribution of interest governance to social order. *European Sociological Review, 1*(2), 119–138.

Tate, J. (2001). *National varieties of standardization*. In: Hall, P. A., and Soskice, D. *Varieties of Capitalism: The Institutional Foundations of Comparative Advantage*. Oxford University Press, 442–473.

Thorhallsson, B. and Kattel, R. (2013). Neo-liberal small states and economic crisis: lessons for democratic corporatism. *Journal of Baltic studies*, *44*(1), 83–103.

Veloso, F. M. (2006). Understanding local content decisions: Economic analysis and an application to the automotive industry. *Journal of Regional Science*, *46*(4), 747–772.

Wade, R. H. (2012). Return of industrial policy? *International Review of Applied Economics*, *26*(2), 223–239.

Wallerstein, I. (1974). *The modern world-system: Capitalist agriculture and the origins of the European world-economy in the sixteenth century* (Vol. 27). Academic Press.

Wallerstein, I. (2004). *World-systems analysis: An introduction*. Duke University Press.

Weber, M. (2019). *Economy and society: A new translation*. Harvard University Press.

Wübbeke, J., Meissner, M., Zenglein, M. J., Ives, J. and Conrad, B. (2016). Made in China 2025. *Mercator Institute for China Studies. Papers on China*, *2*, 74.

Wykrętowicz, S. (2013). *Funkcjonowanie samorządu gospodarczego w wybranych krajach europejskich*, Opinie i Ekspertyzy / Kancelaria Senatu. Biuro Analiz i Dokumentacji.

CHAPTER 5

Models for Managing State Relationships with Stakeholders in the Visegrád Countries

Andrzej Kozina

1 Introduction

The purpose of this chapter is to discuss the author's framework for managing inter-organisational relations at the level of central administration, or more precisely, in the system of state governance, in comparative terms for the four Visegrád countries (V4) in the context of the Fourth Industrial Revolution (4IR). To that end, both the theoretical model of managing these relationships and the actual solutions in this field implemented in the V4 countries will be discussed, justifying the use of the word 'models' in the title of this chapter.

Effective operation of the state, including the coordination of activities of individual actors (interest groups) working within and around the central administration, such as the government and individual departments, depends on how well the process is managed by state institutions responsible for its implementation, and in particular, for their identification, formation, and maintenance.

The chapter starts with an outline of the research framework. The author's original multidimensional model of managing the relationships in question is discussed, including the objectives, scope, resources, structures, processes, and supporting tools that serve as the key theoretical and methodological foundation for the discussion that follows. Selected parts of stakeholder theory and – to a lesser extent – inter-organisational relations theory and the contractual approach are also used as research tools.

In the next section, two categories of critical importance to the topic at hand are explained. To begin, stakeholders (interest groups) are defined as parties to a relationship, i.e. actors both inside and outside the government who are critical to the effective operation of the state. Second, an analysis of stakeholder interactions in terms of their distinctive characteristics is presented.

A more detailed explanation of these relationships follows. The stakeholders in question are classified based on two critical features of their interactions, namely the degree of interest in the operation of the state and the extent to which they influence its governance process.

The next section focuses on preserving and shaping the relationships of interest. It begins by outlining the core concepts of managing stakeholder interactions within the state governance framework. Drawing on these concepts, specific instructions for managing relationships with diverse stakeholder groups are offered and subsequently framed as individual management models for the relationships in question.

As part of empirical research, selected aspects of the proposed relationship management model have been validated taking into consideration the specific features of the Visegrád countries along the five dimensions listed below:

1. The most important stakeholders of the state viewed as representatives of their respective groups.
2. Characteristics of typical stakeholders as representatives of their respective groups.
3. The content and scope of relationships between the state and these groups.
4. The key principles of forming and maintaining these relationships by the state.
5. The main methods (ways) in which the state should manage these relationships.

The data were collected from interviews based on a questionnaire containing five questions directly related to the aforementioned topics. The four Visegrád countries were represented by individuals with extensive expertise in the areas under consideration owing to their positions and duties (not limited to the administrative sector; cf. Table 5.1). Supplementary tools included additional interviews to clarify interpretational problems, legislation analysis, case studies, and discussions led by the research team.

Findings from the empirical study are summarised in subsections. In each case, the contributions of country experts were viewed as supplementary; for this reason, the viewpoints and opposing perspectives were combined. Where considerable differences of opinion among the experts occurred, extra clarification was provided.

The Summary contains an overview of the discussion, including an evaluation of the proposed concept and recommendations for future research.

2   Conceptualisation of Managing the State's Relationships With Its Stakeholders

Managing an organisation's relationships with its stakeholders is one of the emerging topics of focus in contemporary management theory and practice.

TABLE 5.1   Respondents in the study of state–stakeholder relationships in the V4 countries

V4 country	Respondents
Poland	Deputy director of a department of a key ministry. University professor specialising in public management/governance. Former mayor of a medium-sized city, experienced local government official, community activist, and academic. Secretary of a medium-sized urban municipality.
Hungary	Former analyst at the Centre for Euro-Atlantic Integration and Democracy, currently financial analyst. Research fellow at a private economic research institute. Former Member of Parliament, now businessman with interests in media and health care.
Czech Republic	Member of the Southern Moravian Regional Council responsible for science, research and innovation. Director of the Employment Division of the Public Employment Service for Southern Moravia. President of the Czech Chamber of Commerce for Southern Moravia. Director, Secondary Vocational School of Graphics.
Slovakia	Former State Secretary, Ministry of Labour. Junior analyst, Slovak Business Agency. Vice-Dean for Development and Digitalisation, Faculty of Economics, Matej Bel University.

SOURCE: OWN STUDY

A growing number of works on this subject are being published, to mention only Bourne (2009), Cox et al. (2004), Lindgreen (2008), and *Managing Relationships...* (2003). The first and, it appears, finest monograph on the topic under examination, by R. Tyszkiewicz (2017), which covers all the most essential theoretical and methodological issues, is worth recommending, as are the following studies: Koźmiński and Latusek-Jurczak (2014), Piwoni-Krzeszowska (2014), and Kozina (2015).

The issues under discussion have become even more relevant in the context of the global 4IR (Schwab, 2018; Frey, 2019), which fundamentally alters the nature and implementation of fundamental processes, both at the micro level, i.e. in relation to individual organisations, and the macro one, i.e. in the state governance system (Kozłowski and Zygmuntowski, 2017). This also applies to managing stakeholder relationships – a process of interest to us, as it dramatically affects the nature, content and form of these relations due to the rapid development of information technology, particularly the availability and capacity to process large data sets (Mayer-Schonberger and Cukier, 2014; Stephenson, 2020).

A review of the current literature on the interactions between the state and its stakeholders, particularly in the context of managing them, reveals a scarcity of studies that thoroughly and consistently investigate the subject at hand. Methodology-oriented works, in particular, which provide useful tools for researching and shaping the relations in question are few and far between. Some are unoriginal in nature and merely analyse the issue indirectly: in general terms from the perspective of the state as a party to them (Yamak and Suer, 2005); in terms of centralised e-government information systems (Chan, Pan and Tan, 2003); in political and ethical terms (Olsen, 2017); in relation to local administration (Gomes 2004); and finally, in a broader context of the public sector (Hawrysz and Maj, 2017; Kotas, 2012). What is clear, however, is the absence of a thorough understanding of managing state–stakeholder relations. It is thus challenging to find an adequate and clear understanding of the concept of relationship management in light of other concerns. This challenge is made even more difficult in the field of public administration, notably the state governance process. This study aims to at least partially close this theoretical and methodological gap.

In this context, an attempt can be made to develop a special multidimensional model based on an interpretation of the management system proposed by A. Stabryła (1984, pp. 9–13). It considers all of the essential components of this type of system, allowing for a thorough and clear explanation of its special features. The relevant components of the concept were modified for the area at issue, with appropriate dimensions assigned, certain features expanded, and new ones added. In doing so, a different, most commonly cited taxonomy of managerial functions and the breadth of actions performed within their framework was adopted (*Leksykon zarządzania*, 2004, pp. 139–140). As a result, a general model of managing the state–stakeholder relationships was produced (see Table 5.2 for summary).

For the purposes of this discussion, managing relationships in the state governance system can be viewed as a specialised topic of public management/governance theory and practice construed in terms of a model. All of the most important dimensions describing the management system in general can be referred to in order to define its scope, as well as made more specific in order to deal with problems in the field of establishing and shaping relationships with state stakeholders, which require identification and resolution in the realm of public governance.

TABLE 5.2 General model for managing relationships in the state governance system

Aspect	Interpretation
OBJECTIVES (purpose)	The overall (general) objective is to influence stakeholder relationships in such a way that they contribute as much as possible to achieving the required level of efficiency in the operation of the state. In order to achieve this objective, the following two secondary goals must be met: 1. To establish, maintain, strengthen etc. relationships that have a positive impact on the efficiency of the state's functioning, 2. To discontinue, change, weaken etc. relationships that have a negative effect on the above. These secondary goals are affected by the characteristics of the areas of state activity, where it enters into specific relationships with stakeholders or their groups, such as trade unions (to form collective labour relations), or employers (to lay down the conditions for doing business), etc.
SCOPE (substance)	Specific issues addressed as part of the relationships in question and their unique characteristics (scope, intensity, permanence, etc.) are determined by the needs (requirements) of the specific processes, tasks, projects, transactions, where these relations occur, as well as the requirements and expectations of the parties to these relations, i.e. the government and other stakeholders (e.g. creating and verifying budgets with and between ministers, negotiating with the central bank the terms and conditions for a loan including the interest rates), etc.
RESOURCES (subject and object)	*Human resources* (critical) – organisational units in the government responsible for managing relationships and representing it vis-à-vis stakeholders, with a certain range of competencies and potential of knowledge, abilities and skills, including *executive units* – responsible for carrying out these functions and *managerial units* – tasked with supervising them. *Ancillary resources* – created and/or utilised in the performance of the functions under consideration, including *information resources* – databases and knowledge; *financial resources* – expenditure necessary to discharge the responsibilities; *technical resources* – hardware and software, networks and data storage media; and *tangible (physical) resources* – other equipment, materials, time and space.
SYSTEM STRUCTURE (static)	A type of structure in the state management system that determines the scope of action, the objectives and tasks of the various units in terms of managing relationships, such as employment. or industrial policy. Moreover, the structure determines the links between these units, especially the rules of interaction and coordination mechanisms, the form and manner in which these tasks are supervised and the extent to which they are formalised. The tasks in question are in a sense 'inscribed' or embedded in the organisational structure of a cabinet. Their efficient implementation is facilitated by the use of contemporary auxiliary types of structures: networks, processes, and virtual entities.

TABLE 5.2   General model for managing relationships in the state governance system (*cont.*)

Aspect	Interpretation
EXECUTIVE PROCESSES (dynamic – functional)	Managing relationships assists executive processes, including the main ones, i.e. those implemented to meet the requirements of external recipients, and supporting ones to meet the needs of internal units. It is difficult to capture the relationship management process in the strict sense, as the individual tasks carried out within its framework are dispersed amongst the organisation as links in the chain of individual executive processes. At best, they can be described as sub-processes of more extensive activities concerning relationship management, e.g. running social campaigns or the implementation of complex projects, especially EU-funded ones, in cooperation with numerous external institutions.
MANAGEMENT PROCESS (dynamic – functional)	Planning – gathering and analysing data on the current situation of the state and its stakeholders, anticipating changes in this regard, identifying relevant (existing and new) stakeholders and defining the nature and scope of the necessary relationships with them, formulating objectives for managing these relations, specifying activities, allocating the resources required to achieve these objectives, and devising rules to monitor and control their implementation.

Organising – analysing the needs and capacities, particularly the competencies required to meet the stakeholder relationship management objectives; defining and allocating activities relevant to these objectives to people and teams; and providing appropriate guidelines. Giving people/ teams the authority they need to perform these duties and ensuring accountability for their completion. Providing resources to individuals and teams to perform tasks and coordinate relationship management activities.

Leading – establishing an appropriate working environment for subordinate teams and ensuring that they are fully committed to relationship management responsibilities by providing them with the necessary information, explaining, instructing, and training; motivating them with tangible and intangible incentives appropriate to the tasks at hand; identifying and overcoming any difficulties in their performance.

Supervision – establishing the necessary standards for achieving relations management goals and objectives; detecting and explaining potential deviations from these standards, and taking appropriate remedial action. |
| AUXILIARY METHODS (dynamic – instrumental) | Various detailed yet typical tools, such as models, principles, methods, techniques, etc. used to implement specific relations management activities, especially standard data collection techniques such as interviews, surveys and questionnaires, strategic analysis methods, especially stakeholder analysis, PEST, SWOT and scenario methods, strategic balance sheet, etc., process analysis and improvement tools, information management and communication systems, negotiations and mediation, etc. |

SOURCE: OWN STUDY BASED ON (STABRYŁA, 1984, PP. 9–13)

3   The Concept and Types of State Stakeholders

The generic term 'stakeholder' (or interest group) has two distinct interpretations in the literature (Freeman and Reed, 1983):

1.   A broader one, in which it denotes anyone who can influence an organisation, or is influenced by it, is in any way involved in its interests or makes any demands on it. They are thus "groups or individuals who can influence or are influenced by the organisation" (Freeman, 1984, p. 21), who are "directly or indirectly interested in the activities of the organisation in its efforts to achieve its objectives" (Stoner, Freeman and Gilbert, 1997, p. 80). In the area under consideration, these are all kinds of entities that expect benefits, advantages, etc. from the state.

2.   A narrower one, which assumes that it is impossible to meet the expectations of all the stakeholders, hence the focus should be on achieving the objectives of a limited group that has an actual impact on its actions and expect benefits from it. "Diverse interest groups have varying opportunities to influence the organisation, thus they can both pose a serious threat and be of little consequence to it. This is why more recent definitions of interest groups emphasise the prospect of exerting pressure on an organisation as well as making demands on it" (*Leksykon zarządzania*, 2004, pp. 151–152). According to K. Obłój (2007, p. 217), these groups "meet two conditions: first, they have a 'stake' in the organisation's operations, its decisions and their effects; and second, they are capable of exerting effective pressure on it." For example, governments tend to satisfy the material needs of large social groups with high leverage (electoral potential) and ignore the demands of small groups with limited impact in this respect.

Stakeholders are usually divided into two groups:

1.   Internal ones (in the state governance system): legislative and judicial institutions, ministries (departments), government agencies, local government units, managers and employees of these institutions, etc.;

2.   External ones (in the environment of such a system): the media, non-governmental organisations, especially educational and social institutions, formal (organised) and informal social groups, especially employers' and employees' organisations (trade unions), individual citizens, experts and advisors, various pressure and opinion groups, etc.

Further considerations require a more thorough characterisation of the state's stakeholders in order to determine the most significant activities required to appropriately manage relationships with them. Putting aside the complex stakeholder analysis techniques outlined in the extensive literature (e.g. Lisiński, 2004, pp. 80–88; Obłój, 2007, pp. 217ff.), it makes sense to apply two detailed stakeholder identification tools, i.e. the matrix developed by M. Johnson and K. Scholes (1999, p. 216) and C. Eden and F. Ackermann (1998, pp. 121–125, 344–346). The two variables adopted for the description of the stakeholders in question, namely the degree of their interest in the operation of the state and the strength of their influence, were the main principles on which these matrices were originally built. The treatment of the various stakeholder types proposed by the cited authors was also taken into consideration. Given the unique characteristics of the state governance system and its stakeholders, their recommendations and the designations of the different categories of interest groups were amended. The resulting new matrices are presented in Table 5.3 and 5.4.

Special consideration should be given to a certain group of state stakeholders in the context of the global 4IR: dynamic and expansive corporations, particularly multinational ones that create and implement increasingly complex IT solutions. Their impact on the structure and operation of governmental institutions is growing at an unprecedentedly rapid rate. On the one hand, by creating and deploying ever-more complex communication and information management systems, such enterprises have a favourable impact on the state governance structure, particularly its relationships with stakeholders. However, since they enjoy virtually unfettered and direct access to all forms of data in real time, including sensitive information, the influence of IT businesses in this field can be unfavourable and even dangerous, jeopardising the privacy of government entities. Therefore, the latter must work to counteract the increasing power of these corporations, keep their influence in check, effectively

TABLE 5.3   The power of influence/stakeholder interest matrix

Power of influence on state actions	High	Demanding (entitled)	Cooperating (partners)
	Low	Unknown (anonymous)	Interested (observers)
		Low	High
		Level of interest in state actions	

SOURCE: OWN STUDY BASED ON JOHNSON AND SCHOLES (1999, P. 216); EDEN AND ACKERMANN (1998, PP. 121–125, 344–346)

TABLE 5.4   Characteristics of types of state stakeholders

Type	Description
Cooperating (partners)	Very interested in the situation in the state and very influential, especially in the legislature and the judiciary, e.g. political parties represented in parliament.
Demanding (entitled)	Not interested in the situation of the state, but very influential, e.g. local government, influential media, effective and powerful pressure groups.
Interested (observers)	Very interested in the situation in the state, but with little influence on it, e.g. labour offices, charitable institutions, NGOs, political parties outside parliament, businesses, etc.
Unknown (anonymous)	Not interested in the situation of the state and with very little influence on it, e.g. small and weak social groups.

SOURCE: OWN STUDY

'tame' them, but especially guarantee effective data protection. Maintaining the state's key position in the stakeholder management system is not a simple undertaking, though, as it demands the creation and deployment of information systems that become more complex over time, must be continually enhanced, and as a result, the human resource competencies associated with them must be constantly upgraded.

The characteristics of stakeholders in the governance systems used in the Visegrád countries were developed taking into account the four types of stakeholders identified above (Table 5.5) and their characteristics (Table 5.6).

As the description above demonstrates, there is a range of similarities and differences in terms of how the roles of individual stakeholders are perceived in each country and, consequently, how they fit into respective groups. For example, non-governmental organisations in three countries are considered as demanding stakeholders, but in Slovakia some of them are classified as unknown (Sk_4_4). The role of trade unions is also perceived differently. In each country, the importance of the business sphere – both large companies and industrial and commercial organisations – is emphasised, although in Hungary, global corporations are given priority with the SME sector playing a marginal role (Hu_4_4). Only in Slovakia was the important position of EU institutions highlighted (Sk_4_4), in Poland – the media and church institutions (Pl_4_3), whereas in the Czech Republic – the army, although the labelling of the latter stakeholder group as unknown is questionable (Cz_4_3). Conversely,

TABLE 5.5   Types of stakeholders in the V4 countries

Stakeholders/ Country	Poland	Hungary	Czech Republic	Slovakia
Cooperating	Political parties in power (politicians). Business – financial elites, chambers of commerce, banks, investors. The media. Local government.	Friends of key government politicians. Strategically important global companies representing e.g. the oil and automotive sectors. Chambers of industry and commerce.	Government and its agencies. Chambers of industry and commerce. Labour offices. Educational institutions.	Professional and employers' organisations. European Union institutions. Trade unions.
Demanding	Entities with vested interests favouring the government, e.g. trade unions or business organisations. Public sector (reasonably well-organised, striking). Catholic Church. Voters.	Overly politicised business, not limited to large global companies, such as Google or Facebook.	Trade unions.	Ministries and public agencies. Regulatory institutions. Regional governments. Universities and schools.
Interested	Opposition political parties and social organisations that support them. Intellectual elites. Officials. NGOS – through member involvement, appeals, protests, etc.	Large companies influenced by cooperation between the government and oligarchs. NGOS. Trade unions. Advocacy groups.	NGOS. Social movements.	SME sector. Slovak Academy of Sciences. Business organisations outside the tripartite commission.

TABLE 5.5   Types of stakeholders in the v4 countries (*cont.*)

Stakeholders/ Country	Poland	Hungary	Czech Republic	Slovakia
Unknown	Professional groups without strategic significance for the state (budget sphere). People who are economically, socially excluded or discouraged from participating in public life, e.g. the poorly educated, unemployed, unorganised peasants and workers, often young people.	SME sector.	The military. General public.	Marginal areas of the public sector. NGOs providing civic assistance and social services.

SOURCE: OWN STUDY

this very group was aptly characterised by Polish and Slovak respondents who noted its marginal importance to the state.

A number of inconsistencies in recognising the state's primary stakeholder groups were noted in Hungary, where corruption is allegedly the worst in the European Union. Stakeholders simply cannot afford to be uninterested in the state or the current political situation if they want access to politicians and have their demands met, or to win the backing of oligarchs who control huge enterprises and have a monopoly on public procurement and government contracts (Hu_4_4).

The characteristics of both individual and group stakeholders are relevant to their role discussed previously from the perspective of the needs of all the countries considered. As a result, both similarities and differences exhibit a range of specific features. For example, in the Czech Republic, they fall on a continuum from the autocratic nature of cooperating stakeholders to the

TABLE 5.6   Characteristics of stakeholders in the V4 countries

Stakeholders/ Country	Poland	Hungary	Czech Republic	Slovakia
Cooperating	Self-interest, sometimes serving the public good. Not always legitimate financial links. Parties represented in parliament, able to form government. Local government dependent on the party in power. Business – limited trust in the authorities and expectations of a friendly investment climate. Media by virtue of their function.	Have exclusive access to government politicians or reach out to a number of influential people working in institutions that are in good standing with the government.	Authoritarianism. Lack of competence.	Significant economic or institutional power. Embedded in formal structures capable of effectively influencing processes.
Demanding	Organisations representing a significant proportion of a given environment or a significant share of the market. Expect their demands to be met as best and quickly as possible, e.g. trade unions, business, the church (concessions, waivers, grants, etc.).	Global technology companies with government relations offices but no direct access to politicians.	All effort focused on employees. Influence on employment policy and wages.	These actors tend to be gatekeepers who face the challenge of change that could undermine them.

TABLE 5.6   Characteristics of stakeholders in the v4 countries (*cont.*)

Stakeholders/ Country	Poland	Hungary	Czech Republic	Slovakia
Interested	Parties unable to form a government, whether represented in parliament or not. Social organisations contesting the actions of authorities. Middle class attaches importance to peace, family and quality of life. NGOs with little influence on the state.	Individuals and groups who want to influence the functioning of the state but cannot.	Action by leaders in different areas of interest.	Actors usually defined by their business approach or innovative nature or by their long-standing outsider status.
Unknown	Groups with a sense of being ignored by government, focused only on getting things done. Individuals not aligned with organisations, do not participate in elections, do not manifest their views.	Usually high-ranking executives who form interest groups or are active in chambers of industry.	Inactivity, apathy.	They can, at best, act as mediators, trying to take into account various needs and help to improve government operations.

SOURCE: OWN STUDY

passivity of the unknown ones (Cz_4_4). Individual interest groups' characteristics in Slovakia, and to a lesser extent in Hungary, reflect their potential influence on the functioning of the state. When identifying other stakeholder groups, Polish respondents emphasised their demands and expectations from the state.

Certain pathological phenomena were noted again in Hungary, where key stakeholders in the state do not conduct their activities transparently, very little information reaches the public, most transactions are concluded behind closed doors, and ordinary citizens can only accept decisions made without prior consultation (Hu_4_4). Similar concerns were cited by Polish respondents, who emphasised the importance of efficient self-advertising, the capacity to draw attention and persuade, and ambiguous financial arrangements in meeting their vested interests (Pl_4_2). In the Czech Republic, irregularities in the state's dealings with key stakeholders have also been mentioned (Cz_4_4).

In Poland, demanding stakeholders (or groups with a large membership) act on the principle of 'we are stronger as a group' (often at the behest of politicians), limit competition, and tend to advocate for the current employees. On the other hand, they have been able to bring about a number of positive changes – quite often, they successfully resolve pressing issues with a broad impact on society at large (Pl_4_2). On the other hand, in the case of the middle class as one of the stakeholders, a growing aversion to politics was noted due to the need to toe the party line in public. Hence, even though this class has little impact on the state, it may become much stronger one if the intellectual elites start to publicise their views or communicate their position more strongly to the authorities, including the media (Pl_4_2). In democracies, NGOs often play an important role, however their impact on Polish politics is frequently insufficient. Despite the fact that they relieve the state of a lot of responsibilities in times of crisis, they are typically underappreciated (Pl_4_3). Although the majority of unknown stakeholders are people who need to be led rather than are capable of leading themselves, they are often viewed as a mass with the capacity to change everything unless they achieve a decent standard of living and are likely to become even more demanding (Pl_4_2).

4   Characteristics of the Relationships Between the State and Its Stakeholders

When discussing the interpretations of the concept of organisational relationships in the state governance system, i.e. between the state and its stakeholders, it makes sense to start with general definitions of the term relationship as "an association between objects, concepts, quantities, etc.," "the way in which two or more people or things are connected, or the state of being connected" (*Słownik języka...*, 2019).

We shall thus assume that organisational relations between stakeholders in the state governance system includes all kinds of links, associations, dependencies, contacts, interactions etc. that occur between all kinds of entities, institutions, groups that comprise, on the one hand, the subsystems of this system and, on the other, the components of its immediate and distant environment.[1]

The relationships in question rely mainly on the co-creation of tangible and intangible values by the parties involved in them. They include model solutions for jointly implemented processes and activities, founded on recognised and shared social standards as well as a state management philosophy focused on the formation of partnership relations among the key interest groups. This promotes the growth of relational capital (both internal and external) as well as promotes the positive image of a government demonstrating concern for citizens' problems and their well-being. Shared values represent the synergistic effect of engagement in a variety of interactions. This interpretation should be supplemented by a list of the most significant aspects of these interactions, namely the degree of unpredictability, nature, and impact on the state's efficiency.

First and foremost, they are characterised by their number and diversity, which depend on the perceived number and types of stakeholders, as well as their interests, expectations, demands, etc. articulated to the state.

It should also be noted that these relationships have both static (relationships, associations, etc.) and dynamic properties (interactions, contacts, etc.). The fact that they evolve dynamically, nonetheless, allows them to be categorised according to how much changeability or stability they exhibit. They must therefore be continuously observed, and steps must be taken to bring about the desired level of change. As a result, they are frequently difficult to identify, let alone influence.

The nature of the interactions under discussion is another critical aspect. They can be formal, or purposefully shaped, mostly through legal restrictions, or informal, arising naturally, ad hoc, etc. and independently of the current legal system, occasionally as informal connections or agreements. Naturally, the former are the main focus of our interest. The latter may significantly affect the former, although they are difficult to capture and identify.

---

1 A broader discussion of the concept of organisational relationships can be found e.g. in Tyszkiewicz (2017, pp. 37–65).

Moreover, both types of relationships can have a positive, negative or neutral impact on how efficiently the state works. It should be emphasised that relationships within the state governance system and with its environment should generally be positive, particularly with the internal and key external stakeholders due to their function and importance, however, this is not always the case.

The relationships under consideration are in practice complex and multifaceted, i.e. they involve a range of substantive and formal issues, and may be symmetrical or asymmetrical, stronger or weaker, incidental or permanent, etc.

A general overview of the relationships between the state and its stakeholder groups identified above is presented in Table 5.7.

The relationships under discussion are subject to change due to 4IR, particularly the dynamic development of IT. They occur in virtual space far more frequently than in the conventional form, which particularly applies to face-to-face contacts or those involving the traditional media. In fact, they tend to occur digitally, via the Internet, using governmental institution portals, or even social networks, particularly in exchanging evaluations, opinions, or remarks by citizens and their groups. Sometimes these interactions are anonymous

TABLE 5.7   Characteristics of stakeholder relationships in the state governance system

Stakeholder type	Description
Cooperating (partners)	Work closely together across a wide range of issues based on mutual trust, maintain or even strengthen positive relationships with key partners both strategically and operationally, and strive to improve cooperation.
Demanding (entitled)	Maintain satisfaction, give satisfaction through the necessary benefits, encourage favourable exchanges, negotiate their conditions and even cooperation, exploit their strengths, but give in to pressure in extremely difficult situations (non-equivalent exchange).
Interested (observers)	Identify and analyse information needs and communicate on an ongoing basis to the extent necessary, provide reliable, credible, complete, etc. data, and project a positive image to encourage possible cooperation.
Unknown (anonymous)	Involved to a limited extent, minimal effort, but at the same time are carefully monitor and analyse the environment for possibilities to attract potential yet hitherto unidentified partners for cooperation.

SOURCE: OWN STUDY

rather than personalised. The recent pandemic has only made these characteristics more pronounced.

The state–stakeholder relations in the Visegrád countries' governance systems are discussed below using the four-stakeholder model summarised above. Their contents and scope are outlined in Table 5.8.

The respondents share perspectives on some matters and sharply differ on others, with the latter clearly prevailing, as was previously noted with regard to stakeholders and their characteristics. For instance, Polish respondents

TABLE 5.8   Relationships between the state and its stakeholder groups in the v4 countries

Stakeholder\ Country	Poland	Hungary	Czech Republic	Slovakia
Cooperating	Executing the political agenda, developing the state's architecture, and selecting the course of action for state institutions. Relationships with local governments are affected by the economic cycle. The fiscal dimension, mutual investment aims, and values all play important roles in commercial relations.	Usually consulted by government when taking decisions on policy issues, particularly economic ones.	Employment, education policy, budgeting.	Representatives of these groups usually have strong formalised links with the executive that allow them to communicate their needs and preferences to decision-makers.
Demanding	Maintaining a favourable social and economic climate in interactions with state authorities (government). State economic policies include: taxation, anti-inflationary measures, concessions, waivers, etc., church fund.	Public policies affect them, but they are not expected to participate in the creation of state rules.	Working conditions.	Usually linked to power and personal control in the management of an institution. May replicate political power relations.

TABLE 5.8   Relationships between the state and its stakeholder groups in the V4 countries (*cont.*)

Stakeholder\ Country	Poland	Hungary	Czech Republic	Slovakia
Interested	Reviewing or contesting the activities of state authorities (government). Opinion-forming, expert relations between the state and this group.	Policies usually have a detrimental impact on them because they are purposefully implemented in this way or other groups are given preferential treatment.	Mainly environmental issues.	Must rely on personal and informal relationships with decision-makers to influence decisions.
Unknown	No interactions are intended to influence state authorities. Marginalisation of these groups determines their lack of interest in the state; at most, they insist on being appreciated from time to time.	Subject to the impact of rules and regulations, but do not want it to be the case; they simply want to survive.	None.	These groups are usually outside observers.

SOURCE: OWN STUDY

acknowledge that each stakeholder group and the state have different tasks and expectations. Hungarian respondents, on the other hand, tend to focus on the influence of the state on the positions of these groups (Hu_4_4), Czech respondents – on the areas in which these relationships occur (Cz_4_4), whereas in Slovakia, their context tends to be paramount (Sk_4_4).

In Poland, the relationships between the state and its cooperating stakeholders involve mainly the lobbying of politicians by financial and economic elites (Pl_4_2).

A strong middle class acts as a powerful deterrent to oligopolies. With a free press and universal suffrage, these organisations might be replaced if they become overly commercialised (Pl_4_2). Furthermore, too many policies impose obligations and burdens on both local governments and businesses (Pl_4_3). Demanding stakeholders are particularly active in their interactions with state authorities in order to improve their position; this is what they are primarily interested in. They can, however, accomplish a lot of good, and their leaders frequently shift to the first group of stakeholders (Pl_4_2). Furthermore, the Polish state does not place sufficient emphasis on relationships with third-party interest groups. (Pl_4_3). Finally, unknown stakeholders 'vote' with their dissatisfaction, but they frequently require guidance and leadership; for this reason, they tend to be easily exploited by politicians and financial elites. They are often characterised by low influence and passivity, sometimes by tax avoidance and, unless directed otherwise, remain inactive in elections (Pl_4_2). As a result, Polish respondents once again mention a range of phenomena that are far removed from the desirable model of interactions between the state and its stakeholders.

A similar situation persists in Hungary, where the first stakeholder group receives preferential treatment over others due to its privileged position. This is because its members are needed by the state to further its present political and economic interests. Nowadays, the Hungarian state is nearly synonymous with the government; therefore state bodies are essentially tools of the latter, which makes strictly professional dealings with stakeholders nearly impossible. (Hu_4_4).

It should be emphasised that the state should take a proactive and positive stance in managing its relationships with stakeholders, promote cooperation, be receptive to their demands, and even engage them in partnerships. This applies even to those who, at a given moment, appear to be less important, but who could potentially become critical partners, provided that they accept the principles of state operation and engage in the process of co-creating values considered as important for society. The state is able to offer a lot to its stakeholders, but, at the same time, expects a lot from them.

5   General Principles for Managing the State's Relationships with Its Stakeholders

The synthetic description of stakeholders and the steps required to effectively manage interactions with their groups presented in the previous section is insufficient. In fact, explaining how such activities should be carried out by matching particular recommendations to each stakeholder type is necessary before addressing the fundamental issue covered in this chapter. Below, I shall discuss my own relationship management concepts, which were originally applied to business negotiations (Kozina, 2019). Table 5.9 offers a fresh perspective on these ideas, first by presenting them in a more comprehensive format and then by relating them to the unique characteristics of the structure and managing relationships with its constituents.

TABLE 5.9   General principles for managing relationships with stakeholders in the state governance
system

Principle	Description
Sustainability	Characterised by the duration (continuity) of stakeholder relationships and the extent to which the positive experiences of collaboration accumulate. This principle requires the creation and regular updating of the knowledge base of current and potential stakeholders and relationships with them, especially the analysis of insights arising from these relationships, their results and relevance in terms of performance.
Intensity	Refers to the strength of the relationship as measured by two parameters: its relevance to the partners' goals and frequency of interaction over the course of their collaboration. A relationship that is not intense enough may deteriorate or even end, whereas one that is excessively intense may cause preventable problems owing to the negative consequences of routine (mutual boredom).
Shared values	Concerns the declared and actual tangible and intangible values such as loyalty, solidarity, reliability, etc. and defines the potential limits of partnership in their co-creation. Conflicts about values should be avoided – unnecessary conflicts typically result from attempts to impose different values on one another (in politics, this is the rule).
Reciprocity	Specifies whether and to what extent partners in a relationship respond favourably to the positive feedbacks and actions of others, avoid negative actions and rely on a similarity of circumstances in which they find themselves together, according to the old adage 'do unto others as you would have them do unto you.' This involves adopting a co-operative strategy with the partner at the start of each specific relationship, and possibly substituting it with a competitive strategy if the former does not work out.
Credibility	Built on mutual trust and the idea that partners do not engage in misleading, illegal, or immoral behaviour toward one another, even the kinds of discourse known as half-truths or selective communication. They are absolutely dependable, truthful, and predictable to one another. They never disappoint. They know what to expect from one other, and nothing surprises them in the negative sense of the word.
Openness and symmetry of information	Provides that there are no communication barriers between cooperating partners. All relevant data flow freely and without restrictions. Communication channels are sufficiently open. Information exchanged is useful, or authentic, reliable (comes from trusted sources), delivered at the right time and form, in the right quantity and quality, to the right recipients, etc. There are no delays, omissions or misstatements. Partners are 'well informed' and informationally secure.

TABLE 5.9 General principles for managing relationships with stakeholders in the state governance system (*cont.*)

Principle	Description
Mutual support	Reflects the extent to which the actors in an interaction support each other's efforts, especially in difficult or crisis situations, in relations with other actors in the environment, for the purpose of strengthening their bargaining power and credibility, e.g. by supporting bids, providing loan guarantees, references, guaranteeing contracts, etc. Parties to the interaction perceive their roles much more broadly, going beyond the narrow, specific objectives of individual transactions. A shared 'early warning system' for potential challenges and contingencies in the relationship is essential.
Balance	Comprises two sub-principles. The first one is the principle of complementarity, which determines the extent to which the resolution of substantive problems and the formation of mutual relationships benefit each other. The other one is decoupling, which determines the extent to which the two activities mentioned are disconnected, as the effective implementation of one should not have a negative impact on the other and vice versa. It is therefore inadvisable to accept an unfavourable agreement at the price of maintaining a positive relationship with a partner, or to undermine the relationship by seeking short-term benefits at the partner's expense.
Strategic orientation	Determines the extent to which specific transactions can and should only constitute a stage in a long-term cooperation between parties, or even in a strategic partnership. It is based on mutual trust and the assumption that the formulation of the objectives of specific transactions must take as an important reference point the more general intentions arising from the vision and mission pursued. In a given situation, it may not deliver the expected benefits, especially material ones, or even lead to tangible losses. However, it creates or develops a beneficial relationship with the partner and may yield significant advantages later that significantly outweigh any prior loss.
Flexibility	Actors offer one another the greatest possible number of beneficial solutions to problems under consideration while ensuring their utility. They should be sufficiently relevant to the conditions of operation and collaboration so that, in the event of a possible failure to establish a beneficial relationship with one partner, opportunities still exist to enter into other relationships. A sound and comprehensive assessment of individual transactions in a broad market context must therefore be carried out, which requires a considerable potential of competencies, especially of a relational nature.

TABLE 5.9   General principles for managing relationships with stakeholders in the state governance
system (*cont.*)

Principle	Description
Transitivity	Refers to partners' mutual support in establishing and maintaining alliances with other institutions and players in order to form networks of collaborating organisations. As is the case with the reciprocity principle, support should be offered with the goal of attracting new collaborators or even allies through a current partner. Strategic partnerships should reflect the mutual 'pull' of partners with the capacity and good experience to establish cooperation, coalitions, alliances etc. Proven strategic partners are simply more attractive and credible to others.
Selectivity	Reflects the range of potential relationships, especially partnerships, which an organisation establishes and sustains. It is assumed that not all actors should or can form relationships with it, especially the positive ones. Potential partners are identified using stakeholder analysis. Establishing too many and/or unpromising relationships without due consideration may waste the committed organisation's resources. On the other hand, ignoring potentially attractive partners deprives the organisation of considerable opportunities.

SOURCE: OWN STUDY

6   Specific Recommendations for Managing the State's Relationships With Its Stakeholders

The principles described in Table 5.9 can now be applied to the four fundamental groups of state stakeholders identified previously in order to formulate a set of specific recommendations for managing relationships in the state governance system, drawing on the final stage of the conceptualisation (Table 5.10). For individual stakeholder groups, specific recommendations fall on the following spectrum: strategic collaboration – cooperation limited to the exchange of required benefits – cooperation limited to essential communication – none, or possibly seeking cooperation opportunities.

It should also be emphasised that the proposed set of recommendations has a twofold practical application. First, it is diagnostic in the sense that it enables the identification and evaluation of existing stakeholder interactions. Second, it is prognostic as it identifies the risks and opportunities associated with forming and maintaining relationships with new potential stakeholders.

TABLE 5.10   Specific recommendations for managing relationships with stakeholders in the state governance system

Principle \ Stakeholder type	Cooperating (partners)	Demanding (entitled)	Interested (observers)	Unknown (anonymous)
Sustainability	Permanent, regular contacts, established as tradition or custom.	Constant, routine, recurring contacts within the necessary scope of exchange.	Periodic contacts based on established and mutually respected information exchange rules.	Incidental, limited and random interactions.
Intensity	A continuous and strong relationship, routine (in a positive sense), mutual understanding without the need for lengthy explanations.	Medium, usually periodic intensity of relations, depending on the needs.	Medium intensity of irregular relations, reduced to a minimum by the data needed.	Low, one-off, possibly several interactions.
Shared values	Full compatibility of (shared) values, their development and co-creation on the basis of consensus.	Partial divergence of values, their compatibility for the necessary compromise, at an acceptable level.	Prevalence of divergent values or limited consistency in the data provided.	Lack of or incidental compatibility of values.
Reciprocity	Full understanding between partners and mutual acceptance of expectations and requirements.	Acceptance and fulfilment of expectations (requests) to the extent necessary.	Understanding of information needs and acceptance of communication terms and conditions.	Kindness, positive attitude, no need for understanding or acceptance.

TABLE 5.10 Specific recommendations for managing relationships with stakeholders in the state governance system (*cont.*)

Principle\Stakeholder type	Cooperating (partners)	Demanding (entitled)	Interested (observers)	Unknown (anonymous)
Credibility	Complete trust and full credibility, established on the basis of good experiences of cooperation.	Limited credibility, necessary level of trust in the exchange of benefits.	Reliability and usability of data provided; limited trust.	No way of assessing credibility; possible trust fraught with risk.
Openness and symmetry of information	Communication channels fully open, exchange of information at the required level of utility.	Utility of data corresponding to the scope of benefits needed.	Limited usability of data and extent of information exchange – only in response to requests made.	Essentially irrelevant due to incidental nature of contacts; avoiding information traps.
Mutual support	Full mutual support between partners.	Support to the extent necessary to meet needs.	Information-only support as expected.	Polite signals of readiness to contact.
Balance	Balancing the value and importance of the activities under consideration; mutual assistance in this regard.	Dominance of substantive issues over the limited scope of positive relationship building.	Only information support on needed data.	Both substantive issues and relationships are irrelevant.
Strategic orientation	Current needs and mutual expectations of the parties reviewed and met in line with strategic objectives.	Dominance of immediate issues over long-term ones, possibly viewed in terms of future benefits.	Ongoing information and limitation of strategic perspective to projected information needs.	Obvious lack of strategic perspective.
Flexibility	Creating an environment conducive to creative exploration of solution options and their comprehensive analysis.	Limited flexibility, assessed against reported expectations.	Flexibility reduced to the extent of data required and accepted methods and forms of communication.	Possible need for flexibility when seeking potential.

| Transitivity | Establishing and maintaining all relationships necessary for the organisation's objectives in the network of relationships. | Potential to indirectly satisfy the needs of other actors in the interaction chain. | Possible transfer of data to other recipients to the extent agreed by the parties to the interaction. | None, possible brokering of contacts, familiarisation and referrals. |
| Selectivity | All necessary and sufficient relationships with the necessary number of partners justified by the required level of performance. | Minimal control in terms of relationship management, limited to those claiming benefits. | Limited control, in terms of relationship management, to those requesting information. | By their nature, contacts are selective, i.e. ad hoc and unplanned. |

SOURCE: OWN STUDY

Tables 5.11 and 5.12 explain in more detail the techniques (principles and procedures) of effective management of the state's relationships with its stakeholders in the V4 countries.

As was the case with the state's relationships with individual stakeholder groups, the principles vary greatly across countries. According to Polish and, to a lesser extent, Hungarian respondents, the concept of reciprocity is important in shaping these relationships. Although the function of informal interactions with demanding and interested parties was recognised in Slovakia, the idea of

TABLE 5.11   Principles for managing relationships with stakeholder groups in the V4 countries

Stakeholder group\Country	Poland	Hungary	Czech Republic	Slovakia
Cooperating	Achieving and maintaining a parliamentary majority capable of forming a government and implementing a political programme. Elections, codes, regulations, etc. are the basis. Regional, fiscal and economic policies of the state. Principle of mutual aid and administrative facilitation.	Relationships are very pragmatic, economy-oriented to benefit all – the state can announce the results of its actions to the public; stakeholders also benefit from the decisions.	Subject to legal regulation.	Outside of the tripartite agreement and inter-ministerial procedures for commenting on legislation, there is very little formal pressure in which collaborators may voice their concerns.
Demanding	Transactivity. These stakeholders support state authorities insofar as the latter protects or secures their interests. Goal: maximum satisfaction of this stakeholder group.	The live and let live principle.	Tripartite relations.	Formal structures exist in individual ministries with mostly informal relations between key representatives of public agencies.

TABLE 5.11   Characteristics of stakeholders in the V4 countries (*cont.*)

Stakeholder group\Country	Poland	Hungary	Czech Republic	Slovakia
Interested	Pluralism in public debate. The state should build positive relations with them through joint projects and committees or support policies.	Subordination, especially of citizens and their groups; they try to exert pressure on the authorities by pushing their ideas and programmes.	Irregularity.	In practice, these relationships depend on interpersonal favours and ties based on individuals and their shared agenda with the state.
Unknown	Equal rights of citizens in their relations with the authorities. Creating opportunities to meet life's needs.	Indifference.	Lack of cooperation.	Lack of cooperation.

SOURCE: OWN STUDY

formalising these contacts prevails in the other two countries. Except for the Polish respondents, none of the others believe that standards for shaping relationships with unknown interest groups can be developed.

Respondents from Poland identified a number of irregularities in the state's relationships with the first group of stakeholders. In theory, politicians and business elites believe that they play a positive role by creating jobs, but the former frequently seek to exploit voters, while the latter strive to evade taxation, secure an employer's market, and inexpensive labour. They advocate for regulation, but when it comes to governance, they are only concerned with implementation to the extent that they find advantageous. Even though this is the case, it does not imply that it is the right thing to do. Local government and business organisations demand 'transparency' from the government, as well as support for local planning and development. It is necessary for the state to strive to ensure the integrity of the political and economic elites. They should serve as role models for other interest groups, their actions should be

TABLE 5.12   Methods of effective management of relationships with stakeholder groups in the V4
              countries

Stakeholder group\Country	Poland	Hungary	Czech Republic	Slovakia
Cooperating	Provision of a political and electoral framework to stabilise the functioning of state authorities. Selection of credible and reliable politicians and professionals for key state positions. Creation of a friendly investment climate, efficient service, assistance, advice to business. Effective tax policy, investment in the regions, mechanisms for regulating currency value for business, influencing exports, etc.	Several consultative forums exist, but only for those stakeholders who share the values of the state/ government, so only they can achieve some of their objectives.	Bureaucracy.	Government uses existing structures since they effectively bring these stakeholders together, making it possible to share their knowledge and reveal preferences.
Demanding	Transparency of relationships between state authorities and influential stakeholders. Common institutions – platforms for sharing knowledge and dialogue with these groups, informing, providing sound analyses. Support and promotion of local government activities and development plans. Entrepreneurship support through economic missions and trade fairs. Provision of the best and fastest service, streamlining administrative procedures.	Limited consultation, usually not for negotiation purposes, but for recognising the outcomes of actions.	Bargaining.	These institutions are usually used as leverage based on the preferences of those in power.

TABLE 5.12   Methods of effective management of relationships with stakeholder groups in the V4 countries (*cont.*)

Stakeholder group\Country	Poland	Hungary	Czech Republic	Slovakia
Interested	The state enables the presentation of views and positions critical of the authorities and observes democratic principles of transfer of power (elections). Joint central–local government committees, partnership relations with chambers of economic self-government. Government support policy for self-government and business support sectors.	When citizens' initiatives achieve a certain level of interest and/or popularity, the state either rejects them or treats stakeholders as unequal negotiating parties mainly through various traditional and social media channels.	Bargaining.	Government usually contacts these actors when it needs specific advice and expertise in a specific area in order to make policy decisions.
Unknown	Measures intended to include excluded people in public and social life and encourage them to be more active.	No genuine relationships exist.	No genuine relationships exist.	No genuine relationships exist.

SOURCE: OWN STUDY

transparent, they should support general development not only their own interest, act in the belief that the long-term welfare of the general public is in their best interest. Then they will govern for a long time and achieve their own benefits through higher incomes for the general public and demand for their services and products. The ineffectiveness of serfdom as well as other forms of exploitation, and their demise shows that the most important thing is to improve the wellbeing of all, even if it cannot reproduce the communist system, in which people were expected to deliver greater productivity and effort for no extra pay (this was also the case under serfdom – all surplus was taken away from the serfs). The foundation of a successful state is a large, prosperous middle class and equality of opportunity (Pl_4_2).

Dialogue and negotiation with organised groups, presenting their demands in a more general context, acknowledging problems (e.g. hard work at low wages), but also the need to take into account the interests of others (e.g. environmental pollution by mines, increased risk of death) is essential for demanding stakeholders. These groups must not be ignored (Pl_4_2). It is also vital to capitalise on the potential of another group of stakeholders, recognising their arguments and solutions they may offer to enhance policies or economic activities as well as appreciating their role in educating and civilising society and the economy as a whole (Pl_4_2). The relationships between the state and unknown stakeholders should also be improved, since they are mostly occasional and based at best on political interests of those in power. It is necessary to create opportunities for these stakeholders so that they are self-sufficient, able to support themselves (vocational training and other conditions), and avoid exploitation by the more powerful. Appropriate rules must be introduced to that effect (Pl_4_2).

Relationships with significant stakeholders in Hungary are mostly pragmatic, albeit often based on corruption whereby stakeholders are expected to pursue a politicians' political goals (e.g. by way of participating in his/her campaign or financial contribution). The state and demanding stakeholders are not at odds. Stakeholders representing the third group are most likely to be consulted on the implementation of various programmes and initiatives only when it is politically advantageous for the state to do so. The state has no relationship with the last stakeholder group. (Hu_4_4).

In general, the practical approaches to interacting with specific stakeholder groups in the V4 countries significantly differ from the model concepts outlined in Table 5.9. Some of them are only applied in Poland. Considerable efforts should thus be undertaken in each of the countries under consideration to improve the way in which state institutions manage their interactions with stakeholders.

As regards the respondents' perception of effective methods of managing relationships with stakeholders, the situation is identical to that outlined above.

Only Polish respondents explored the topic at hand in any depth (in contrast to other respondents), i.e. did not ignore the unknown stakeholders (as was done by the representatives of other countries). Not only did they identify the methods for managing relationships with specific stakeholder groups, but also established the circumstances required for these methods to be effective. In the case of interacting stakeholders, it is crucial to design true democratic processes rather than assume that only 10% of the population is aware of what is going on.

It is critical to be able to bring out the best in everyone, to provide equitable opportunities for all, and to support the middle class. Legal accountability for one's actions is required. People with integrity and moral compass must be elected to positions of power. People at large must be defended against fake news that distorts the image of reality; all activities should be informed by sound analysis instead of 'playing to the grandstand.' It is vital to prevent economic oligopolisation, to offer opportunities to new entrepreneurs, and to foster technological growth and innovation. Unanimity in party voting should be prohibited – each MP regardless of their party affiliation should be driven by his/her own conscience – what is needed is a real democracy, not a parliamentary oligopoly. Conflict escalation through the media should be avoided when dealing with demanding stakeholders. It is important not to take decisions based exclusively on media coverage, which frequently exaggerates and presents numerous situations in a false or distorted light. A fair and objective exchange of opinions with stakeholders is required to ensure proper stakeholder relationship management. Given the positive external effects on society as a whole of intellectual, educational, and innovative activities, tax incentives should be offered to encourage them. For this is the breeding ground for future leaders, who ought to be trustworthy. In order to prevent assessments, recommendations, and expert opinions from being produced in the interest of, say, a specific law or interest group, care must also be taken to ensure their impartiality and integrity. The state should effectively reach out to unidentified stakeholders by appropriate policies ensuring equal opportunity, education, support, and preventing abuse by more powerful organisations (Pl_4_2).

Although there are consultation tools in place in Hungary, they have proved to be limited and inadequate in practice. Instead, they should be designed to benefit both the state and these stakeholders. Regular meetings with economically significant stakeholders are held, but the public is largely unaware of them (Hu_4_4).

In Slovakia, the needs of the state ten to be prioritised, whereas stakeholders collaborate with the state bodies when it is hesitant to make changes in order to speed them up (Sk_4_4). In the Czech Republic, bargaining with individual stakeholder groups predominates (Cz_4_4).

7   Summary

Stakeholder management is undeniably one of the most significant, albeit auxiliary, aspects of state governance. This is due to the fact that it has a significant

impact on process implementation efficiency, particularly in terms of cooperation and entering into written and unwritten contracts with both internal
stakeholders and interest groups from the distant and close environment, and
thus determines the overall performance of state institutions.

Table 5.13 summarises the findings of the research intended to provide partial empirical validation of the proposed model for managing relationships
with stakeholders in the Visegrád countries along its five dimensions.

TABLE 5.13   Empirical findings

Dimensions of the state–stakeholder relationship management model	Research findings
Key state stakeholders representing respective groups.	Similarities and differences in the recognition of the significance of individual stakeholder groups across the v4 countries. Examples of stakeholders given preferential treatment in some of these countries. Prevalence of corruption in Hungary.
Specific features of typical stakeholders and their groups.	Stakeholder characteristics correspond to their place and role in the state. Differences in the description of characteristics by respondents from each country. Pathological phenomena in Hungary and irregularities in Poland.
Content and scope of relationships between the state these groups.	Predominance of differences in defining stakeholder relationships among the v4 countries. Recognition of the needs of both parties to the relationship in Poland. Influence of the state underscored in Hungary, the scope of relationships in the Czech Republic, and their context in Slovakia.
Key principles for shaping and maintaining these relationships by the state	Predominance of differences in defining these principles across the v4 countries. Significant differences between the model principles and those applied in practice. The principle of reciprocity emphasised in Poland and partly in Hungary. Predominance of formal principles in the Czech Republic and Slovakia. Apart from Poland, lack of cooperation with unknown stakeholders.

TABLE 5.13   Empirical findings (*cont.*)

Dimensions of the state– stakeholder relationship management model	Research findings
Main methods (ways) of effectively managing these relationships.	The same situation as in the case of principles of relationship formation. Specific and comprehensive methods applied in Poland. Predominance of consultations in Hungary, state needs in Slovakia, and bargaining in Czech Republic. Apart from Poland, lack of cooperation with unknown stakeholders.

SOURCE: OWN STUDY

It should be noted that the proposed concept of managing the relationships discussed above is universal and comprehensive in nature, as it embraces all the dimensions and features of the management area under consideration. One may even argue that it has the potential to serve as an effective instrument for describing, analysing, and influencing these relationships in real-world situations.

Information on stakeholders in the state governance system as well as the interactions among them should be reviewed and updated on a regular basis. Their description should be as accurate and objective as possible, taking into account all of their features, even those that appear to be of minor importance. It should also be dynamic in nature, include present and potential stakeholders, their current and possible relationships, and the hypothetical or desirable (model) ones to enable anticipating their behaviours. By analogy, the state must be viewed as a current or potential stakeholder in the interests of other actors, particularly in terms of attaining its own objectives and influencing the viewpoints of its partners (the so-called dual analysis problem). All data about stakeholders, including the findings of analyses, should be collected, processed, and disseminated by all the subsystems of the state in the form of a knowledge base. These requirements are especially relevant in the context of 4IR, particularly given the growing importance of dynamically developing information technology, which poses considerable challenges to state institutions in terms of engaging in appropriate interactions with their stakeholders.

However, these ideas are still preliminary and need to be refined by the author as part of his in-depth research effort, notably in terms of improving detailed methodological tools, especially quantitative ones. Developing effective procedures and instruments for identifying and analysing stakeholder goals and preferences is a key part of it. The proposed theory must be tested much more rigorously in a comparative empirical research setting, taking into consideration the Visegrád countries' extensive links with diverse stakeholders in their governance systems.

Bibliography

Bourne, L. (2009). *Stakeholder Relationship Management. A Maturity Model for Organisational Implementation*, Gower.

Chan, C., Pan, S. and Tan, Ch-W. (2003). *Managing Stakeholder Relationships in an E-Government Project*, Americas Conference on Information Systems Proceedings, paper 98.

Cox, A., Lonsdale, C., Sanderson, J. and Watson, G. (2004). *Business Relationships for Competitive Advantage*, Palgrave MacMillan.

Eden, C. and Ackermann, F. (1998). *Making Strategy: The Journey of Strategic Management*, Sage Publications.

Freeman, R. E. (1984). *Strategic Management: A Stakeholder Approach*. Pitman.

Freeman, R. E. and Reed, D. J. (1983). Stakeholders and Shareholders: A New Perspective on Corporate Governance, *California Management Review*, xxv, 2.

Frey, C. B. (2019). *The Technology Trap. Capital, Labor, and Power in the Age of Automation*, Princeton University Press.

Gomes, R.C. (2004). Who Are the Relevant Stakeholders to The Local Government Context? Empirical Evidences on Environmental Influences in The Decision-Making Process of English Local Authorities, *Brazilian Administration Review*, 1(1), 34–52. https://doi.org/10.1590/S1807-76922004000100004

Hawrysz, L. and Maj, J. (2017). Identification of Stakeholders of Public Interest Organisations, *Sustainability*, 9(9), 1609, https://doi.org/10.3390/su9091609

Johnson, G. and Scholes, K. (1999). *Exploring Corporate Strategy. Text and Cases*. Prentice Hall.

Kotas, M. (2012). Building Relationships with Stakeholders – As a Key Success Factor in Public Sector Organizations, *Olsztyn Economic Journal*, 7(1), 51–61. https://doi.org/10.31648/oej.3372

Kozina, A. (Ed.) (2015). *Wybrane problemy zarządzania relacjami w przedsiębiorstwie*. Mfiles.pl. Encyklopedia zarządzania, Kraków.

Kozłowski, K. and Zygmuntowski, J. J. (Eds.) (2017). *FutureIsights: Technologie 4.0 a przemiany społeczno-gospodarcze*, Oficyna Wydawnicza SGH.

Koźmiński, A. K. and Latusek-Jurczak, D. (Eds.). (2014). *Relacje międzyorganizacyjne w naukach o zarządzaniu*. Oficyna Wolters Kluwer Business.

Leksykon zarządzania (2004), Difin.

Lindgreen, A. (2008). *Managing Market Relationships. Methodological and Empirical Insights*. Gower Publishing Ltd.

Lisiński, M. (2004). *Metody planowania strategicznego*. PWE.

Managing Relationships at Work (2003). *Institute of Leadership & Management Series*, Pergamon Flexible Learning, Oxford.

Mayer-Schonberger, V. and Cukier, K. (2014). *Big Data. Rewolucja, która zmieni nasze myślenie, pracę i życie*. MT Biznes.

Obłój, K. (2007). *Strategia organizacji. W poszukiwaniu trwałej przewagi konkurencyjnej*. PWE.

Olsen, T. D. (2017). Political Stakeholder Theory: The State, Legitimacy, and the Ethics of Microfinance in Emerging Economies, *Business Ethics Quarterly*, 27(1), 71–98. https://doi.org/10.1017/beq.2016.59

Piwoni-Krzeszowska, E. (2014). *Zarządzanie wartością relacji przedsiębiorstwa z rynkowymi interesariuszami*. Monografie i Opracowania, nr 249. Wydawnictwo Uniwersytetu Ekonomicznego we Wrocławiu.

Schwab, K. (2018). *Czwarta rewolucja przemysłowa*. Studio Emka.

Słownik języka polskiego (2019). https://sjp.pwn.pl/slowniki/relacja.html

Stabryła, A. (1984). *Analiza systemowa procesu zarządzania*. Ossolineum.

Stephenson, D. (2020). *Big Data, nauka o danych i AI bez tajemnic*. Helion.

Stoner, J. A. F., Freeman, R. E. and Gilbert, D., R. (1997). *Kierowanie*. PWE.

Tyszkiewicz, R. (2017). *Zarządzanie relacjami z interesariuszami organizacji*. Wydawnictwo Placet.

Yamak, S. and Süer, Ö. (2005). State as a Stakeholder. *Corporate Governance*, 5(2), 111–120. https://doi.org/10.1108/14720700510562695

The Development of e-Services in the Evolution of e-Government in the V4 Countries

Marcin Kędzierski and Pavel Horák

1 Introduction

The concept of the Fourth Industrial Revolution (4IR) is still fairly new. Originally, the idea of Industry 4.0 was proposed in 2011 by German government experts who used it for the first time in their strategy to develop a technologically advanced economy (Industrie 4.0). But even for those working with new technologies it has been more of an appealing packing box and PR notion than a well-defined concept. The same applies to public administration and the entire debate on e-government. Can we consider the dynamic computerisation of public administration that occurred in the V4 countries at the turn of the 21st century to be the first stage of 4IR? Although it should not be perceived as such in the absence of the Internet, public e-services would be impossible without prior computerisation.

If we define the Internet as a model of relations between various actors, we may characterise the impact of 4IR on public administration by describing the evolution of e-government with special reference to the V4 countries. The emphasis will be on identifying the new, virtual, and digital nature of relationships not only between various public institutions/their representatives (government to government – G2G; administration to administration – A2A, and government/public administration to business – G/A2B) but also – and perhaps more importantly – those between the government/public administration and citizens; or, more recently, the government and employees (G/A2E).

The V4 countries are currently implementing strategic policies to advance e-government in a number of public areas, including cybersecurity, e-education, e-health, and crucially, e-administration. A later section will highlight e-services as a special example of interaction between the government and the public administration. Next, we shall attempt to categorise diverse public e-services and their development in the V4 countries using case studies.

Finally, we would like to answer the question: How has the evolution of public e-services informed the recent revision of the public administration code of conduct in the v4?

2   The Evolution of e-Government With a Special Focus on the V4 Countries

According to a widely held belief, the creation of the first public websites in the early 1990s marked the beginning of e-government. However, since the 1960s and 1970s, we have seen breakthrough developments in internal computer networks that have enabled new forms of communication among various actors in public administration. Initially, the process affected the military and public R&D sectors (such as ARPANET in 1969), but since the 1970s, it spread to other civilian public organisations (basic G2G communication). However, the advent of the Internet and the World Wide Web in 1990 opened up entirely new opportunities for e-government, expanding internal communication and providing a platform for the growth of G2B, G2C, and most recently G2E interactions (cf. Grönlund and Horan, 2004; Dawes, 2008; Ranga Rao, 2011).

The origins of e-government demonstrate its adaptability to technological advances. Even though the Internet was built with public funds, governments were more interested in responding to social expectations and technological revolutions rather than creating or fostering them (see e.g. UN, 2011; Trotta, 2018). This remark is still true of the present-day evolution of public e-services for citizens. In fact, the development of e-government follows the technological revolution and takes advantage of new opportunities ushered in by technology.

This evolution can be divided into seven stages (Gil-Garcia and Martinez-Moyano, 2007, pp. 269–270):

1.   Initial presence – A small number of discrete government websites make up the official online presence of a government body (mostly developed by single governmental agencies). At this stage, governments normally provide static information and a limited number of services to citizens and private organisations.

2.   Extended presence – Governments offer more specialised, regularly updated information scattered over a number of websites. The official website of a country's government may act as a portal with links to the websites of other government agencies, departments, and subnational administrative entities. Some governments may start interacting with residents, corporations, and other stakeholders via email or search engines.

3. Interactive presence – Governments employ a national or state portal as the main landing page for services across many agencies. At this level, there is more contact between the public and the various government entities (e.g. e-mail, forums, etc.). Information is accessible to both individuals and corporations, depending on their interests. Passwords can occasionally be required to gain access to more customised and secure services.

4. Transactional presence – Citizens and businesses can personalise or customise a national or state-wide portal, which becomes a unique showcase of all the governmental services available in the relevant area of interest. The primary criteria for portal design and access are the needs of many constituents (government structure and functions are only secondary). The site enables secure electronic payments, including taxes, fines, and fees for services.

5. Vertical integration – Integration of similar services provided by various levels of government, which can be virtual, physical, or both. Therefore, this stage does not refer solely to an incipient integration in the form of government websites but to the change and reconstruction of the processes and/or governmental structures.

6. Horizontal integration – Integration among a variety of governmental services must exist for citizens and other stakeholders to have access to all the potential IT-associated benefits. Therefore, at this stage government agencies need to cross organisational boundaries and develop a comprehensive and integral vision of government as a whole. Vertical and horizontal integration do not necessarily happen together or sequentially.

7. Totally integrated presence – All government services are fully integrated vertically and horizontally. Citizens have access to a variety of functionalities via a single portal using a unique ID and password. All services can be accessed from the same web page and can be paid for in a consolidated bill. Unbeknownst to the general public, a revolution has occurred, and services are now physically as well as technologically arranged according to processes and constituencies. Governments implement institutional and administrative reforms at this stage that fully utilise the potential of information technologies.

The first two stages were primarily centred on the dynamic computerisation of public administration and mainly involved one-way Internet-based communication from the government to corporations, people, and employees. Stages 3 through 7 are much more intricately linked to the development of extensive mutualisation of communication between the government and outside actors, on the one hand, and the adoption of brand-new systems for data gathering and processing, on the other. In fact, the notion of 4IR and its designations (personalisation/customisation, automation, digitalisation, etc.) can only to some extent be used to identify the later stages. While the governments were putting various technological solutions into use, none of these stages were inherently progressive or mutually incompatible. While in some public policy areas new solutions were implemented at once, in others it took considerably more time or even did not happen at all.

It is interesting to note that even though the V4 countries were unable to establish modern, democratic state structures due to their communist background until 1989, they underwent political and economic change at the same time as the Internet was invented. Therefore, despite the major institutional gaps between the V4 and Western European nations, Czechoslovakia (since 1993, the Czech Republic and Slovakia), Hungary, and Poland may have taken advantage of the Internet in their transformation efforts before their accession to the EU in order to fulfil their obligations under the acquis communautaire (see Kapsa and Musiał-Karg, 2021).

This may account for the relatively minor disparities in the development of e-government among the V4 countries. Paradoxically, entering the Internet era provided them with the opportunity to implement solutions that had previously been difficult to introduce in a number of Western countries, such as Germany, due to path dependence, most notably in mobile banking (and

TABLE 6.1   Evolution of e-government in the V4 countries

Stage	Czech Republic	Hungary	Poland	Slovakia
Initial presence	Mid-1990s (e.g. Czech government's website www. vlada.cz, 1996)	Early 2000s (official central website on Hungary: magyarorszag. hu launched in 1st February, 2003)	Late 1990s (e.g. Polish Parliament's website www. sejm.gov.pl)	Late 1990s (e.g. the foundation of the topic and ownership by government institutions)
Extended presence	Since early 2000s (e.g. Website of the Ministry of the Interior www.mvczr.cz, 2000; website of the Ministry of Labour and Social Affairs www.mpsv. cz, 2000)	2005 (Ügyfélkapu (Client Gate), the e-governance portal launches, used mainly for interactions, but as a rule services can be used, whenever possible)	Since early 2000s (official Public Information Bulletin, BIP; 2001)	Since 2004 the government had a dedicated representative for the topic ofe-government

TABLE 6.1   Evolution of e-government in the V4 countries (*cont.*)

Stage	Czech Republic	Hungary	Poland	Slovakia
Interactive presence	Since middle 2000s (Portál veřejné správy/Public Administration Portal, 2004)	2005 (on paper at least), late 2000s in practice	Since late 2000s (e-Platform for Public Administration Services, ePUAP; 2008)	Since late 2000s (the central portal of the public administration was created in 2007)
Transactional presence	Since late 2010's (Portál občana/Citizen's Portal; Portál Národní identifikační autorita/National Identity Authority Portal, 2018)	2013 (first instance companies can make electronic payment for Ministry of Justice, later expanded to include more online payments (EFER system for online payments)	Since late 2010s (e.g. e-PIT; 2019)	For businesses, there was some activity in early 2010s, for the citizens, the services became more active in 2019
Vertical integration	n/a	Ügyfélkapu (Client Gate) was always the main e-government portal. The change in the structure and competencies of municipalities (and centralization of administration) after 2010 eased a more centralized e-administration as well	n/a (despite some pilot implementations)	Portal Slovensko. sk attempts to centralise different services and integrate different levels of services in one place since 2019

TABLE 6.1   Evolution of e-government in the V4 countries (*cont.*)

Stage	Czech Republic	Hungary	Poland	Slovakia
Horizontal integration	Since early 2020's (Digitalni-urad. cz, 2021)	2018 (Pursuant to the e-Administration Act, from 1 January 2018, the cooperating bodies involved in administrative processes shall obtain information (data or documents) from another cooperating body rather than asking the customer (citizen or business) to resubmit it)	Since early 2020s (Obywatel.gov.pl and mObywatel, advanced versions of e-Platform of Public Administration Services	Since 2018, the government has been pushing the principle one-time-is-enough to integrate horizontally different sites to minimise information gathering
Totally integrated presence	n/a	Arguably from 2018	n/a	n/a

SOURCE: OWN STUDY

mobile business services, including e-commerce) and in e-administration (more recently, the so-called mobile administration).

It would be fair to say that all the V4 countries have made some progress in digitalising public services (Stage 4: transactional presence) owing to the pandemic and the revolution it triggered. Public administration, which had been attempting to postpone digitalisation before 2020, was forced to change its approach almost overnight. Some procedures that were not digitalised for years became digital in a matter of weeks (Pl_6_1).

The question, however, remains whether and if so, when the V4 countries may be able to introduce both vertical and horizontal integration that goes beyond simple digitalisation of particular public services. To address it, we would like to review their current strategic policy responses to digitalisation challenges.

3   Development of Advanced e-Government as a Strategic Policy Goal
       of the V4 Countries

Since its inception, e-government has expanded in a variety of policy areas. Education, health, security, social services, and last but not least public administration were all heavily impacted by digitalisation. It must be noted that governments responded quickly to the prevailing social and commercial trends. As a result, digital solutions in areas such as education or health policy were typically implemented in response to mounting social and commercial pressure. Moreover, the EU began emphasising the importance of e-government in the creation of a new economic model in the early 2000s and with the adoption of the Lisbon Strategy (EURactiv, 2005).

The digitalisation of public administration thus became a strategic priority for all the V4 countries. However, the process did not accelerate until the late 2000s/early 2010s due in part to the emergence of the new perspective of 4IR and its attendant innovations, such as customisation and personalisation of services (see Maksimova, Solvak and Krimmer, 2021). In fact, it gave rise to completely new social expectations. At the time, the V4 governments attempted to meet them by establishing dedicated agencies, government plenipotentiaries, or even ministries in charge of digitalisation:

- Czech Republic: Since 2021, a Deputy Prime Minister has been in charge of digitalisation as a horizontal policy (previously as a government plenipotentiary, currently as the Minister of Regional Development); prior to 2021, the Interior Ministry, the Ministry of Trade and Economy, and the Ministry of Culture shared responsibility for digital policy (moreover, a Ministry of Computerisation existed from 2003 to 2007);
- Hungary: Since 2010, the Ministry of the Interior and the Prime Minister's Chancellery have shared responsibility for digital policy. In 2014, that responsibility was transferred to the Ministry of Innovation and Technology. As of 2022, a special government commissioner has been assigned to oversee digital policy;
- Poland: the Ministry of Administration and Digitalisation (2011–2015), followed by the Ministry of Digital Affairs (2015–2020); as of 2020, the Prime Minister's Chancellery now oversees digitalisation as a horizontal strategy (under the Minister of Digital Affairs);
- Slovakia: the Deputy Prime Minister has been responsible for Investment and Computerisation (since 2016); as well as the Ministry of Investment, Regional Development and Computerisation (since 2020).

However, according to EU's *eGovernment Benchmark 2021*, the level of digitalisation of public services in the V4 remains below the EU average (71%): 63% in Czech Republic and Hungary, 61% in Slovakia, and 58% in Poland. Furthermore, despite the fact that Poland was the first V4 country to establish a Ministry of Digital Affairs, it still has a relatively low penetration of e-services – only 48% compared with the EU average of 67% (Czech Republic 64%, Hungary 70%, Slovakia 68%), even though the European Commission rated Poland as "on track" with its recent policies. Nonetheless, Poland outperforms its V4 peers in terms of the most important criterion of user-centricity.

As a result of the relative underperformance of e-government across the V4, their governments, partially overseen by the European Commission, have recently adopted a number of policies designed to encourage the implementation of more advanced solutions. The primary, current strategic documents in the area of digitalisation from each of the V4 countries, which focus mostly on completing the Stage 4 (transactional presence) and advancing toward vertical and horizontal integration, are described below.

3.1 Czech Republic

The main document that charts the process of Czech Republic's digitalisation is the Digital Czech Republic Strategy 2018–2030 (Digitální Česko, DČ). It is a collection of strategic papers and implementation plans that should help to accelerate the process of creating optimal conditions for the ongoing 4IR. The primary goal of DČ is to ensure that the public administration, private sector, and citizens are prepared for the changes brought about by the digital revolution.

The strategy is comprised of three strategic documents representing three distinct pillars:

- Czech Republic in Digital Europe (2018) – focuses on the Digital Single Market (DSM) in Europe and sets the main and partial goals of the Czech Republic in the area of negotiating digital agendas (implementation – Government of the Czech Republic);
- Information Concept of the Czech Republic (2018, act. 2020) (*Informační Koncepce České Republiky*, IKČR) – outlines the goals and general tenets of the acquisition, development, management, and operation of public information systems in the Czech Republic (implementation – Ministry of the Interior);
- Digital Economy and Society Concept (2018) (*Koncepce Digitální ekonomika a společnost*) – intends to ensure the harmonisation of objectives spanning across public administration, economic and social partners, academia, and the professional community, covering all areas of the digital economy and society. This strategic document implicitly includes all the projects currently underway, such as Industry 4.0, Construction 4.0, Society 4.0, Work 4.0, Education 4.0, as well as all potential new initiatives such as Culture 4.0, Healthcare 4.0 and Agriculture 4.0 (implementation – Ministry of Industry and Trade).

Other strategic documents focused on digitalisation and associated with DČ include:

- Strategic Framework for the Development of Public Administration in the Czech Republic for the Period 2014–2020 (Ministry of the Interior of Czech Republic, 2016); implementation – Ministry of the Interior;
- Client-oriented public administration of the Czech Republic 2030 (*Klientsky orientovaná veřejná správa 2030*) (Ministry of the Interior of Czech Republic, 2020) – a plan outlining themes for the next stage of modernisation and development of public administration and e-government in the Czech Republic, with a focus on streamlining and improving the operation of public institutions in compliance with European Commission strategic papers (Europe 2020) and the Czech government (The International Competitiveness Strategy for the Czech Republic 2012–2020 and The National Reform Programme of the Czech Republic 2021; implemented by the Ministry of the Interior);
- The National Cyber Security Strategy of the Czech Republic 2021–2025 (*Akční plán k Národní strategii kybernetické bezpečnosti České republiky na období let 2021 až 2025*) (2020); implemented by the Ministry of Foreign Affairs (together with the Ministry of the Interior, Security Information Service, National Cyber and Information Security Agency, Ministry of Defence and Armed Forces);
- Strategic Framework Czech Republic 2030 (Office of the Government of the Czech Republic, 2017) – a document intended to support the digitalisation of the economy and society (particularly in the fields of work and education), which replaced the previous Strategic Framework of Sustainable Development; implemented by the Ministry of the Environment;
- The National eHealth Strategy of the Czech Republic 2016–2026 (*Národní strategie elektronického zdravotnictví ČR 2016–2026*) (Ministry of Health of Czech Republic; 2016) implemented by the Ministry of Health.

In conclusion, the concept of e-government is a specific policy within DČ that falls under the purview of the Ministry of the Interior. It should be emphasised, however, that the said ministry is in charge of all the key initiatives pursued under the Digital Czech Republic/e-government and put into operation by other ministries/public institutions. Organising and implementing the digitalisation of public administration is the responsibility of the open data task force – part of the Department of Chief Architect of e-Government at the Ministry of the Interior.

The Prime Minister and representatives of individual ministries make up the Government Council for the Information Society, which, among other tasks, monitors adherence to the principles of digital data, manages the open data system, and prevents potential data duplication.

3.2 Hungary

The Digital Success Programme, which was launched in 2015 and covers all the digital programmes, recommendations, and strategies, lay down successive steps of the process in Hungary. The following are the key documents, strategies, and initiatives in the field of public administration:

- Digital Success Programme (*Digitális Jólét Program*, DJP) (Ministry for Innovation and Technology of Hungary, n.d.);
- National Infocommunication Strategy (*Nemzeti Infokommunikációs Stratégia*, NIS) (European Commission, 2014) – the primary document outlining the computerisation and digitalisation of various areas (infrastructure, competencies, economy, and state); it focuses on, among other things, the provision of internal IT services supporting the operation of government, electronic public administration services for the general public and corporate target groups, and other electronic services within the purview of the state (such as those related to health, education, libraries, cultural heritage, division of state data and information assets);
- Artificial Intelligence Strategy (*Magyarország Mesterséges Intelligencia Stratégiája*) (Ministry for Innovation and Technology of Hungary, 2020);
- Public Services and Public Administration Development Operational Programme (*Közigazgatás -és Közszolgáltatásfejlesztési Operatív Program*) (European Commission, n.d.), supported by the European Social Fund and the Cohesion Fund;
- NAV 2.0 (*Nemzeti Adó- és Vámhivatal*) (National Tax and Customs Administration of Hungary, n.d.) – digitalisation of the National Tax Authority.

As the strategies represent holistic, interdisciplinary, and inter-institutional approaches, their implementation is delegated to various ministries. For example, the Digital Agricultural Strategy (*Magyarország Digitális Agrár Stratégiája*, DAS) developed under DJP assigns tasks to the Ministry of Agriculture and the Ministry of Human Resources, and recommends requesting the involvement of selected universities in conjunction with the Agricultural Cluster. Nonetheless, even though digitalisation implementation strategies involve other ministries, chambers, universities, and stakeholders, the Ministry for Innovation and Technology is the primary institution responsible for digitalisation (and DJP implementation). It should be noted, however, that the Ministry of the Interior is in charge of e-government.

The Client Gate – the country's official central electronic administration website – is the crucial e-government tool. Its online functionalities include services for employers and employees (on-line tax declarations, company registration via an attorney-at-law, electronic provision of statistical data, e-procurement, etc.; 160 out of 920 official procedures can be completed on-line). Despite the fact that the general public can access a variety of services online, its use is actually constrained due to low levels of digital literacy, even though the COVID-19 pandemic brought significant improvements in this field.

3.3   Poland

The main document that describes the process of digitalisation is the State Informatisation Strategy (*Strategia Informatyzacji Państwa*, SIP; Ministry of Digital Affairs of the Republic of Poland, n.d. a). SIP is a sub-sectoral strategy that builds upon the former Integrated State Computerisation Programme (*Program Zintegrowanej Informatyzacji Państwa*, PZIP) (Ministry of Digital Affairs of the Republic of Poland. (n.d. e), which constituted the operationalisation of the sectoral Efficient State 2020 Strategy (*Strategia Sprawne Państwo 2020*) and its follow-up – the Efficient and Modern State 2030 Strategy (*Strategia Sprawne i Nowoczesne Państwo 2030*) (Ministry of Home Affairs of the Republic of Poland. n.d.).

The main goal of PZIP/SIP is to improve public administration and government performance through computerisation. It is important to note that the PZIP for the 2019–2022 planning period was replaced by SIP in 2021 following a mid-term evaluation due to the lack of adequate integration of various computerisation and digitalisation-related initiatives as well as a lack of emphasis on the citizens' perspective. The new SIP specifically provides that citizens should come first thanks to improved public services as a result of the computerisation of public administration, development of e-administration (digital administration, including e-services), and access to the open public data. Decision-makers agreed to incorporate new projects, initiatives, and products into SIP in order to facilitate the development of an integrated IT model for the State Information Architecture (*Architektura Informacyjna Państwa*, AIP; Ministry of Digital Affairs of the Republic of Poland, n.d. b). Every single project in the field of computerisation/digitalisation implemented by any public institution can apply for funding e.g. from the Operational Programme Digital Poland (*Program Operacyjny Polska Cyfrowa*, POPC) that distributes EU funds provided that it is aligned with the AIP (Ministry of Digital Affairs of the Republic of Poland, n.d. d). The key institution responsible for integrating the public IT infrastructure (hardware), systems (software), and other resources under the AIP is the Chief IT Specialist of the State (*Główny Informatyk Kraju*, GIK). It should be made clear that GIK is not a single individual but rather a set of systems and procedures that facilitate the coordination of IT projects carried out by various public institutions (Ministry of Digital Affairs of the Republic of Poland, n.d. c).

The following are the main SIP-derived programmes:

- Gov.pl – the official internet platform of the Republic of Poland and its institutions with a uniform visual identity;
- eID – a pan-European e-authorisation system allowing access to public services for both citizens and public administration;
- System of Public Registers (*System Rejestrów Państwowych*, SRP);
- National System of Electronic Document Flow (*Elektroniczne Zarządzanie Dokumentacją*, EZD RP);
- Services and Data Integration Platform (*Platforma Integracji Usług i Danych*) – a nationwide register for monitoring the availability of services and data;
- Integrated Analytical Platform (*Zintegrowana Platforma Analityczna*, ZPA) – a tool for managing public registers and data held by ministries/other government agencies;
- Centre for IT Competencies in Public Administration (*Centrum Kompetencyjne Administracji*, CKA) (Ministry of Digital Affairs of the Republic of Poland, n.d. a).

Furthermore, the Strategy aims to integrate and standardise national and regional/local IT solutions in public administration.

Other important documents in the field of digitalisation include the Strategy (SIP) and the AIP as a broad category. Two of them play a crucial role – the Policy for the development of artificial intelligence in Poland from 2020 (*Polityka dla rozwoju sztucznej inteligencji w Polsce od 2020 roku*) and the Cybersecurity Strategy of the Republic of Poland for 2019–2024 (*Strategia Cyberbezpieczeństwa Rzeczypospolitej Polskiej na lata 2019–2024*, SC RP) (Ministry of Digital Affairs of the Republic of Poland, 2019). As was the case with SIP and PZIP, the current Strategy replaced the previous one before its maturity (originally planned for 2017–2022), which demonstrates both the dynamic nature of the challenges (even before the COVID-19 pandemic) and insufficient progress made by public administration in addressing them.

Regardless of the strategies and documents, the institutional setup consists of state and non-state actors involved in developing and implementing computerisation and digitalisation policies. The Ministry of Digitalisation is the primary institution in charge of these policies. For a number of years, it used to be a separate institution before being incorporated into the Prime Ministers' Chancellery in 2020 (and the Prime Minister officially became the Minister of Digitalisation). As a result, the Chancellery of the Prime Minister of the Republic of Poland is now the key institution responsible for digitalisation.

Despite the fact that there are still several sectoral agendas in charge of digitalisation, such as the e-Health Centre (Ministry of Health) and the Centre for

Data Processing State Research Institute (Ministry of Education and Science), they are subsumed under AIK and SIP.

3.4   Slovakia

Slovakia's current position in relation to the digital agenda is best described in terms of prior initiatives and participatory processes aimed at identifying issues and priorities in the country's digital space as well as a review of relevant strategic documents at the national level. In 2017, the Digital Single Market Opportunity for Slovakia Action Plan was developed, which identified priority areas in the field of informatisation, defined the key objectives, and set ambitious legislative and non-legislative steps for their implementation. This document not only emphasised the need for new activities, but also listed all the existing strategies, plans, and projects that required a new dimension. This initiative is continued as part of the Action Plan for Slovakia's Digital Transformation for 2019–2022 (Action Plan... 2019).

The following schemes have been launched since its inception:
– National Concept of e-Government (*Národná koncepcia informatisácie verejnej správy*, NKIVS) – an action plan for electronic public administration and the creation of a government cloud;
– First activities of the Data Office with a focus on enhancing the use of data in public administration and implementing the concept of My Data;
– The Office of Behavioural Innovations;
– Action Plan for the Implementation of the Concept of Cybersecurity.

The main actor responsible for the coordination of digital policy in Slovakia is the Informatisation Management Section of the Ministry of Investment, Regional Development and Informatisation (MIRDI). It develops company informatisation concepts, draws up legislation in the field of IT for public administration, and issues standards for public administration information systems. It also monitors the process of digitalisation of public and private sectors, and enhances the development of public administration information systems. Finally, it addresses the management of public administration resources in the field of IT as well as the implementation of priority axis 7 of the Operational Programme Integrated Infrastructure.

The Council of the Government of the Slovak Republic for the Digitalisation of Public Administration and the Digital Single Market (the Council) is another major player in the process. The council serves as the Government of the Slovak Republic's advisory, coordinating, and initiative body for matters pertaining to information technology, the digital single market and the digitalisation of government with a focus on delivering electronic public administration services to both individuals and legal entities. It also deals with electronic e-government systems and economic development in Slovakia in the context of the digital economy.

As the MIRDI is a new ministry, its institutional relationships with other government entities sometimes tend to be informal. Previously, the Ministry of the Economy handled its obligations; as a result, these relationships have been particularly stormy due to political nominations that have resulted in a lack of foresight on the part of various MIRDI actors. As a result, the Council adopts a more apolitical stance and seeks input from outside sources.

4   Digitalisation of Public Services as a Key Driver for e-Government Development in the V4 Countries

It is still too early to assess the performance of strategies mentioned in the previous section. However, since the individual stages of e-government upgrade are mutually exclusive, there is no direct transition from Stage 4 (transactional presence) to Stages 5 or 6 (vertical and horizontal integration). Paradoxically, even if some e-services developed by a public institution are of a high quality, they may overlap or interfere with others; as a result, the existing ones must be modified at some point, which may entail taking a step back in order to proceed (Pl_6_2). This is the case e.g. with the establishment of a new IT architecture for Poland mentioned above.

Naturally, it is debatable whether progress toward vertical and horizontal integration is even conceivable without stepping back. The mindset of public administration appears to be vital for establishing e-government, so in our view every single public institution must go through the process of digitalisation and experience it on its own, even at a very basic level, to prepare for greater digital integration.

The lockdown experience has had a considerable impact on this way of thinking. In fact, particularly in the wake of the pandemic, all the V4 countries are entering a new stage of e-government that affects not only specific public services but also the fundamental tenets of public administration as a whole through both horizontal and vertical integration. The development of data-driven policy that supports the process of automating/customising public services for citizens (e.g. auto-filling of personal data in a variety of forms) as well as advances in the digitalisation of various public services (sometimes after prior revisions) available at cross-institutional platforms forced various public institutions to work together to integrate their databases and procedures (Pl_6_3). Some examples of recent e-service implementations are provided in Table 6.2.

TABLE 6.2   Recent e-service implementations by area in the v4 countries

Area	Czech Republic	Hungary	Poland	Slovakia
Civil affairs (ID, passports, driving licenses, etc.)	Portál občana (access to online government services and the provision of information such as data boxes, replacement of driving licenses, information from registers (driver penalty points, criminal record, trade register, road vehicle register, land and mortgage register), access to applications (eRecept, Vaccination Portal) and portals (trade license processing, completion of tax returns, incapacity for work, pension insurance, services and benefits of the Labour Office (portals of municipalities, cities and regions, 2018) eDalnice (electronic motorway vignette)	Ügyfélkapu (e.g. to report stolen passports, but if a new one is needed, the online platform is only good for making in-person appointments)	mObywatel (mobile access to personal documents: ID, driving licence, COVID certificate, Large Family Card, etc; 2017) e-ID (2019) mPojazd (vehicle registration, 2019) On-line childbirth notification (2020)	Slovensko.sk created a section for the services for citizens and requests from government institutions, which include: e-ID (2017) electronic vehicle registration (2015) Online registry (birth, death, etc.) (2016)

Entrepreneurship	ARES (Administrative register of economic entities, 2013) RES (register of economic entities) RŽP (trade register, 2008, updated electronic submission of an application for the establishment or change of a trade, 2019)	Ügyfélkapu (includes adding new services for tax purposes to your business) Setting up a new business usually requires a lawyer and non-fully integrated systems mostly only the lawyers are permitted to use. Some businesses can be registered online at Ügyfélkapu. Relevant ministries can provide information of businesses online on their own dedicated websites	CEIDG (Central Register and Information on Economic Activity); on-line business registration	Section for entrepreneurs on Slovensko.sk with services for entrepreneurs (2014)
Health	eNeschopenka (sick leave 2020) eRecept (prescription 2011) Tečka (applications containing Vaccination certificate, Test Certificate, or Certificate of past illness COVID-19)	www.eeszt.gov.hu/ (prescriptions, referrals, diagnoses, healthcare data, medical history, documents)	eZwolnienie (sick leave, 2018) eRecepta (prescription, 2019)	eZdravie (electronic sick leave, health documentation, e-prescription – 2018)

TABLE 6.2   Recent e-service implementations by area in the v4 countries (*cont.*)

Area	Czech Republic	Hungary	Poland	Slovakia
Judiciary	eJustice (submission of a proposal to initiate court proceedings /ePodatelna/, online monitoring of the status of court proceedings /info Soud/, extracts from the Commercial Register, Insolvency Register, Criminal Register, 2007)	Ügyfélkapu enables administration online at countries, prosecutors office etc.	e-KRS (National Court Register, 2021) e-Sąd (court of law, 2010)	Electronic information about the judicial decisions at personal email account – at Slovensko.sk (2016)
Public Procurement	Věstník veřejných zakázek (Public Procurement, 2016)	at Ügyfélkapu	e-Zamówienie (Public Procurement, 2021)	e-Zákazky (Electronic public procurement and auctions, 2021)
Social policy	On-line application for all kind of benefits provided by the Ministry of Labour and Social Affairs and the Czech Social Security Administration thorough ISDS (Information system of data boxes) or NIA (National Identification Authority) (2019)	Ügyfélkapu enables online administration	On-line application for parental benefits 500+ (2016)	On-line service portal of the Social Insurance Agency
Tax and Tariffs	Myto cz.eu (electronic toll collection system, 2021) Mojedaně (system for tax submission and electronic sales records, 2021)	Ügyfélkapu for declaring taxes and various tax and tariffs related administration through the integrated system of the tax authority of Hungary	e-Clo (e-Tariff, 2014) ePIT (2019)	Financial services (Tax and Tariffs, 2013)

SOURCE: OWN STUDY

We believe that the COVID-19 pandemic, the lockdowns in particular, significantly accelerated the process in question. Business has been the main force behind e-government since its inception (the computerisation of public institutions); nevertheless, in the early 2010s, non-governmental organisations that deal with digital concerns started to push governments in this direction (Pl_6_2). However, it was only after the epidemic that the general attitude of government administration changed, and eventually, some procedures that had been in place for many years became operational.

The fundamental question now is whether public administration is ready to play a proactive rather than a reactive role in developing e-government. Although the digitalisation of particular procedures/services may eventually lead to a vertical and horizontal integration, it will not happen without the initiative of public agencies (Pl_6_1). Furthermore, functional digital integration may provide a good opportunity for many public institutions to overcome the tyranny of the status quo, in which existing actors continue to protect their political or corporate interests and structural integration is difficult to achieve. As an example let us cite Poland's food safety control system: even if the European Commission-recommended structural integration of public agencies fails, there is still opportunity for functional integration through digitalisation and integration of discrete databases and procedures (see Kędzierski, 2022).

5 Conclusion

Although the term Fourth Industrial Revolution was not coined until 2016, numerous countries were already well on their way to implementing e-government in the early 2010s. The development of new technologies, including greater service customisation, had a profound impact on public administration and the services provided by it. Indeed, many governments, having launched multiple e-solutions in the first decade of the new millennium were forced to upgrade them. Despite their ups and downs, these upgrades have profoundly changed the attitude of business, society, and public administration to digitalisation and e-government. Following a period of experiments, successes, and failures, the V4 countries have now made progress not only in building cross-institutional platforms for citizens and adopting data-driven policies, but also in horizontal and vertical integration of all government services. The COVID-19 pandemic undoubtedly had a considerable impact on public administration's mindset, which was essential before moving forward with more advanced forms of e-government. The process of digital integration is widely acknowledged to be the most difficult challenge for the 2020s in this area, as evidenced in the strategies adopted by all the V4 countries.

Furthermore, the EU's post-pandemic policy, including the Next Generation EU Programme, aims to accelerate the digitalisation of both the economy and the state. All the EU Member States have committed themselves to significant investments and reforms in this area. Due to political tensions, it is unclear whether all the V4 countries will eventually take advantage of this opportunity, since Poland and particularly Hungary may face difficulties in accessing the EU funds earmarked for this purpose. Nonetheless, whether or not these funds eventually become available, business and social expectations to develop e-government will most likely be decisive. This is bound to have a considerable impact on public administration and its logic of operation – sooner or later, these expectations will influence its code of conduct, causing it to adopt a more citizen-friendly approach.

Bibliography

Dawes, S. (2008). The Evolution and Continuing Challenges of E-Governance, *Public Administration Review*, 68(1), 86–102. https://doi.org/10.1111/j.1540-6210.2008.00981.x

European Commission (2021). *eGovernment Benchmark 2021*. https://op.europa.eu/pl/publication-detail/-/publication/d30dcae1-436f-11ec-89db-01aa75ed71a1

Gil-Garcia, J. and Martinez-Moyano, I. (2007). Understanding the evolution of e-government: The influence of systems of rules on public sector dynamics, *Government Information Quarterly*, 24(2), 266–290. https://doi.org/10.1016/j.giq.2006.04.005

Grönlund, A. and Horan, T. (2004). Introducing e-Gov: History, Definitions, and Issues, *Communications of the Association for Information Systems*, 15, 713–729. https://doi.org/10.17705/1CAIS.01539

Kapsa, I. and Musiał-Karg, M. (2021). *The Internet Users' Opinions on Public E-Services. Empirical analysis*. https://repozytorium.amu.edu.pl/bitstream/10593/26670/1/The%20Internet%20Users%E2%80%99%20Opinions%20on%20Public%20E-Services.pdf

Kędzierski, M. (2022). *Integracja czy połączenie. Analiza możliwości zwiększenia efektywności działania inspekcji weterynaryjnej oraz ochrony roślin i nasiennictwa*, Europejski Fundusz Rozwoju Wsi Polskiej. www.efrwp.pl/dir_upload/site/files/Raport_FIR__30.05.2022.pdf

Maksimova, M., Solvak, M. and Krimmer, R. (2021). Data-Driven Personalised E-government Services: Literature Review and Case Study, In: *Electronic Participation. ePart 2021. Lecture Notes in Computer Science*, 12849. Springer, Cham. https://doi.org/10.1007/978-3-030-82824-0_12

Ranga Rao, V. (2011). Collaborative government to employee (G2E): Issues and challenges to E-government, *Journal of E-Governance*, *34*(4), 214–229.

Trotta, A. (2018). *Advances in E-Governance. Theory and Application of Technological Initiatives*, Routledge.

UN (2011). *e-government and New Technologies: Towards better citizen engagement for development*, Department of Economic and Social Affairs. https://publicadministration.un.org/publications/content/PDFs/E-Library%20Archives/2011%20EGM_e-Goverment%20and%20New%20Technologies.pdf

Internet Sources

Action plan for the digital transformation of Slovakia for 2019–2022. (2019). www.mirri.gov.sk/wp-content/uploads/2019/10/AP-DT-English-Version-FINAL.pdf

Digitalni Cesko (n.d.). www.digitalnicesko.cz

EURactiv. (2007). *EU recommends re-focusing e-government strategy on Lisbon objectives*. www.euractiv.com/section/economy-jobs/news/eu-recommends-re-focusing-e-government-strategy-on-lisbon-objectives

European Commission. (n.d.) *Public Administration and Civil Service Development OP*. https://ec.europa.eu/regional_policy/en/atlas/programmes/2014-2020/hungary/2014hu05m3op001

European Commission. (2014). *National Infocommunication Strategy 2014–2020*. https://joinup.ec.europa.eu/sites/default/files/document/2016-11/nis_en_clear.pdf

Hungarian COVID application (n.d.). www.eeszt.gov.hu

Ministry for Innovation and Technology of Hungary (n.d.) *Digital success programme*. https://digitalisjoletprogram.hu/en

Ministry for Innovation and Technology of Hungary (2020) *Hungary's Artificial Intelligence Strategy 2020–2030*. https://ai-hungary.com/api/v1/companies/15/files/146074/view

Ministry of Digital Affairs of the Republic of Poland (n.d. a) *Strategia Informatyzacji Państwa*. http://archiwum.mc.gov.pl/konsultacje/program-zintegrowanej-informatyzacji-panstwa/zalacznik-1-strategia-informatyzacji-panstwa-plan-dzialan-ministra-cyfryzacji

Ministry of Digital Affairs of the Republic of Poland (n.d.b). *Architektura informacyjna państwa*. www.gov.pl/web/cyfryzacja/architektura-informacyjna-panstwa

Ministry of Digital Affairs of the Republic of Poland (n.d.c). *Główny informatyk kraju*. www.gov.pl/web/cyfryzacja/gik-glowny-informatyk-kraju

Ministry of Digital Affairs of the Republic of Poland (n.d.d). *Program Operacyjny Polska Cyfrowa*. www.gov.pl/web/cyfryzacja/program-operacyjny-polska-cyfrowa

Ministry of Digital Affairs of the Republic of Poland (n.d.e). *Program Zintegrowa-nej Informatyzacji Państwa.* www.gov.pl/web/cyfryzacja/program-zintegrowanej -informatyzacji-panstwa

Ministry of Digital Affairs of the Republic of Poland (2019). *Strategia Cyberbezpieczeń-stwa Rzeczypospolitej Polskiej na lata 2019–2024.* www.gov.pl/web/cyfryzacja/strate-gia-cyberbezpieczenstwa-rzeczypospolitej-polskiej-na-lata-2019-2024

Ministry of Health of Czech Republic (2016). *The National eHealth Strategy of the Czech Republic.* www.dataplan.info/img_upload/7bdb1584e3b8a53d337518d988763f8d /national_ehealth_strategy__vo.2_en.pdf

Ministry of Home Affairs of the Republic of Poland (n.d.). *Uchwała Rady Ministrów w sprawie przyjęcia strategii „Sprawne i nowoczesne państwo."* www.gov.pl/web /mswia/projekt-uchwaly-rady-ministrow-w-sprawie-przyjecia-strategii-sprawne-i -nowoczesne-panstwo-2030

Ministry of Interior of Czech Republic (2016). *The strategic framework for the develop-ment of public administration in the Czech Republic for the period 2014–2020.* www .dataplan.info/img_upload/7bdb1584e3b8a53d337518d988763f8d/strategic_frame work_for_the_development_of_public_administration_in_the_cz_for_2014-2020 .pdf

Ministry of the Interior of Czech Republic (2020). *Client-oriented public administration 2030.* www.mvcr.cz/soubor/client-oriented-public-administration-2030.aspx

National Cyber Security Strategy of the Czech Republic (2020) www.dataplan.info/img _upload/7bdb1584e3b8a53d337518d988763f8d/nscs_2021_2025_eng.pdf

National Tax and Customs Administration of Hungary (n.d.). https://kkk.nav.gov.hu /eles/2/web/

Office of the Government of the Czech Republic (2017). *Strategic Framework Czech Republic 2030.* www.vlada.cz/assets/ppov/udrzitelny-rozvoj/projekt-OPZ/Strategic _Framework_CZ2030.pdf

CHAPTER 7

The Management and Regulation of Data and Information Flows in the V4 Countries

Bartłomiej Biga

1 Introduction

This chapter examines the potential for collaboration between public administrations in the Visegrád countries and large technology companies. This is a fascinating issue, particularly in light of the fact that the regulated entities (big tech corporations) are more powerful than the regulators in a number of ways; hence the latter cannot enforce administrative authority on the former. The state administration must thus seek other ways of cooperation, bearing in mind the relative weakness of semi-peripheral countries vis-à-vis technology firms. The discussion in this chapter is based on the most recent research, the available data, and in-depth interviews (IDI) with representatives of various stakeholder groups from all the V4 countries.

Data is a valuable resource for business (Faccia, 2019) and public policies (Studinka and Guenduez, 2018), therefore gathering it is important from the perspectives of both the central and local governments. Interestingly, public authorities have an advantage in this regard, since they control a number of databases characterised by universality, which is difficult to achieve for private actors. Examples include taxpayer data maintained by finance ministries and tax services (Cz_5_2).

Global technology companies, on the other hand, have found ways to collect new categories of data. Their main motivation is associated with commercial needs, specifically, the capacity to accurately target personalised advertising. However, the public sector is increasingly recognising the utility of this data in the context of public policies (Bhardosa et al., 2013, pp. 9–18). Furthermore, it is possible to greatly simplify the design and implementation of state actions based on low-sensitivity data. Aggregated data that lacks information that may be used to specifically identify a person is often sufficient for this purpose.

Semi-peripheral countries are thus faced with a serious dilemma. On the one hand, they must address public concerns about data protection and deliver ever-improving public services. On the other, they cannot afford to hit the IT giants too hard, because even their partial withdrawal from a country would not be well received by the populace, moreover, the latter are mostly outside of their jurisdiction. Even so, for economic reasons, this would be extremely unlikely. A greater threat derives from the fact that these corporations have a significant influence on public debate, including the potential to interfere with democratic processes. The governments of semi-peripheral countries therefore have a strong incentive to seek the best possible relationships with technology giants, even though they are currently too weak to negotiate from a position of equality.

As a result, cooperation between large technology firms and state institutions (especially in the semi-peripheral ones) is very weak (Moore, 2021), which is confirmed by individual in-depth interviews (IDIs) conducted for the purposes of this study. They also reveal that the lack of satisfactory collaboration can be blamed on both sides. Certain obstacles appear to be difficult to overcome. For instance, it would be simpler to plan and manage public transportation if businesses such as Uber or Bolt provided local authorities with aggregated data on resident movements. Individual transportation may thus become less competitive, which would be problematic for the businesses that originally provided such invaluable information. However, in reality, these firms tend not to view public transportation as a rival because their top priority is to outperform other similar firms (Smith, 2016). There is also a broad range of situations in which sharing information, even hypothetically, does not jeopardise a company's competitive advantage. After all, firms such as Google and Apple do not face this risk when sharing population movement data because they operate under a fundamentally different business model (Keen and Williams, 2013).

According to the interviewees, administrations in the Visegrád countries lack sufficiently developed competences to enter into cooperation with technology giants even where there is no threat to their competitive advantages and these companies are willing to collaborate. The comments we received prevent us from being able to definitively state whether these shortcomings in public administration can be addressed in the near future.

2   Traditional and New Information Flows

The prospect of harnessing data and information from the commercial sector for public initiatives is clearly attracting considerable attention. The approach known as Information-Based-Regulation (IBR), which some see as a compromise between the two extreme methods of market-based and command-and-control, is particularly popular. IBR basically mandates that food manufacturers disclose to restaurateurs how food hygiene inspectors evaluated the level of sanitation on their premises or to reveal the ingredients of their products (Bowen and Panagiotopoulos, 2020, pp. 203–221).

However, this represents only a small proportion of the information flows possible under IBR and should be classified as traditional circulation, which is fundamentally different from the new approach mentioned in the Introduction. Figure 7.1 depicts information flows in IBR that have occurred for a long time between distinct sets of actors (public, private, and civil society). As a result, concerns about specific categories of data being made available by public authorities are mostly unwarranted; on the contrary, such practices are well established, and technical developments are merely accelerating them. The digital economy has enabled the acquisition and processing of considerably larger databases.

It is important to recall that, as M. Mazzucato (2011) points out, the public sector, as a rule, does not seek to take over (or, as some argue unjustifiably capture) the value generated by the private sector. According to the author, most technologies that enabled corporations such as Google or Apple to create products and services collecting such valuable data were originally conceived and developed by public institutions. Consequently, sharing in the benefits acquired from this source is nothing more than sharing in the profits due as a reward for successful investment. Moreover, there are examples of thriving, usually bottom-up projects based on data sharing, such as Linux and Wikipedia. In their case, there was no excessive capture of value by technology companies.

In her next book, Mazzucato (2018) contends that if anyone is involved in undue value capture, it is the private sector (rather than the public one so frequently accused in the ongoing debate). As a rule, private enterprises do not participate in the early stages of invention development (i.e. primary innovation), which are the most risky and capital intensive. Technology firms typically join in only at the implementation stage of advanced solutions, where extraordinarily high revenues can be made with relatively small outlays. This is not a bad thing in and of itself, because the roles played by different actors at successive stages of innovation development naturally result from the inherent distinctions between the commercial and public sectors. Ultimately, such an allocation leads to good results; the only problem that remains is fair profit-sharing.

From the perspective of semi-peripheral countries, this issue is even more complicated since they are not usually active as players in the field of technological innovation (Mazzucato, 2018). The public sector in the United States

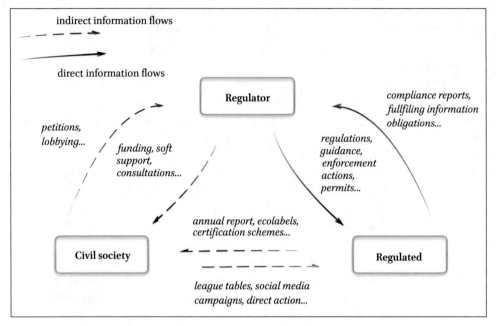

FIGURE 7.1   Indicative information flows in IBR
SOURCE: BOWEN AND PANAGIOTOPOULOS (2020, PP. 203–221)

and in several other developed countries is overwhelmingly responsible for
the creation of a range of key inventions implemented into mobile phones
(which effectively turned them into smartphones). It is therefore more difficult to justify the transfer of data by technology companies to the public sector
in countries such as Poland, the Czech Republic, Slovakia or Hungary. In this
case, the right to obtain data may be understood as a specific share in profits.
Still, one should bear in mind that many promising start-ups, which are being
established in semi-peripheral countries (Gosztonyi, 2022), are promptly taken
over by the existing US giants. In this way, the v4 countries also indirectly contribute to innovations that underlie big-tech's power.

   Consequently, it seems necessary to invoke other arguments, which may
arise from where the data is sourced and the infrastructural support that even
semi-peripheral countries can provide. Moreover, data, or intellectual property
in general, is so distinct from tangible property that its possible capture by the
state carries a wholly different weight. When the state takes over a good of this
type, it restricts the ability of private entities to use it, which is an inherent

feature of tangible property. In the case of intellectual property, however, there is no issue of scarcity – the same databases can be used concurrently. Of course, this begs the question of whether the competitive edge of businesses that rely on data collection will suffer as a result.

Thus, in order to facilitate the acquisition of certain intellectual assets for public policy purposes, a kind of de-propertisation[1] of this asset class is necessary. The requirement to treat intellectual property independently (rather than automatically invoke procedures that apply to tangible property) derives from four fundamental differences. The first one is the previously mentioned scarcity of goods (which is a typical feature of the material world; in the intellectual world, it can only be created artificially). The second one is the notification difficulty – informing who the owner is and that a certain piece of information is protected by an exclusive right at all. The third one is that intellectual property has much fuzzier boundaries, whereas the fourth one arises from the difficulty to enforce intellectual property rights by the courts. This is because such cases are much more unpredictable (Biga, 2017, pp. 18–29). Easier data extraction for public use necessitates a shift away from the traditional definition of intellectual property with its focus on rights, and must be supplemented by the issue of obligations (in the legal sense) and duties (in a broader sense).

Interestingly, the perception of data harvested by digital giants as an opportunity to improve public policies has emerged only recently. Initially, the discussion tended to be dominated by issues of risk, mainly to children and young people, as these groups were the first to become active users of at least social media (Libingstone and Brake, 2010, pp. 75–83). Threats are currently viewed in the context of a violation of privacy as a value in itself.

It is impossible to say if society's concern for privacy is increasing or decreasing. On the one hand, customers are pressuring technology companies to change their policies (e.g. Apple introduced the option to turn off the permission to track the owner in its iOS). The coronavirus outbreak, on the other hand, pushed some people over the edge, making them more willing to trade substantial chunks of their privacy for a greater sense of security. In the context of this chapter, the recent tendency could be reversed if privacy is taken more seriously. Even aggregated and anonymised data may be impacted by privacy issues, which could result in a considerable reduction in the amount of data available for public policy purposes.

---

1   The opposite of 'propertisation' as described by M. Lemley (2004).

3   Co-creation and the Commons

A significant proportion of data generated by large technology companies should be considered in terms of the commons (Buck 2017), since the very process of their sourcing is a model example of co-creation (Hein 2019, pp. 503–518) for even when they are collected by private companies, they track the activities of individual users. The rapid growth of technology giants was made possible by involving millions of users in the process of value co-creation (Birkinbine, 2020, pp. 33–43). Naturally, it can be argued that a sufficient benefit to individuals from providing this data is the ability to access (often free of charge) the services provided by technology giants. However, such a position appears radical not only in light of the aforementioned research by Mazzucatto, who proved that the collection tools themselves were also largely developed outside the commercial sector.

Sound management of the commons requires several basic conditions discussed by E. Ostrom (1990) to be met. The first one is the clarity of legal regulations (who is entitled to what, who can impose what penalties). Moreover, these regulations must be universally accepted by the community, which in turn requires the creation of tools for collective, democratic decision-making by all those using the resources in question. Secondly, conflict resolution mechanisms must be both local and public. The participation of community members is essential, as they have the greatest interest in making governance effective and know best how to circumvent the common rules. Thirdly, these rules must not conflict with higher-order principles. Clearly, these solutions break out of the two-dimensional state – private property mould.

The FRAND – fair, reasonable, and non-discriminatory – licensing formula may offer inspiration for coordinating access to data. Its use in licences is enforced by standardisation organisations which aim to ensure the compatibility of devices produced by different companies. The formula covers key patents for some technology that, under an agreed standard, is intended to be usable in products made by multiple companies (Teece, 2017). In practice, interpreting each parameter of the FRAND formula can be difficult and lead to unexpected results. It does, however, allow for some degree of standardisation. The term 'fair' is understood in the context of antitrust law, the adjective 'reasonable' means requiring non-exclusive licencing and basing all material parts of licencing agreements on valid, objective reasons, whereas 'non-discriminatory' indicates that licensees cannot be chosen arbitrarily (i.e. must be based on objective criteria), and that licence agreements cannot be changed at will.

The weakness of semi-peripheral countries discussed in the above-mentioned book leads us to focus on voluntary forms of cooperation between the public sector and business in the area of the commons. As a result, proposals to include access rights to development resources or intellectual property in constitutional rights appear to have a primarily symbolic value. In fact, they are unlikely to provide an effective barrier to over-privatisation. Such a privatisation of critical resources can be extremely risky to society and, in the long run, detrimental to economic development. Semi-peripheral states, however, must rely heavily on voluntary actions. They are frequently forced to invoke the concept of responsibility, which extends beyond formal legal requirements. This is also a natural consequence of the challenge outlined in the Introduction, namely, attempting to reconcile the public interest (better public services, privacy) with the expectations of the digital giants (which demand freedom to act). The disadvantageous negotiating position of the public side thus forces it to seek recourse in non-legal categories.

The foregoing should not be taken to imply that efforts to create effective institutional barriers against the most egregious infractions of the norms should be completely abandoned. They are necessary, particularly in light of the rising trend towards monopsony, or a situation in which a single company acts as an intermediary between numerous producers and recipients. Because the data held by firms such as Amazon, Booking, or Uber is totally exclusive, it would be difficult to undercut or even attempt to counterbalance their power as the sole distributors. As a result, recognising their data as a public good that may be exploited by competitors as well as public authorities is a critical step in modern antitrust operations. Although such measures appear to be extremely difficult to enforce from the perspective of semi-peripheral countries, one ally is the very nature of data, which, as an intangible resource, cannot be entirely controlled by enterprises.

4   Examples of Collaboration with Technology Companies

Essentially, the v4 countries engage in this form of collaboration for three reasons (from the public policy perspective):
1.   To collect data;
2.   To test public policies and gather feedback;
3.   To promote the collaboration of experts with the commercial sector;
4.   To provide services to businesses and residents.

Cities are one of the most obvious areas for collaboration between governments and technology firms since they are characterised by the highest data collection density (e.g. those sourced from mobile phones). Local governments can offer certain resources (mostly infrastructure) that are especially valuable for businesses in the early stages of implementation (e.g. testing prototypes). In exchange, municipal authorities expect access to the data generated by such a project. A good illustration of such collaboration is the City Lab in Bratislava (Sk_3_4), which seeks access to data on the use of public transport infrastructure (public transport, bike rental, parking spaces), consumption of utilities (to improve network design, reduce water use, etc.), and air quality monitoring.

In some circumstances, simply making data public (even if the knowledge obtained thereby is not used to design public policies) can be beneficial for citizens. One example is the publication of property price statistics on the website of the Brno City Hall (Cz_5_1). If a corporation does not fear that disclosing specific kinds of information will undermine its competitive advantage, as is the case here, it cooperates with local authorities without compulsion and at no cost. In many cases, broad or highly aggregated statistics are useful for local administration (e.g. average rents in a certain district, number of taxi service starts and stops in a given area at a given time, etc.) (Cz_5_1).

It is worth remembering that the flow of data and information between administration and business does not have to be unidirectional. As noted by the representative of the Czech Ministry of Health (Cz_3_3), what is needed is the so-called secondary data sharing. For example, data from X-rays used in individual treatments may be made accessible to private firms to calibrate artificial intelligence specialised in interpreting such images. Another example of knowledge transfer between government and business is geographically distributed data on education (specific competences), which is extremely valuable for job placement services.

This data flow direction may have a significant impact on how regions respond to global issues like climate change. The effectiveness of such programmes depends on coordination, which only public bodies can provide. In this regard, they also have an advantage owing to the open nature of meteorological services in general. However, such coalitions are not being formed, as evidenced by the Hungarian Ministry of National Development and the Ministry of the Interior, which have not collaborated with any private actors on climate change or sustainability (Hu_5_2).

The example of the Polish NGO sector (Pl_5_1) demonstrates that the provision of data by private firms for public policy purposes is frequently motivated by their corporate PR needs. In particular, in emergency situations, such as the recent pandemic, they were ready to supply accurate data on user mobility, which enabled the authorities to assess the effectiveness of pandemic restrictions. The data in question were also supported by information from banks on recorded payment card transactions. Apart from evaluating compliance, they also provided an opportunity to more effectively target financial assistance (known in Poland as shields) to firms thanks to more accurate information regarding the decline in turnover in individual sectors of the economy.

The growing conflict of interests could also be a major challenge to cooperation. Data sourced from organisations such as Airbnb would be highly useful in eliminating inefficiencies in the housing sector; however, drawing attention to this issue is not in the best interests of the company. Airbnb is willing to enter into negotiations with municipal officials. Its 2019 agreement with Krakow authorities was based on the city's proclamation of commitment to sustainable tourism. Although the letter of intent implied some data sharing, the partnership has so far remained primarily declarative.

5   Sustaining Competitive Advantages

In considering the acquisition of data and information from technology companies, it is necessary to permit them to retain certain competitive advantages. This means that unrestricted data acquisition along the lines of China's security services is out of the question. However, it is not easy to analyse this issue from the perspective of justice. Even though capturing private resources should be subject to very strict limitations, the legitimacy of IT corporations' data ownership (or more specifically, private ownership of certain categories of data) is also questionable.

Without resolving this issue, it is worth noting another source of competitive advantage that companies will retain even if they decide to share a large proportion of their data in some form. After all, algorithms are often a much more valuable resource than the data themselves as they facilitate the development of viable business models even when using fully publicly available data (Breidbach, Maglio 2020). A good example is Google's search engine that relies on a top-secret ranking algorithm.

It is important to realise that a variety of business models are based on fairly broad, conditional intellectual property sharing. Examples include Google's distribution of Android and collaboration between firms based on standards licenced through patent pools (e.g. Bluetooth). Typically, these strategies are intended to achieve the broadest possible reach, which, with transaction costs near nil, is quite appealing. They frequently consist in selling extra goods and services, which thus form the company's primary source of revenue.

The experience of Bratislava (Sk_3_4) also shows that cooperation with local government institutions helps companies build their competitive advantage, often thanks to access to municipal infrastructure. For many enterprises, the opportunity to test their solutions in a controlled and relatively safe environment is also valuable. Interesting experiences in this area were reported by the city of Brno (Cz_3_1, Cz_5_1), where bike sharing/rental platforms are open to broad collaboration as long as all players in a given market share the same types of data. This demonstrates that providing data to local governments is no longer an issue – instead, the major concern is the relative level of competition. The flow of data and knowledge is not inherently risky; however, it may cause problems if the burdens are not evenly distributed.

In some cases, making data available for public policies may actually boost a company's competitive advantage. This is especially true in education policy, which, when combined with company-specific data, may expand the pool of candidates who are a better match to its recruitment needs.

However, there is no denying that in some cases, making data available to the public sector may result in a loss of a company's competitive advantage. In such circumstances, there have been recommendations to institute compensation (Pl_5_1), but this presents the issue of determining the amount of fees whether officially imposed or negotiated on the basis of the principle of equality of parties. The latter possibility may be difficult to achieve in practice since, on the one hand, the administration has very specialised leverage (regulation) and, on the other, technology corporations actually enjoy a monopolistic (or rather monopsonistic) status.

6   Willingness to Improve Collaboration

Staffing shortfalls in state administration constitute the most typical hindrance to more effective collaboration with technology companies. Respondents cited a variety of obstacles, including the lack of available teams to engage in such collaboration and a shortage of required competencies. Difficulties are both conceptual (ideas for how technology companies could improve public policy implementation) and practical (different work cultures) in nature (Arunchand and Ramanathan, 2013).

This shows that even the public sector recognises significant shortcomings on this front, which contradicts the widely held belief that the major problem is a lack of transparency on the part of technology firms. It is commonly assumed that companies are unwilling to collaborate with public administration units since the latter add little value to their business models, whilst thinking in terms of the common good is intrinsically antithetical to corporate logic.

However, this does not imply that the administration is unwilling to cooperate. For example, despite the fact that it does not consider it necessary to collect any specific types of data, the Czech Ministry of Finance (Cz_5_2) is ready to discuss the matter with representatives of technology firms. Furthermore, it offers to pay for such cooperation on condition that it takes place in accordance with the public procurement regulations in force.

Administrations in the Visegrád countries vary in their digitalisation levels. Without a doubt, this is a crucial precondition for collaboration with technology companies. Experts from Hungary highlighted their country's undeveloped e-government, which was acutely felt during the pandemic. On the other hand, despite a host of structural challenges, Poland's government is distinguished by the implementation of several cutting-edge digital solutions. Figure 7.2 compares the digitalisation levels of the V4 countries to those of other European countries.

7 Regulatory Opportunities

The Digital Services and Digital Markets Act – a package of regulations designed by the European Commission to respond to the challenges posed by the dominant market position of a small group of digital service providers – was met with high expectations owing to the belief that national legislation has so far proved powerless in this regard. Respondents also noted that avoidance of national legislation by technology businesses does not always stem from a lack of goodwill, but is rather a natural by-product of regulatory fragmentation, which is difficult to reconcile with services based on standardisation. As a result, at least in theory, these EU restrictions can benefit technology companies.

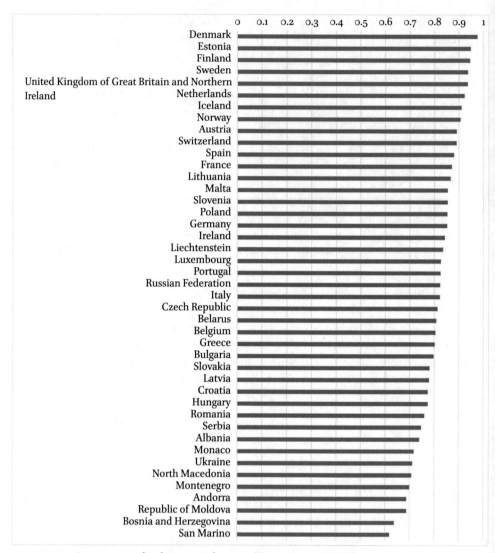

FIGURE 7.2   E-government development index 2020 (European countries)
SOURCE: HTTPS://PUBLICADMINISTRATION,UN,ORG/EGOVKB/EN-US/DATA-CENTER

However, it should be acknowledged that in semi-peripheral countries such as Poland, Slovakia, the Czech Republic, and Hungary, local subsidiaries of technology giants are nothing more than a conveyor belt for policies formulated in California. This is especially evident during discussions on draft legislation, where the staff of these companies use materials (slides, brochures) prepared by the headquarters. Such a passive attitude contrasts dramatically with these people's high competencies (Pl_5_1).

8   Conclusion

According to the interviews conducted for the purpose of this study, the administration's lack of imagination frequently impedes cooperation between technology companies and public authorities. In many cases, the latter do not even consider what kinds of data might be relevant for their policies. This implies that the problem faced by the studied countries is far more serious than the disparities in the strength of their negotiating positions with technological giants would suggest.

In spite of this, the intangible nature of data and information as well as the ease with which it may be shared allow for cooperation in some areas. This is the case particularly where technology companies do not perceive it as a challenge to their competitive advantages – improving public services is rarely viewed as a threat to their business model. What matters more is competition between individual enterprises. In other words, improving public transport based on data provided by online taxi platforms is less problematic than inconsistent disclosures by individual companies. In the latter situation, it would result in competing for the same customer who prefers taxis to public transportation (often for reasons other than poor planning).

It should also be noted that the problem of insufficient data flow from technology corporations to public administration cannot be resolved by legislation alone. The question of jurisdiction (due to asset dispersion) may generate major complications in the case this business activity. Moreover, as demonstrated by the Chinese experience, overly intrusive regulations requiring full access of state agencies to data kept by technology corporations create a slew of issues (Aho and Duffield, 2020). China is a huge market that cannot be ignored by Western technology companies; as a result, they are willing to make drastic concessions in order to sell their products in the Middle Kingdom. By contrast, the Visegrád countries' bargaining power is far too small to demand such flexibility in their approach to user privacy.

The People's Republic of China's policies grant its officials unrestricted access to data held on its territory. Furthermore, technology firms cannot avoid this obligation by using overseas servers since their employees in China are compelled by law to disclose all the necessary information to representatives of the authorities. This enables local security services to collect information about foreign nationals. Users in Europe and North America are well aware of this risk, which makes Chinese providers of IT products and services much less attractive.

Without coordinated regulatory action (e.g. at EU level), semi-peripheral countries must rely on the goodwill of technology giants. Even if the competencies of public sector staff are improved, effective application of hard legislation in this area will be extremely challenging. Fortunately, according to the report, technology companies freely agree to some forms of collaboration. This means that by and large, the data they collect can be used for public policy purposes in the Visegrád countries.

It should be borne in mind that merely mandating technology companies to share data will not facilitate public initiatives if the administration remains unprepared. The first step should therefore involve training up the latter for new ways of doing things. However, as this is a sensitive area of staff skills, which are also valuable to the private sector, we expect that without a considerable increase in remuneration, the public sector will continue to be unable to collaborate meaningfully with technology companies.

Bibliography

Aho, B. and Duffield, R. (2020). Beyond surveillance capitalism: Privacy, regulation and big data in Europe and China. *Economy and Society*, *49*(2), 187–212. https://doi.org/1 0.1080/03085147.2019.1690275

Arunchand, C. H. and Ramanathan, H. N. (2013). Organizational culture and employee morale: A public sector enterprise experience. *Journal of Strategic Human Resource Management*, *2*(1), 1.

Biga, B. (2017). Ekonomiczna analiza odmienności własności intelektualnej i materialnej na przykładzie patentu. *Studia Ekonomiczne*, *312*, 18–29.

Birkinbine, B. J. (2020). Political economy of peer production. *The Handbook of Peer Production*, 33–43.

Bharosa, N., Janssen, M., van Wijk, R., de Winne, N., Van Der Voort, H., Hulstijn, J. and Tan, Y. H. (2013). Tapping into existing information flows: The transformation to compliance by design in business-to-government information exchange. *Government Information Quarterly*, *30*, S9–S18.

Bowen, F., and Panagiotopoulos, P. (2020). Regulatory roles and functions in information-based regulation: a systematic review. *International Review of Administrative Sciences*, *86*(2), 203–221. https://doi.org/10.1177/0020852318778775

Breidbach, C. F. and Maglio, P. (2020). Accountable algorithms? The ethical implications of data-driven business models. *Journal of Service Management*, *31*(2), 163–185. https://doi.org/10.1108/JOSM-03-2019-0073

Buck, S. J. (2017). *The global commons: an introduction*. Routledge.

Faccia, A. (2019, August). Data and Information Flows: Assessing Threads and Opportunities to Ensure Privacy and Investment Returns. In: *Proceedings of the 2019 3rd International Conference on Cloud and Big Data Computing*, 54–59.

Gosztonyi, M. (2022). Self-Identification of Start-Ups. *Economic and Social Development: Book of Proceedings*, 157–169.

Hein, A., Weking, J., Schreieck, M., Wiesche, M., Böhm, M. and Krcmar, H. (2019). Value co-creation practices in business-to-business platform ecosystems. *Electronic Markets*, *29*(3), 503–518. https://doi.org/10.1007/s12525-019-00337-y

Keen, P. and Williams, R. (2013). Value architectures for digital business: beyond the business model. *Mis Quarterly*, *37*(2), 643–647.

Lemley, M. A. (2004). Property, intellectual property, and free riding. *Tex L. Rev.*, *83*, 1031.

Livingstone, S. and Brake, D. R. (2010). On the rapid rise of social networking sites: New findings and policy implications. *Children & society*, *24*(1), 75–83. https://doi.org/10.1111/j.1099-0860.2009.00243.x

Mazzucato, M. (2011). The entrepreneurial state. *Soundings*, *49*(49), 131–142. https://doi.org/10.3898/136266211798411183

Mazzucato, M. (2018). *The value of everything: Making and taking in the global economy*. Hachette.

Moore, M. (2021). *Regulating Big Tech: Policy Responses to Digital Dominance*. Oxford University Press.

Ostrom, E. (1990). *Governing the commons: The evolution of institutions for collective action*. Cambridge University Press.

Smith, J. W. (2016). The Uber-all economy of the future. *The Independent Review*, *20*(3), 383–390.

Studinka, J. and Guenduez, A. A. (2018). *The Use of Big Data in the Public Policy Process-Paving the Way for Evidence-Based Governance*. EGPA Conf.

Teece, D. J. (2017). The tragedy of the anticommons fallacy: a law and economics analysis of patent thickets and FRAND licensing. *Berkeley Tech. LJ*, *32*(4), 1489–1526. https://doi.org/10.15779/Z38RR1PM7N https://publicadministration.un.org/egovkb/en-us/data-center

CHAPTER 8

Open Data Policy as a Response of the V4 Countries to the Technological Shift

Marek Oramus

1 Introduction

The main focus of this chapter is to compare open data policies pursued by the Visegrád Group (V4) countries. According to reports such as the Open Data Maturity benchmark study (ODM 2020; 2021) published annually by the European Data Portal (EDP), there are significant disparities between these countries in this regard. According to its findings, Poland is the most advanced of the four, the Czech Republic is working hard to catch up to the leaders, while Hungary and Slovakia are struggling to meet European standards. The comparison is based on the revised open data policy cycle framework developed by Zuiderwijk and Janssen (2014; Charalabidis et al., 2018), which consists of 5 stages: policy environment and context, content, implementation, evaluation, and change or termination. The author takes into consideration the distinctive qualities of the V4 countries, which were covered in the previous chapter in relation to semi-peripheral countries and may have a substantial impact on open data policy. The chapter ends with conclusions on similarities and differences between individual national open data policies.

2 Increasing Importance of Opening Data by Governments

In recent decades, the idea of making the data collected by various public institutions available to a wide range of stakeholders (central and local government units, the private sector, NGOs, the academia, individual users) has been gaining popularity among those in power. One of the main driving forces behind this strategy is the development of information and communication technologies (ICT), which has also been reflected in public policy research by, among other things, concepts such as digital era governance (Dunleavy et al., 2006) and smart city (Townsend, 2014). Open data initiatives are now viewed as one of the key components of the Fourth Industrial Revolution (4IR). Real-time processing of enormous amounts of unstructured data, also known as big data, has become increasingly important in this context (Beyer and Laney, 2012). As more and more open data policies are adopted, public institutions are having a greater impact on the current socioeconomic changes.

The term itself can be defined in a variety of ways. According to M. Kassen (2019, p. 1), open data, also known as open government data (OGD), is used to refer to collections of various types of information (including statistics) that are made available to the general public in specialised digital repositories in machine-readable formats. It is important to keep in mind that the scope of open data has been expanding recently with a greater focus on re-use as more and more private organisations make their data available.

In their methodology, the authors of the Open Data Maturity study adopt the following definition (ODM Method Paper, 2021, p. 3):

> Open (government) data refers to the information collected, produced or paid for by the public bodies (also referred to as Public Sector Information) and made freely available for re-use for any purpose.

The term re-use in this definition should be understood as (PL Guide 2019, p. 18):

> Use of public sector information by natural persons, legal entities and organisational units without legal personality, for commercial or non-commercial purposes, which are other than the original purpose for which the information was generated.

The focus on data reuse can be seen as the next stage of policy development; following that in which policymakers seek to make as much structured public data available as possible. The stage that follows should focus on maximising impact, putting forward creative solutions, and identifying novel phenomena and trends. Therefore, the model employed also takes into account this aspect of open data policy.

Both open data theorists and practitioners cite a number of advantages to the adoption of this strategy. Janssen, Charalabidis, and Zuiderwijk (2012; Charalabidis et al., 2018, pp. 7–8) cite the following benefits: political and democratic (e.g. greater transparency and accountability of governments, increased trust, increased public participation or improved public policy-making); organisational (improving the image of data providers, increasing citizen satisfaction, use of the wisdom of the crowds); innovative (stimulation of knowledge development, new insight, new social services); economic (stimulation of competitiveness and innovation, economic growth, information for investors and companies); as well as operational and technical (reuse of data, improving its quality, new data). Over the years, there have also been efforts to commercialise the advantages of open data, although it is challenging to accurately measure them. In this regard, it is worth citing the EDP report entitled *The Economic Impact of Open Data Opportunities for value creation in Europe* (Economic Impact EDP, 2020), where the savings to the public sector from administrative improvements are expected to be between €0.25bn and €1.48bn, while the decrease in labour expenses thanks to real-time traffic navigation is estimated at up to €20bn.

However, the implementation of open data policy is fraught with complications and risks, particularly if the process is poorly designed. Individual institutional factors impeding the process include (PL Guide 2019, p. 28): lack of a clear plan for open data, overly rigid hierarchical structures, insufficient knowledge among officials about the regulations or the benefits of implementing the policy, lack of an inspiring coordinator or an interdisciplinary team responsible for the process. The first of these issues derives from the fact that government policies on open data are frequently framed in highly abstract terms or are primarily concerned with the goals rather than the tools to be used (Charalabidis et al., 2018, p. 56), which makes implementation difficult. Even if these limitations are overcome (ibid. p. 9), legislative (non-compliant laws, privacy), governance (responsibilities, maintaining quality), interpretation (bias, misinterpretation of ambiguities), and data quality risks (poor data quality, timeliness) must be kept in mind. The fact that those in power seek to make the broadest data sets available in accordance with stakeholder expectations whilst paying insufficient attention to policy provisions and the above-mentioned risks only serves to exacerbate these issues (Zuiderwijk and Janssen, 2014, p. 26). As a result, it is vital to review the laws governing public open data in each country, and the findings of this study should serve as a starting point for a detailed investigation of the areas in most need of improvement.

3   Methodology

A structured approach based on identifying and analysing individual policy stages was pioneered in the 1950s by Laswell (1956) and later developed by Jones (1970) and Anderson (1975), among others. The present study is based on Charalabidis and Zuiderwijk's (2018) original concept, which comprises the following five stages (Stewart et al. 2008):
1.   Problem identification and agenda setting;
2.   Policy formulation;

3. Policy implementation and enforcement;
4. Policy evaluation;
5. Policy change or termination.

Using this approach as a basis for their analysis Zuiderwijk and Janssen (2014) presented the following open data policy model (Figure 8.1).

In this study of the Visegrád countries, a model comprised of 35 public policy components was used (Charalabidis et al., 2018). However, it should be borne in mind that the original case study discussed by the authors focused on the juxtaposition of Dutch policies at the national level with those implemented by the key actors (e.g. ministries). With such a perspective, there was less scope for the use of quantifiable indicators to identify more accurately the discrepancies among the various actors studied. For this reason, other internationally recognised frameworks such as Open Data Maturity (ODM, 2021) released annually by the European Data Portal and the Open Data Barometer prepared by the World Wide Web Foundation, among others, were also applied.

The summaries of policy milestones provided in the next section were compiled using information from a variety of sources, including national strategic and programme documents, current legislation, data from governmental websites, and other organisations with responsibility for open data policy. They were supplemented with findings from international studies by the European Data Portal and the OECD. National open data portals were also tapped as one

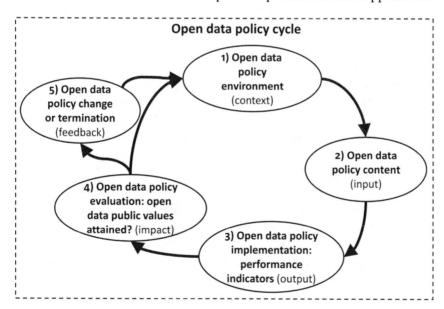

FIGURE 8.1   Open data policy cycle

SOURCE: CHARALABIDIS, ZUIDERWIJK ET AL. (2018)

of the key data sources, since the evaluation of their advancement is one of the indicators of how a country leverages its potential in this area.

The author personally gathered data on Poland's open data policy. In order to obtain comparable information from other Visegrád countries, the following researchers were consulted: Pavel Horák (Masaryk University, Czech Republic), Máté Hajba (Free Market Foundation, Hungary) and Martin Reguli (F. A. Hayek Foundation, Slovakia). These specialists also assisted in compiling nation-specific study findings presented in tabular summaries throughout this chapter (cited as V4 expert opinions).

4 Policy Environment

It must be borne in mind that the European Union has a major impact on national public policies concerning data availability, particularly in the case of the Visegrád countries. E-confederalism in this context is provided by the operation of international platforms such as the European Data Portal (Kassen, 2018). Different local, regional, and national portals coexist, but strive to follow the guidelines set forth at the EU level. The EU Member States are currently guided in their decision-making by Directive (EU) 2019/1024 of the European Parliament and of the Council, which mandates all countries to publish all data and documents in an open format, with some clearly established exceptions (e.g. documents subject to third-party intellectual property rights or concerning critical infrastructure). This represents yet another step forward on the path outlined by the 2003 Directive (2003/98/EC).

The first stage of the open data public policy cycle focuses on its context and the environment that determines its design. Every public policy (not only open data) is affected by a number of factors that are not always controlled by those responsible for its preparation. The implementation of advanced information and communication technology (ICT) solutions requires not only adequate financial but also infrastructural facilities as well as access to knowledge and appropriately qualified civil servants. Therefore, factors like socio-cultural legacies which translate into how the authorities make decisions, or the resources available to the state, should be taken into account.

When examining the model's social aspect, its creators (Charalabidis et al., 2018) explore policymaking in various countries using Pollitt and Bouckaert's observations (2011). In search of alternatives for the V4 countries, the author of this chapter chose a recent study on public administration in Central Europe by Mazur (2020). As shown in Table 8.1, there are major differences in the respective social and political histories of the Visegrád countries, which will have a significant impact on the progress of open data legislation, as the subsequent

TABLE 8.1   Stage 1: Open data policy environment

Policy element	Czech Republic	Hungary	Poland	Slovakia
Social context	Policymaking is consensus-based with little participation of non-state actors at the state level; government agencies tend to be closed to outside influence. Reforms proceed slowly, but more importantly, only when they cannot be avoided due to pressing critical strategic decisions (Mazur, 2020).	Policymaking and coordination of efforts are of rather poor quality as are the indicators reflecting the effectiveness of the Hungarian government's social consultations, use of evidence-based policy, enactment of laws, and accountability procedures (Mazur, 2020). Digitalisation policy is consensus-based.	Reforms and their outcomes are rarely subject to systematic research or evaluation. As a consequence, the potential for systemic and organisational learning, especially as regards administrative reforms, is quite low. A non-linear process of change consists in reversing the effects of previously implemented reforms. This process is characterised by selectivity, lack of cohesion and an unspecified vision of the target model (Mazur, 2020).	The differences between public agencies in the quality and scope of participatory processes are too significant to argue that the commitment to participation has higher than a marginal impact on open government legislation to date (Žuffová, 2020).

TABLE 8.1   Stage 1: Open data policy environment (*cont.*)

Policy element	Czech Republic	Hungary	Poland	Slovakia
Political context	Unitary, fairly decentralised state, where the government (usually formed by fragile coalitions) has a leading role in state administration and its rules of procedure are in line with majoritarian decision-making.	Unitary, highly centralised state. With the current governing party's supermajority in the parliament, it adopted a new constitution which has been amended several times since. Currently, decision making exclusively depends on the governing party.	Unitary, fairly decentralised state. However, the government's plans to centralise authority in recent years are obvious. The processes for developing and implementing public policies and initiatives are of poor quality. Problems usually affect coordination procedures (Mazur, 2020).	Unitary, fairly decentralised state. The oligarchisation of Slovak politics may lead to a change in government and subsequent reforms in the near future. The politicisation of the civil service persists, and strenuous efforts to promote public e-government have yet to reduce the administrative burden placed on citizens (Mazur, 2020).
Economic context	GDP: 250.68 billion dollars in 2019 (World Bank, 2020).	GDP: 163.47 billion dollars in 2019 (World Bank, 2020).	GDP: 595.86 billion dollars in 2019 (World Bank, 2020).	GDP: 105.08 billion dollars in 2019 (World Bank, 2020).

| Legislation and regulatory context | Strategic Framework Czech Republic 2030; Digital Czechia Strategy: Free Access to Information Act (Act No. 106/1999 Coll.), (cf. Government Regulation No. 425/2016 Coll. for the list of information published as open data). | National Digitalisation Strategy 2021–2030; National Infocommunication Strategy 2014–2020; Hungary's Artificial Intelligence Strategy 2020–2030.(Act CXII of 2011 Informational Self-determination and Freedom of Information Government Decree 305/2005) (XII. 25.) | Efficient State Strategy 2020 (objective 1); Efficient and Modern State 2030 (objective III) (draft, not yet adopted); Open Data Programme (ODP) for 2021–2027 (2021); Integrated State Digitalisation Programme. | Action Plan for the Digital Transformation of Slovakia for the Years 2019–2022 (Resolution of the Government of the Slovak Republic No. 337/2019, Document of the Action Plan); Strategic document for the growth of digital services and the area of next generation access network infrastructure 2014–2020. |

TABLE 8.1   Stage 1: Open data policy environment (*cont.*)

Policy element	Czech Republic	Hungary	Poland	Slovakia
Culture and country	Population ca. 10,6 million (2019). Cultural characteristics: The family is the centre of the social structure. Czechs value forward thinking, are logical, practical, and efficient. Careful planning, in both one's business and personal life, provides a sense of security. Rules and regulations help people understand what is expected of them and plan their lives accordingly. Czechs are private people, tend to be formal and reserved, Once you develop a personal relationship they open up a bit, but they are never overly emotional (Commisceo Global, 2021).	Population ca. 9.77 million (2019). Cultural characteristics: Traditional values play a key role in Hungarian society, with an emphasis on preserving the unique culture of the country. According to Hofstede Insights, Hungary is an individualistic and masculine society with a tendency to avoid uncertainty. Hungarians have a proclivity for cynicism and pessimism (Commisceo Global, 2021).	Population ca. 38 million (2019). Cultural characteristics: A hierarchical society, people accept a hierarchical order in which everybody has a place and which needs no further justification. Individualist society: high preference for a loosely-knit social framework. A masculine society, where people 'live in order to work,' an emphasis on equity, competition, and performance. There is a strong propensity towards avoiding uncertainty. Thinking that is more normative than pragmatic. A restricted society with a proclivity for scepticism and pessimism (Commisceo Global, 2021).	Population ca. 5.5 million (2019). Cultural characteristics: Many of the customs, laws and conventions are still deeply influenced by past rulers: Czechs, Hungarians and the Austrian Habsburgs. Slovaks value privacy. It takes a while for them to open up to and trust new people. As a result they can seem overly formal and reserved. The society is less individualistic and the family is the centre of the social structure. (Commisceo Global, 2021).

	Country (national).	Country (national).	Country (national).	Country (national).
Geographic level				
Type of data providing organisations	Ministries, central administrative institutions, regional offices, municipalities with extended powers and other municipalities (B2G portals).	Governmental organisation, public administration, ministries, municipalities; other organisations, such as research institutes and universities.	Ministries, central administrative institutions, municipalities, and other governmental organisations.	Ministries, provinces, municipalities, and other governmental organisations.
Key motivations and policy objectives	To ensure the readiness of entrepreneurs, public sector, and citizens for rapid implementation and changes caused by digitisation, connectivity and digital structure and trust in the digital environment. (European Commission, 2019).	To ensure democracy and democratic control, to ensure efficiency and help innovation.	To increase the supply and improve the quality of data available at dane.gov.pl for each user and for re-use; to create an environment in which the economic and social benefits of open data are noticed and translate into the new services, products, business models and new jobs; to support strategic decision-making (ODP, 2021).	Better customer-oriented e-services; approach to data as a valuable national resource and a strategic asset (data driven state); data ownership, data sharing with creative communities and businesses and better usage of data in the policy-making and regulatory process.

TABLE 8.1   Stage 1: Open data policy environment (*cont.*)

Policy element	Czech Republic	Hungary	Poland	Slovakia
Mission type	Mainly strategic focus on transparency, access to information (including availability, easy and unlimited sharing), civic participation, public accountability (and thus support of democracy /e-democracy/ and open governance /e-governance) (opendata.gov.cz).	Economic importance of data in aiding competitiveness and effectiveness. Challenges to society, such as automation. The strategy focuses on commercial aspects and effectiveness in terms of open data and data in general while also emphasizing transparency.	Strategic focus on better access to open data by increasing their volume and quality. This should translate into a more effective public administration, wider engagement of citizens and private stakeholders in the re-use process and as a result to higher quality of life and more innovative environment.	Mainly strategic, focus on transparency, access to information, civic participation and public accountability (Žuffová, 2020).
Available resources	Professional central coordinating team, a range of databases maintained by providers, and data providers from state bodies with varying levels of qualifications. Individual pillars of the Digital Czechia Strategy were built with contributions from the EU Structural Funds.	Human resources and IT resources (Hungary's Artificial Intelligence Strategy 2020–2030 and http://kozadattar.hu).	Human resources: task team supporting Committee of the Council of Ministers, a network of data openness representatives at the government administration level (in every ministry and NSO). Financial resource: ODP for 2021–2027 is funded mainly by EU funds with support of the state budget.	The e-government Strategy of the Slovak Republic lays down the criteria and procedures for e-government funding which combine state budget funds with resources from the EU Structural Funds.

Available open data platform	One national open data platform has been created: https://opendata.gov.cz	National open data platform: http://kozadattar.hu Hungarian Central Statistics Office: www.ksh.hu	One national open data platform: https://dane.gov.pl. Various other open data portals are available, e.g. in individual municipalities.	One national open data platform has been developed: https://data.gov.sk
Resource allocation	Human resources: at the national level to support the opening process and to provide education to different ministries and other organisations inside and outside the public administration. IT resources: a national portal	Human resources: at the national level to support the opening process. IT resources: a national portal	Human resources: at the national level. When the Ministry of Digital Affairs was abolished, its responsibilities were transferred to the Prime Minister's Chancellery. This unit is also in charge of the national open data portal.	Human resources: at the national level to support the opening process and to provide education to different ministries. Partnership and dialogue between public authorities, citizens and NGOs. IT resources: a national portal.

SOURCE: OWN STUDY BASED ON CHARALABIDIS, ZUIDERWIJK ET AL. (2018) AND V4 EXPERT OPINIONS

discussion will demonstrate. All four are unitary states, but they differ in terms of decentralisation; moreover, Hungary and Poland exhibit tendencies toward power centralisation at the expense of local governments.

World Bank data for 2019 were used to assess the individual countries' economic potential, since 2020 marked a departure from the multi-year trend due to the pandemic crisis and its negative effect on the economies at large. Considerable disparities exist between the GDPs of the Visegrád countries, particularly between Poland and the other countries (more than fivefold difference); it should be noted, however, that even small countries with relatively small economies (e.g. Estonia with USD 31 trillion; World Bank 2020) are capable of successfully implementing innovative public policies.

The fact that all the V4 countries are members of the European Union and operate under its legal framework is essential in terms of regulation. As a result, when implementing the most recent solutions, they are guided, among other things, by the aforementioned EU Directive 2019/1024, which serves as the model for their own documents. Poland, for example, is now implementing a new Open Data Programme (ODP) for 2021–2027, and most other countries have long-term strategies in place that incorporate open data as one of their goals.

As this comparative analysis focuses on the implementation of open data policies at the national level, regional and local levels have been excluded for the sake of greater clarity, even though the actors representing the latter two levels of administration also play an important role in the provision of data for the national portals. Apart from ministries, statistical offices, and other entities operating at the central level, local governments make a broad range of data available for use by local activists.

It is important to note the main goals and motivations outlined in each Visegrád country's open data policy. The Czech Republic is working to create a digital landscape that will allow all stakeholders to adjust to the continuing technology change as easily as possible (European Commission, 2019). In the case of Hungary, the focus on democracy and civic control is rather dubious, considering Viktor Orbán's government's measures aimed at suppressing free speech and crushing the opposition. In Poland, the emphasis is on increasing the availability of high-quality data and, like in the Czech Republic, developing a space that allows for its broadest possible re-use. Similar goals have been set by Slovakia, which intends to build a comprehensive platform to encourage greater user participation. Generally speaking, all these strategic plans demonstrate an intention to promote public data accessibility in order to increase the transparency of activities. The Czech and Polish authorities particularly emphasise the importance of opening data to improve the quality of public services provided to citizens.

Significant resources, including human, financial, and infrastructural ones, are required to implement full data openness as outlined in the respective programme documents (Welle Donker, 2019). An important impetus needed for these measures to succeed is provided by support from the European funds – the EU not only sets certain standards for the development of this policy, but also ensures financial assistance to facilitate their achievement (with contributions from national budgets). Employing competent implementers is a separate issue. The traditional obstacle in this case is the disparity in pay between the public and private sectors, particularly for ICT professionals.

In terms of organisational arrangements, a central team made up of an external IT professional and a national coordinator was established in the Czech Republic, while in Poland a special task force was set up at the Committee of the Council of Ministers as a result of the abolition of the Ministry of Digitalisation and the transfer of its responsibilities directly to the Prime Minister and his close associates. A Data Management Department exists in the Prime Minister's Office, and representatives accountable for the data opening procedure have been designated in all ministries and other key government bodies. Resources are therefore predominantly allocated at central government level, with regional and municipal levels receiving less funding.

In each of the countries surveyed, there is a main web portal that serves as a central data repository. As a rule, it aggregates data from other portals, such as government statistical offices, making them the first choice for people looking for public data. Their evaluation is based on international reports such as the ODM, but there are also scholarly investigations into the question of comparability of the offered solutions. In their study of 41 national portals, Nikiforova and McBride (2021) discovered that Slovakia had the best usability of any Visegrád country, while Poland, Hungary, and the Czech Republic ranked significantly lower. A more in-depth discussion of these portals' capabilities follows under the subsequent stages of the public policy cycle.

5   Policy Content

In terms of the content of the open data policy itself (which can be referred to as input), two sets of elements have been identified: those related to the process of opening data and those related to data management. In the former case, the model comprises, among other things, a summary of the documents dealing with the open data policy in question, the main objectives or stakeholder lists obtained from them as well as the technical requirements needed to implement such a policy. The latter group of elements includes a description of standards set for both data development and data sharing with

TABLE 8.2   Stage 2: Open data policy content

Policy element	Czech Republic	Hungary	Poland	Slovakia
Policy strategy and principles	Most kinds of data are provided in an open format. The original principle of 'transparency' of state administration (as an anti-corruption tool) has currently been replaced by the principle of 'digitalisation.'	According to ODM 2020, Hungary was the only EU country without the ability to request data sets on the national portal, however, it has changed in ODM 2021.	Most kinds of data are provided in an open format. National agencies are advised to use the strategies 'open by design' and 'open by default' (ODP 2021–2027).	Most kinds of data are provided in an open format.
Actors involved in opening data	Governmental organisations, IT providers, regional and local governments; the key actors involve specialized experts from the Open data task force team, who are part of the Department of Chief Architect of e-government at the Ministry of the Interior, and local data providers.	Governmental organisations, collecting and creating data, IT providers, regional and local governments, institutes joining the open data portal.	The main actor is Chancellery of the Prime Minister which took over the responsibilities of the abolished Ministry of Digital Affairs. It cooperates with open data representatives from national agencies and other data providers including local governments, NGOs and private sector.	Governmental organisations collecting and creating data, IT providers, regional and local governments.

Targeted open data users	Anyone, but primarily citizens, entrepreneurs, businesses, as well as NGOS, universities, companies, students, and the automotive industry.	Anyone, but especially citizens and entrepreneurs.	Wide group of stakeholders: government administration, local government, private sector, the academia, NGOS, individual users (ODP 2021–2027).	Anyone, but especially citizens, entrepreneurs, businesses, NGOS and journalists.
Types of data opened and not opened	Open data include a wide range of subjects relating to various areas of interest to citizens. Different sources (ministries) contribute open data to varying degrees. Only data sets from state institutions are registered in the national open database due to the risk that NGOS may add undesirable data that cannot yet be removed.	Open data on a range of topics (e.g. administration, economy, finance, migration). Upon request, public administration bodies must provide data related to its operation, unless it is private. Restricted access: sensitive data, data that should not be disclosed e.g. due to national security concerns.	13 categories of open data available on the national open data portal. Most data sets are connected with the government and the public sector (almost 500), economy and finance (over 200) and regions and cities (almost 200). Unrestricted reuse is permitted for anonymised, resigned rights-based, or Public Statistics Act-based data sets. Data sets that do not meet specific security, legal and technical standards are not made open.	Open data on a range of topics: the Open Data Cloud is formed by data sets from the Statistics Office, Business Register, Statistics Office of the Organisations, and some others (Slovensko.digital 2016).

TABLE 8.2   Stage 2: Open data policy content (*cont.*)

Policy element	Czech Republic	Hungary	Poland	Slovakia
Policy measures and instruments	All central elements of the Digital Czechia and e-government are under the control of the Ministry of the Interior; they are managed by various Ministerial subdivisions. The open data task force team is part of the Department of Chief Architect of e-Government at the Ministry of the Interior. It serves a supraministerial function and is in charge of coordinating and putting the digitalisation of public administration into action.	The Digital Success Programme (https://digitalisjoletprogram. hu/en/) supports the government through various strategies, such as the Artificial Intelligence Strategy 2020–2030, Digital success Programme 2.0, and Digital success Programme 2030. These fall under the responsibilities of the Ministry for Innovation and Technology, but the strategies also demand cooperation with other ministries. The Artificial Intelligence Strategy deals more specifically with open data and data policy elaborating on its goals.	Numerous policy measures and instruments are listed in ODP 2021–2027, including indicators for every policy goal in order to measure its progress. Most of these indicators are based on statistics from the national open data portal. Progress reports are published annually.	E-government is a specific policy under the overall information society strategy and falls under the responsibility of the Ministry of Finance. The Ministry is in charge of all central aspects of the Information Society and e-government, which are handled by various ministerial subdivisions.

Provision of (technical) support for opening data	Technical support is provided through seminars, courses, manuals, and regulations governing the licensing of data sets.	The National Infocommunications Service Company Ltd. which operates the open data portal provides the necessary support.	Manuals, video guides, and other tools accessible to help data providers are available on the national data portal. Training workshops are planned annually, mostly for officials in the central administration (30 sessions for 513 officials in 2019).	State institutions cooperate with one another and with relevant actors from the academy, civil society, NGOs, the business sector and the public.
Provision of (technical) support for open data use	The Open Data Portal provides data collected for the National Catalogue of Open Data. Open data task force team offers of full-time, online or e-learning training, workshops and consultations (Data.gov.cz).	The open data portal supports both institutions that join as data owners and users. The Digital Education Strategy of Hungary includes the Digital Success Program for digital education.	The major focus of technical support is on opening data; in the case of data re-use, hackathons and other events are organised to promote open data use. Additionally, re-users may publish their applications on national open data portals.	The Open Data Portal provides a support app for the organisations where access to open data is mandated. Training is provided to all the public administration staff (Data.gov.sk).
Type of engagement of and interaction between data providers and users	Instruction presentations are available for users and data providers to obtain support from the open data portal (Data.gov.cz). Regular annual conferences, fairs, irregular hackathons (hackujstat.cz).	Instructions are available for both data owners and users on open data platform as well as on the website of the Hungarian Central Statistical Office.	Open data portal aggregates information about data providers and allows data users to visit their websites. There is also a feedback form on specific data sets. Seminars, workshops and hackathons are organised.	Instruction presentations available and contact forms present for users and providers of data to get support from the open data portal (Data.gov.sk).

TABLE 8.2   Stage 2: Open data policy content (*cont.*)

Policy element	Czech Republic	Hungary	Poland	Slovakia
Promotion of data and metadata	Promotion through various national organisations, NGOs, national and local data portals.	Hungary is among the 3 EU countries that do not promote open data use on social media. Promotion is limited mostly to a few events (ODM 2021).	Dissemination tasks targeting citizens, entrepreneurs, NGOs, academia, and administration. Focus is on internet campaigns and organising events.	Promotion through various national organisations, private and NGO data portals as well as local administration sites.
Data processing before opening	The data submitted should be as raw as possible. Opening data involves deciding which data sets can be opened and when.	The open data portal is operated by the National Infocommunications Service Company Ltd. as appointed by the relevant ministry, but data providers are responsible for their accuracy.	Based on Tim Berners-Lee's classification, technical standards recommend providing data suitable for re-use: structured and in one of the open data formats.	The National Agency for Network and Electronic Services is the administrator of the data.gov.sk portal, but is not responsible for the data supplied by individual providers and/or owners (Data.gov.sk).

Data quality	This commitment has been adopted to conduct training for civil servants to improve the quality of published data sets. The levels of data literacy in public administration vary, and a more unified approach to open data is required. Ranked 8th (89%) in Data Quality rating (ODM 2021).	Ranked 31st (43%) in Data Quality rating (ODM 2021).	In 2020, Poland implemented updated standards for open data in order to improve their quality in four areas: API, security, technical, and regulatory.New tools and improvements for the national open data portal are incrementally implemented, such as validators and submitting notifications about incorrect data in 2019 (Report PODP, 2019). Ranked 9th (86%) in Data Quality rating (ODM 2021).	This commitment has been adopted to conduct training for public servants to improve the quality of published data sets. Stakeholders interviewed for the IRM Design Report and this report agree that the levels of data literacy in public administration vary (Žuffová, 2020). Ranked 25th (70%) in Data Quality rating (ODM 2021).
Selected open data license and use conditions	All information is subject to licensing. Except where explicitly stated otherwise, the contents are licensed under CC Attribution 4.0 International.	The data is licensed under The Open Data Commons – Public Domain Dedication & Licence The Hungarian Central Statistical Office (HCSO).	Every data set is accompanied by information on use conditions along with license type (for about 2/3 of data sets, CC BY 4.0, and the remaining 1/3 CC0 1.0).	All information is subject to the license terms of the Creative Commons Attribution Licence (CC–BY) 4.0. (Statistics Office of the Slovak Republic 2020b).

TABLE 8.2   Stage 2: Open data policy content (*cont.*)

Policy element	Czech Republic	Hungary	Poland	Slovakia
Data and metadata provision	Data is made available via the National open data portal (NKOD.gov.cz). It is possible to search for and download data sets as well as provide input; however, it is not possible to directly contribute to the data portal.	Data is made available via the national data portal. Hungary is the only EU country without the ability to request data sets on the national portal.	Poland launched a new multifunctional search engine that enables searching according to multiple criteria, both in the resource metadata and in the content of structured data (ODM, 2020). About 450 APIs are available. Possibility to give feedback. Only users with permission from data provider can publish data.	The Statistical Office of the Slovak Republic creates classifications and code lists, ensures their harmonisation with international norms and standards. The classifications and selected code lists are created in collaboration with ministries and state organisations. (Statistics Office of the Slovak Republic, 2020a).
Numbers or percentages of opened data sets	About 141,000 data sets from 248 providers available at data.gov.cz (May 2022).	About 205,000 records from 3522 institutions (May 2022).	About 26,000 data sets from 189 providers available (May 2022) at open data portal dane.gov.pl.	About 3,000 data sets from 93 providers available (May 2022). Out of these data sets, 33% is provided by Statistics Office of the Slovak Republic (Data.gov.sk).

Data access and availability	Data offered through various portals, often duplicated. Registration or login is usually not required.	Data offered through the open data portal and the Hungarian Central Statistical Office. Registration is not required and access is free. The Statistical Office charges a fee only for extra services.	Data offered mainly through dane.gov.pl portal and National Statistical Office portal which do not require registration or login in order to access data. Similar approach is used by other data portals.	Data offered through various portals, often duplicated. Registration or login is usually not required.
Way of presenting data and metadata to users	National portal provides data sets in XML, CSV and RDF formats. A uniform standard for data cataloguing (DCAT–AP–CZ 2.0.0) is used, as well as standards for specific data sets specified in Czech legislation (so- called Open Formal Standards).	The open data portal presents data in a format provided by individual data owners. The Statistical Office provides data viewable in a browser or in XLSX and CSV formats.	Open data portal recognizes data about 70 file formats. In Poland, the technical standard published on dane.gov.pl has been supplemented with the implementation of the standardised DCAT–AP metadata schema (Open Data Maturity 2020). Statistics Poland offers different visualisation tools depending on data type.	Code lists and classifications can be downloaded as XML or CSV formats. The basic code lists are released through central meta-information system of public administration – MetaIS (Statistics Office of the Slovak Republic 2020a).
Data update frequency	Differs by data provider and portal; usually every year.	The open data portal provides data whenever their owners do so. The Statistical Office creates reports, the frequency of which depends on the category.	Differs by data provider and portal, e.g. the NSO Portal provides data sets in a more organised way. Longer delays are possible on the national ODP portal.	Generally depends on when the data becomes available, which differs by data provider and portal (Žuffová, 2020).

SOURCE: OWN STUDY BASED ON CHARALABIDIS ET AL. (2018) AND V4 EXPERT OPINIONS

stakeholders. The main focus of this stage is to present the assumptions of a given open data policy as intended by its creators.

In terms of the key principles of the open data policy approach, all the countries surveyed strive to provide as much data as possible in open formats. How the rationale for opening data has evolved over the years is best illustrated by the example of the Czech Republic – originally, the idea was to make state actions as transparent as possible. It was thus a response to the serious corruption problem that countries in the region have been dealing with for years. With improving corruption indicators over the last decade (albeit Transparency International's rating for the Czech Republic has deteriorated again since 2019), the Open Data policy has placed a greater emphasis on digitalisation and supporting economic development through the use of innovative technologies. Poland's Open Data Programme 2021–2027 highlights the importance of two overarching principles promoted by the European Union: 'open by design' (a given resource should be open from the moment it is designed through all subsequent stages of its life cycle; such a provision at an early stage of policy development can potentially broaden the scope of data that can be made available), and 'open by default' (all public data should be open and in a format that does not limit its free use, including for commercial purposes; the only exceptions involve security or privacy considerations).

As was previously indicated in the description of the resources planned for the open data policy, each V4 country has established bodies in charge of the reform's successful implementation. Teams responsible for coordinating efforts to that effect may be affiliated with specific units within a ministry (such as the Ministry of the Interior in the Czech Republic) or may be directly answerable to the Prime Minister (as is the case in Poland, where it is currently the task of the Prime Minister's Chancellery).

The policies of all the Visegrád countries broadly define the potential open data recipients, which fits quite well with their summaries presented in the literature (cf. Charalabidis et al., 2018, p. 5). The prevailing view is that all interested parties should have access to the data in order for the policy to have the most impact. In Poland's open data policy, the central and local governments are listed as the main stakeholders. It is crucial to bear in mind that open data policies should not just target the public at large, but they should also provide added value to other public sector institutions, which can use them to implement their own policies and streamline the bureaucratic processes required to request access to such data.

There are minimal differences amongst the V4 countries in terms of the range of data made available, and they do not significantly differ from other EU Member States. National portals usually provide data from a broad range of topical areas that are typically related to specific ministries. This broad scope is also due to the fact that they comprise data from local government databases and national statistical offices. Data tagged as not intended to be made open include those that meet the risk criteria mentioned above. According to Poland's ODP 2021–2027 and the guidelines for the organisations tasked with carrying it out, resources that do not meet specific technical requirements and would be difficult to reuse should likewise remain unavailable. It is noteworthy that in the Czech Republic, organisations from the private or social sectors are not permitted to upload their own data sets on the official portal. This decision was dictated by the fear of publishing controversial material, which, combined with the technical limitations that prevent their easy removal, was considered too risky.

For the sake of implementing open data policies, which are typically outlined in national digitalisation strategies or open data programmes, individual countries are assumed to employ comparable instruments and measures as shown in Table 8.2. As was mentioned in an earlier section devoted to the actors and resources involved, these include special task teams established under the government, a specific ministry or designated open data coordinators.

To ensure the successful implementation of open data policies, appropriate support, including technical assistance, must be provided at both the opening and subsequent use stages. Workshops, trainings, and promotional activities aimed at boosting awareness of the capabilities of the technology under consideration are quite popular in all countries. In Poland, for example, in 2019, 513 officials participated in 30 training workshops devoted to these issues (Report PODP, 2019). An important role is also played by the main portal, which should include extensive tools in the form of guides, tutorials and instructions. In Hungary, the National Infocommunications Service Company Ltd. is the principal actor in charge of assisting data providers. Slovakia emphasises the collaboration of diverse public, corporate, and civic actors. Ministries and central agencies are responsible for the implementation of departmental initiatives and are assisted in this by the E-government Architecture Office. In general, greater support tends to be directed towards individuals interested in opening up data rather than those involved in using it. For example, the needs of the latter group are usually addressed at events such as hackathons, which, however, mostly involve dissemination activities.

Activities aimed at fostering collaboration between data producers and recipients are typically limited in scope and generally involve attendance at conferences or similar events, as well as access to contact information for the resource's developers via the portal. For example, the Polish service allows users to comment on specific data sets, allowing them to be improved if data gaps or other errors are discovered.

In order to expand the reach of open data policy, intensive dissemination campaigns are required. In this regard, Hungary and Slovakia stand out negatively, since they rarely use social media to promote projects in this area, even though it is an important communication channel via which potential audiences can be reached at a fairly low cost.

Data processing frequently falls outside the purview of national open data portal operators, and is instead the duty of resource suppliers. The Czech Republic demands that such data should be submitted as raw as feasible. In Poland, Tim Berners-Lee's five-star rating of linked open data (for more information on this idea see Vetro et al., 2016) requires that it should be properly structured, delivered in one of the preferred open data formats, and each individual piece of data should be standardised (e.g. phone numbers or addresses) to make it easier to process it.

This brings us to one of the crucial indicators of how sophisticated a policy is, namely data quality. Based on this, potential users form opinions about the usefulness of the available resources, such as whether they can be easily processed or used for other purposes, such as designing a new application. A focus on quality also sends a positive message that a government cares about more than just supplying as much data as possible, which may have little added value for policy. The Open Data Maturity 2021 quality criteria reveal significant differences across the V4 nations.

The Czech Republic performs the best in this regard and comes 8th in the ranking. Its policies are guided by, among other things, the FAIR principles (findability, accessibility, interoperability, and reuse of digital assets; cf. Wilkinson et al., 2016). Moreover, the system is capable of flagging problems with particular data sets and publishing examples of bad practice to avoid replication by other providers. Poland achieved a similar result (advancing from 18th to 9th place), among other things, thanks to adopting new API, security, technical and regulatory standards in 2020, which provide a good starting point for further improvement in the future. Slovakia and Hungary were the worst performers. (ranked 25th and 31st, respectively), with the former scoring poorly on (meta)data completeness and timeliness, and the latter failing to meet the DCAT-AP standard, which was created by the European Commission as an expansion of DCAT from the W3C on interoperability of data sets.

It should be remembered that the reuse of open data is restricted to some extent by licensing. As a rule, all the countries in question rely on Creative Commons licences, the most popular being CC-BY 4.0, which permits any processing and use of data as long as the resultant work is appropriately referenced in terms of provider, licence and/or processing (Khayyat and Bannister, 2015). This is the default licence in the Czech Republic and Slovakia, whereas in Poland it covers about 2/3 of the data sets (the remaining 1/3 is covered by the most favourable CC0 1.0 licence from the point of view of the recipients, tantamount to a complete waiver of copyright protection).

Data and metadata are made available primarily through national open data portals. Individual countries are trying to refine their search tools, for example, a new multi-criteria search engine has been implemented in Poland and new APIs (Application Programming Interface) for advanced data analysis are being made available to users on a regular basis. To increase transparency and standardise solutions in individual countries, e.g. in Slovakia, classifications and code lists in line with international standards are being implemented. The amount of resources supplied considerably varies among portals, but as was already mentioned, considering such a quantitative indication without looking more closely at data quality is of limited utility. National statistical offices are typically the largest suppliers of data that can be downloaded without registering or logging in.

Along with the effort to unify the solutions used to comply with EU rules, the V4 countries, like the other EU Member States, are working to standardise the file formats made available. Formats such as CSV, XML, or XLSX are commonly used, even though others are acceptable depending on the sort of data involved. Files that are difficult to edit, such as PDF, are generally avoided, though they do appear every now and then. The fact that the most recent Polish technical standards define over seventy different file formats, including DCAT-AP, best demonstrates the diversity of the available resources. Another useful feature is the ability to visualise the data, which is not yet standard in all national open data portals due to, inter alia, the diversity of data types, hence such pilot schemes as the economic dashboard developed by Statistics Poland (https://dashboard.stat.gov.pl), which is unfortunately not updated on a regular basis.

The last component to be evaluated in the second stage of the open data policy cycle is the frequency of updates. Automating the process of adding new resources to the site continues to pose the most serious problems. Delays and gaps are essentially unavoidable without the automation of file sharing if we consider that, for instance, the data.gov.pl website hosts data sets from more than 140 providers and that it is their responsibility to regularly update them. This affects not just semi-peripheral nations like the V4 and substantial resources will be needed to address it.

6   Policy Implementation

This output stage comprises indicators that measure the open data policy's implementation level. The primary, performance-oriented ones include the

TABLE 8.3   Stage 3: Open data policy implementation

Policy element	Czech Republic	Hungary	Poland	Slovakia
Performance indicators on open data provision (e.g. number of data sets opened, machine-readability of data).	Performance in open data provision is measured especially as the number of data sets uploaded to the National open data portal. Performance is scored using international benchmarks: the Global Open Data Index (index.okfn.org) and the Open Data Monitor.	No sustainability strategy for the portal (ODM 2020), although the country wants to improve access to data by creating new agencies and portals. Performance indicators are set forth in Hungary's Artificial Intelligence Strategy (Hungary AI, 2020), however, they focus on impact rather than on provision.	Indicators on open data provision through the dane.gov.pl portal (number of data providers and data sets) are published in annual reports on the implementation of the open data program. The number of available data sets can be accessed using the portal's search tool.	Performance in open data provision is measured in various ways, e.g. the number of opened data sets compared to the number of available ones, the opening of municipal high-value data sets, scores in international benchmarks, research by the National Audit office (Algemene Rekenkamer, 2015, 2016).
Performance indicators on open data use (e.g. the number of data users, number of data set downloads, type of data use)	Performance in open data provision is measured mainly by the Open Data Barometer.	Hungary has no sustainability strategy for the portal. "There is no clear overview on how open data is being re-used in the country. [..] Open data is being used in decision- and policymaking processes, however the use is not measured." (ODM, 2020)	Apart from the Open Data Barometer, the indicators on open data use statistics (number of data providers, data sets, downloads) are published in annual reports. They also include the number of applications available for the public to access or reuse data.	Performance in open data provision is measured mainly by scores in international benchmarks: the Open Data Barometer, and the Global Open Data Index.

SOURCE: OWN STUDY BASED ON CHARALABIDIS ET AL. (2018), AND V4 EXPERT OPINIONS

number of available data sets and whether they meet all the standards set forth at earlier stages; whether it is possible to observe how frequently a resource has been accessed, and how detailed the user statistics are. As a result, it may be said that the third stage of the cycle evaluates the outcomes of the actions taken, as opposed to the fourth stage, which focuses on the impact (long-term effects).

The first set of indices under comparison concerns data provision and includes the basic quantitative metrics. The authors of the above-mentioned public policies recognise the significance of international benchmarks such as the Open Data Maturity employed in this analysis, the Open Data Barometer or (the Global Open Data Index in Slovakia, among others), and documents prepared by respective national audit offices. These are all taken into consideration when evaluating implementation progress. It is vital that the indicators are assessed and updated on a regular basis for this solution to be effective. Poland, for example, produces annual reports on ODP implementation that include all actions taken during the timeframe, including dissemination.

The second set of performance measures refers to data reuse and is essentially the key predictor of the effectiveness of the policy being implemented. They also permit policymakers to measure the level of interest and, as a result, demand for this type of public service, which can provide recommendations on the desired functionalities to be developed. In this sense, Hungary's policy falls short of expectations: while decision-makers in charge of implementing various government programmes occasionally exploit open data, there is little feedback on its actual use (ODM, 2020). It is unclear whether new uses are found for these resources, because the kozadat.hu portal lacks a section devoted to examples of apps created by external parties using the data made available via it. The Czech portal also lacks a catalogue comparable to those available on the Polish or Slovak portals. Metrics that can be easily obtained using national tools are typically supplemented with international reports (historically, they have comprised the Open Data Barometer and Open Data Maturity).

The final impacts of open data policy are technological and operational. To a large extent, they reflect the previously mentioned functionalities of national repositories, the quality of data made available to stakeholders, and the presence of technical constraints that limit their long-term capacity to generate added value for society. With very low ODM 2021 quality metrics, Hungary and Slovakia have the greatest ground to make up. In Hungary, in particular, there are substantial deficiencies in both data resources and how they are made available to users. Poland has an opportunity to reduce the gap with Europe provided that the new technical standards adopted in 2020 are broadly implemented.

7   Policy Evaluation

One of the most difficult issues in the public open data policy cycle is determining whether the objectives specified by relevant programme documents,
which are frequently qualitative in character, have been achieved. The model
adopted for this study relies on impact evaluation by characterising political,
social, economic, technological, and operational added value. As was previously stated, efforts have been made in recent years to monetise the benefits
of open data policies, such as in the framework of the EDP report (Economic
Impact EDP, 2020). Even though such commercialisation initiatives are frequently controversial, they have the advantage of being analysed using the
same methodology in all the Visegrád countries.

A study of the effects of open data legislation in the nations studied demonstrates disparities in the benefits brought about by resource availability, which
corresponds to the quality and efficacy of the actions undertaken in this field.
ODM 2021 defines political impact as the effect of open data on the public
sector and citizen participation, or how it translates into improved internal
administrative processes, greater transparency, and fact-based service delivery. Poland, with a score of 100%, is considerably ahead of Hungary, whose
score of 58% is significantly lower than the EU average of 80%. Both the Czech
Republic and Slovakia are at the bottom of the list, which agrees with previous findings on their generally low progress in measuring the long-term policy
impacts. The second, social aspect refers to the extent to which these policies
address the challenges faced by citizens, such as social inequality, support for
the excluded, and demographic issues. In this area, there is a huge gap between
Poland and Slovakia, which scored 100% and 25% respectively, indicating that
the latter's institutional activity in measuring policy outcomes is insufficient.

The issue of the economic impact of open data policies was already raised
in this study in the context of commercialisation problems. To calculate this
indicator, the authors of the ODM 2021 report asked respondents about their
opinions on measuring this kind of impact in their country, whether they
thought this policy had any economic impact on the macro and micro levels
of the economy and the administration's operation, whether any research was
available on this topic, and what kinds of effects were identified. Poland again
received the maximum possible score, and its System of Local Government
Analyses, a crucial tool that assists local government units with public policies
and development, was one of the good practices mentioned in the review. Slovakia scored a zero for this aspect of impact assessment.

TABLE 8.4   Stage 4: Open data policy evaluation

Policy element	Czech Republic	Hungary	Poland	Slovakia
Political and social value (e.g. increased transparency)	According to the ODM 2021 report, the political impact score is 25% (critically low in comparison with the EU average of 80%) and social impact is 63% (below the EU average of 75%).	According to the ODM 2021 report, the political impact score is 58% (below the EU average of 80%) and social impact is 44% (significantly below the EU average of 75%).	According to the ODM 2021 report, the political impact score is 100% (well above the EU average of 80%) and social impact is 100% (well above the EU average of 75%).	According to the ODM 2021 report, the political impact score is 17% (critically low in comparison with the EU average of 80%) and social impact is 25% (critically low in comparison with the EU average of 75%).
Economic value (e.g. economic growth)	According to the ODM 2021 report, the economic impact score is 31% (significantly below the EU average of 61%).	According to the ODM 2021 report, the economic impact score is 56% (slightly below the EU average of 61%).	According to the ODM 2021 report, the economic impact score is 100% (well above the EU average of 61%).	According to the ODM 2021 report, the economic impact score is 0% (critically low in comparison with the EU average of 61%).

TABLE 8.4 Stage 4: Open data policy evaluation (*cont.*)

Policy element	Czech Republic	Hungary	Poland	Slovakia
Technical and operational value (e.g. ability to reuse data)	According to the Open Data Monitor (2015), the Overall Quality Score is 26%, with 0% for open licenses, 65% for machine readability, 17% for metadata availability, and 22% for metadata completeness. According to the Open Data Portal, open data are freely available on the web as data files for download in an open machine-readable format, accompanied by documentation, and prepared with the goal of making machine processing by software writers simple and feasible (data.gov.cz).	According to the Open Data Monitor (2015), the Overall Quality Score is 51%, with 35% for open licenses, 60% for machine readability, 66% for availability, and 44% for metadata completeness.	According to the Open Data Monitor (2015), the Overall Quality Score is 39%, with 0% for open licenses, 39% for machine readability, 63% for availability, and 54% for metadata completeness.	According to the Open Data Monitor (2015), the Overall Quality Score is 26 %, with 0% for open licenses, 65% for machine readability, 17% for availability, and 22% for metadata completeness. According to the Open Data Portal, open data are freely available on the web as data files for download in in an open machine-readable format, accompanied by documentation, and prepared with the goal of making machine processing by software writers simple and feasible (data.gov.cz).

SOURCE: OWN STUDY BASED ON CHARALABIDIS, ZUIDERWIJK ET AL. (2018), AND V4 EXPERT OPINIONS

8 Policy Change or Termination

Although the final stage of the public open data policy cycle is the least developed (i.e. no subcomponents have been identified), it is critical for maintaining the continuity of ongoing open data operations and the gradual introduction of improvements. If substantial flaws or limitations are discovered, it may even lead to a decision to interrupt and restart the entire process e.g. as a result of recognising an opportunity to make a major technical leap and reject outdated solutions.

Pursuing an innovative open data policy poses a major challenge especially for semi-peripheral countries with limited resources. Implementing revolutionary changes is particularly challenging due to obstacles such as limited resources and the requirement to organise tenders for specialised businesses with the know-how to apply new technology. Even more so is abandoning the current model and starting from scratch. As a result, an incremental approach prevails in the Visegrád countries, where multi-annual digitalisation policies

TABLE 8.5   Stage 5: Open data policy change or termination

Policy element	Czech Republic	Hungary	Poland	Slovakia
Policy change and termination	Gradual development of open data policy. Several policy documents have been prepared. The government plans to create a National Data Fund, which would link data across the Czech public administration and improve its quality.	Several digitalisation strategies exist. The latest one, with a mandate until 2030, is the Artificial Intelligence Strategy 2020–2030.	Every few years, new open data policy documents are produced. New ODP for 2021–2027 is an evolution of previous one for 2016–2020 intended to ensure continuity of activities in accordance with EU legislation and recommendations. Changes are implemented incrementally.	Gradual development of open data documents (from 2013 onwards). Several policy documents have been prepared. The government portal INSPIRE, provides a full list of the documents and the key links (Inspire.gov.sk).

SOURCE: OWN STUDY BASED ON CHARALABIDIS ET AL. (2018) AND V4 EXPERT OPINIONS

with a time horizon of around ten years are being designed, including programmes explicitly committed to data opening. In this context, the European
Union's pressure, which sets the pace of transformation through the adoption
of successive directives, is critical. To meet the EU's expectations, a considerable emphasis is placed on incremental improvements in the form of new
standards or functionalities in national open data portals, particularly in the
Czech Republic and Poland, which are the most advanced V4 states in this
regard. EDP reports also provide a good stimulus, encouraging constructive
rivalry among countries. For example, the Czech Republic is considering establishing a National Data Fund to work on integrating and increasing the quality
of multiple data sets generated by its administration. Moreover, the plan also
involves assessing impacts, identifying users, and introducing the concept of
high-level data sets. Policymakers in Poland, on the other hand, rely heavily
on a widespread adoption of new API, security, technical, and legal standards.

9   Conclusion

The analysis uncovered significant differences in the open data policies pursued by the Czech Republic, Hungary, Poland, and Slovakia. These are further
complicated by the fact that all of these countries are subject to EU legislation,
which, as was repeatedly noted throughout this chapter, plays an important
role in pressing individual Member States to reform and raise standards. Meanwhile, two groups of countries have emerged within the V4.

The Czech Republic and Poland comprise the first one. Decision-makers
in these countries clearly recognise the pro-development nature of these programmes, which they see as one of the hallmarks of innovation and hence a
way to join the ranks of established Western European economies. Even the rise
of populist regimes that place little value on transparency has not prompted
them to reverse course. This bodes well for the possibility of achieving long-
term goals, even if the administration changes after the next elections.

Open data policies enacted by Hungary and Slovakia stand in stark contrast
to the preceding and hence place them at the bottom of European rankings.
Although Hungary's KPIs improved significantly in the ODM 2021 report as
compared with ODM 2020, the country's open data policy lags behind European leaders. However, based on the analysis of present political contexts, it
is possible to speculate that the reasons for this state of affairs differ. Hungary
lacks strategic thinking on open data (despite the fact that the issue is listed in
Hungary's Artificial Intelligence Strategy 2020–2030), the authorities tend to
ignore this issue and only perform the tasks that are absolutely necessary or

do not require significant commitment. Meanwhile, Slovakia pursues a number of initiatives aimed at catching up with more developed countries, but the shortage of capital renders them less effective.

Given the importance of open data policy in the context of the Fourth Industrial Revolution, efforts in this area must be intensified. A pro-active approach by policymakers and authorities can provide a key stimulus in terms of innovation to all stakeholders, including market and civic actors. As a result, a country's international status improves, which is critical for semi-peripheral nations aspiring to become core countries.

Bibliography

Act CXII of 2011 Informational Self-determination and Freedom of Information Government Decree 305/2005.

Algemene Rekenkamer (2015). *Trendrapport open data 2015*. www.reken-kamer.nl/publicaties/rapporten/2015/03/31/trendrapport-open-data-2015.

Algemene Rekenkamer (2016). *Trendrapport open data 2016*. www.reken-kamer.nl/publicaties/rapporten/2016/03/24/trendrapport-open-data-2016.

Anderson, J. E. (1975). *Public Policy-making*. Praeger, Holt.

Beyer, M., Laney, D. (2012). *The Importance of 'Big data': A Definition*. Source: www.gartner.com/doc/2057415/importance–big–data–definition (06.05.2022).

Charalabidis, Y., Zuiderwijk, A., Alexopoulos, Ch., Janssen, M., Lampoltshammer, T. and Ferro, E. (2018). *The World of Open Data. Concepts, Methods, Tools and Experiences*. Springer.

Commisceo Global (2021). *Country reports and guides*. www.commisceo–global.com/resources/country–guides/ (20.09.2021).

Directive 2003/98/EC of the European Parliament and of the Council of 17 November 2003 on the re-use of public sector information.

Directive (EU) 2019/1024 of the European Parliament and of the Council of 20 June 2019 on open data and the re-use of public sector information.

Dunleavy, P., Margetts, H., Bastow, S. and Tinkler, J. (2006). *Digital Era Governance: IT Corporations, the State, and e–Government*. Oxford University Press.

Economic Impact EDP (2020). *The Economic Impact of Open Data. Opportunities for value creation in Europe*. Publications Office of the European Union.

European Commission (2019). *Digital Government Factsheet, Czech Republic*. https://joinup.ec.europa.eu/sites/default/files/inline-files/Digital_Government_Factsheets_Czech%20Republic_2019.pdf.

Free Access to Information Act (Act No. 106/1999 Coll.), cf. Government Regulation No. 425/2016 Coll. for the list of information published as open data.

Hungary AI (2020). *Hungary's Artificial Intelligence Strategy 2020–2030*. Source: https:// ai–hungary.com/api/v1/companies/15/files/146074/download (23.09.2021).

Janssen, M., Charalabidis, Y. and Zuiderwijk, A. (2012). Benefits, Adoption Barriers and Myths of Open Data and Open Government. *Information Systems Management*, *29*(4), 258–268.

Jones, C. (1970). *An Introduction to the Study of Public Policy*. Wadsworth Publishing Company.

Kassen, M. (2018). Open data and its intermediaries: A cross–country perspective on participatory movement among independent developers. *Knowledge Management Research & Practice*, *16*(3), 327–342.

Kassen, M. (2019). *Open Data Politics. A Case Study on Estonia and Kazakhstan*. Springer.

Khayyat, M. and Bannister, F. (2015). Open data licensing: More than meets the eye. *Information Polity*, *20*(4), 231–252.

Laswell, H. D. (1956). *The Decision Process*. Bureau of Governmental Research, University of Maryland.

Mazur, S. (Ed.). (2020). *Public Administration in Central Europe. Ideas as Causes of Reforms*. Routledge.

Nikiforova, A. and McBride, K. (2021). Open government data portal usability: A user–centred usability analysis of 41 open government data portals. *Telematics and Informatics*, *58*.

ODM (2020). *Open Data Maturity Report 2020*. Luxembourg: Publications Office of the European Union.

ODM (2021). *Open Data Maturity Report 2021*. Luxembourg: Publications Office of the European Union.

ODM Method Paper (2021). *European Data Portal. Measuring open data maturity. Seventh edition.* Source: https://data.europa.eu/sites/default/files/method–paper_ insights–report_n7_2021.pdf (13.05.2022).

ODP 2021–2027 (2021). *Uchwała Rady Ministrów nr 28 z dn. 18 lutego 2021 r. w sprawie Programu otwierania danych na lata 2021–2027*. Monitor Polski. 23.03.2021. poz. 290.

PL Guide (2019). *Data opening. Good Practice Guide*. Source: https://dane.gov.pl/media/ ckeditor/2019/07/04/open–data–good–practice–guide.pdf (20.09.2021).

Pollitt, Ch. and Bouckaert, G. (2011). *Public Management Reform: A Comparative Analysis – New Public Management, Governance, and the Neo–Weberian State*. Oxford University Press.

Report PODP (2019). *Raport nt. rezultatów wdrażania programu otwierania danych publicznych. Okres sprawozdawczy: 01.01–31.12.2019 r.* https://mc.bip.gov.pl/fobjects/ download/797770/sprawozdanie-podp-za-2019-r-pdf.html

Resolution of the Government of the Slovak Republic No. 337/2019.

Slovensko.digital (2016). *LOD Slovakia*, Slovensko.digital, January 2016. Source: https://platforma.slovensko.digital/t/lod–slovakia–linked–open–data–cloud/1392 (20.09.2021).

Statistics Office of the Slovak Republic (2020a). *Metadata, Statistics Office of the Slovak Republic.* https://slovak.statistics.sk/wps/portal/ext/metadata/!ut/p/z1 (20.09.2021).

Statistics Office of the Slovak Republic (2020b). *API Open data SO SR, Statistics Office of the Slovak Republic.* https://slovak.statistics.sk/wps/portal/ext/Databases/Open_data/!ut/p/z1 (20.09.2021).

Stewart, J., Jr., Hedge, D. M. and Lester, J. P. (2008). *Public policy: An evolutionary approach.* Wadsworth Thomson Learning.

Townsend, A. (2014). *Smart Cities: Big data, Civic Hackers, and the Quest for a New Utopia.* W. W. Norton & Company.

Vetrò, A., Canova, L., Torchiano, M., Minotas, C. O., Iemma, R. and Morando, F. (2016). Open data quality measurement framework: Definition and application to Open Government Data. *Government Information Quarterly, 33*(2), 325–337.

Welle Donker, F. (2018). Funding Open Data. [In:] B. van Loenen, G. Vancauwenberghe, J. Crompvoets (Eds.). Open Data Exposed. *Information Technology and Law Series, 30.* T.M.C. Asser Press.

Wilkinson, M. D., Dumontier, M., Aalbersberg, I. J., Appleton, G., Axton, M., Baak, A., Blomberg, N., Boiten, J.-W., da Silva Santos, L. B., Bourne, P. E., Bouwman, J., Brookes, A. J., Clark, T., Crosas, M., Dillo, I., Dumon, O., Edmunds, S., Evelo, C. T., Finkers, R.,... Mons, B.(2016). The FAIR Guiding Principles for scientific data management and stewardship. *Sci Data 3*, 160018.

World Bank (2020), data from country profiles. https://data.worldbank.org/country/ (20.09.2021).

Žuffová, M. (2020). *Independent Reporting Mechanism* (IRM)*: Slovakia Implementation Report 2017–2019, OpenGov Partnership.* www.opengovpartnership.org/wp–content/uploads/2020/03/Slovakia_Implementation_Report_2017–2019_EN_for–public–comment.pdf; www.opengovpartnership.org/documents/slovakia–implementation–report–2017–2019–for–public–comment/ (20.09.2021).

Zuiderwijk, A. and Janssen, M. (2014). Open data policies, their implementation and impact: A framework for comparison. *Government Information Quarterly, 31*(1), 17–29.

CHAPTER 9

Communication Management – the Approach of the Visegrád Countries to Fake Narratives and News

Michał Żabiński *and Máté Hajba*

1 Introduction

The unprecedented development of information and communication technologies (ICT) and the resulting expansion of social media offer people access to a wealth of data and the ability to share it with others. The fact that content can be created to be further used by others in real time as part of the Fourth Industrial Revolution (4IR) has many positive consequences, but it also poses a serious threat to individuals, society, the state, and the democratic system (Pomerantsev, 2019); a threat to which democratic states seem ill-equipped and powerless to respond (Aro, 2019). This raises the question of the appropriate countermeasures and remedies to be taken at the state and international public policy levels.

This chapter examines a number of issues concerning propaganda and disinformation in the modern world, with a particular emphasis on the Visegrád countries, specifically, how their respective administrations respond to these challenges. The study is based on interviews with government officials and independent experts from each country.

The paradox of social media is that, due to their pervasive presence, they are both necessary for the preservation of our democratic liberties and pose a threat to them. Free expression and communication are critical components of democratic governance systems. We interpret our reality, communicate facts, opinions, and emotions through social media, all of which have a significant impact on how we think and vote. Today, it appears that social media are more important than the radio, television, and newspapers combined. These older media, however, have two distinctive qualities: civic accountability and a sense of duty. We can assess the credibility of contents provided through more traditional channels, or at the very least we know the profile of the media in question and the values advocated by certain authors. Even if this approach is not always clear or effective, we have adapted to the rules of the game.

In conventional media, anonymity is limited, and there are various barriers in place to disinformation and manipulation. State (public policy) and social rules apply and are sometimes represented as codes of conduct. Even though these rules keep evolving, we usually know what can be shown or said in those media. Regrettably, nothing of the kind holds true for contemporary social media. National and international laws serve as the legal foundation for media activities and defend freedom, independence, and the expression of ideas through the media (Ronkova, 2016).

We live in an era of mistrust and individualism (Krastev, 2013). We doubt our governments, elites, and media, and we distrust the established institutions. Locked in our information bubbles, we seek knowledge online from people we trust and who hold the same views as we do. We express our thoughts and opinions seeking praise and 'likes' without realising how dangerous the environment actually is. We believe that the anonymity of the Internet protects us without realising that it is a double-edged sword in that it actually prevents us from finding out who is on the other side of our computer screen or where this screen is actually located. This gives rise to the challenge of misinformation and manipulation, which likely poses the most serious threat to contemporary society and democratic principles. The perception of misinformation varies by country: in Europe, it tends to depend on geographical and demographic factors. The Baltic States with their high proportion of Russian-speaking population were the first to experience massive foreign propaganda activity on the Internet. As a result, these countries are regarded as the most advanced in terms of institutional safeguards and state intervention capacity against propaganda as well as the most cognizant of the risks involved. However, as the United Kingdom's experience with the Brexit referendum painfully demonstrated, they are not the only nations being attacked (Aro, 2019).

2   Theoretical Aspects of Modern Disinformation (Propaganda)

To properly appreciate the risks and threats of modern-day propaganda and disinformation, we must first explore the phenomenon of social media and explain the concepts loosely used above. Online media (including social media) are accessed by 82% of people to seek news compared to 64% for TV (Chaffey, 2021), which means that the Internet has become the primary source of information. The role of social media in the interchange and flow of information is enormous. In 2020, 57% of people between the ages of 16 and 74 used social networks compared with 87% of those in the 16–24 age band (Eurostat, 2021).

According to a poll conducted in January 2021, active social network penetration has reached 53.6% of the global population. United Arab Emirates tops the list of surveyed countries with the penetration rate of 99%, followed by South Korea (89.3%), Taiwan (88.1%), and the Netherlands (88%). In the Visegrád Group, Hungary (62%), the Czech Republic (53%), Slovakia (51%), and Poland (50%) had the greatest active social media penetration in 2020. In the EU Code of Practice on Disinformation, which is the first worldwide self-regulatory standard based on voluntary participation developed specifically to combat disinformation on social media, the main risk is considered to be "the exposure of citizens to large-scale disinformation, including misleading or outright false information" and a serious risk to open democratic societies (European Commission, 2018). Social networks are a powerful tool for influencing people, but no other technology has been weaponised to such an extent (Ong and Cabañes, 2018).

To realise the seriousness of the situation, we should invoke the agenda-setting theory, according to which the frequency with which information appears in the media is correlated with its relevance, and thus may affect both public and political programmes (Bevan and Jennings 2019). The media have the power to affect and determine the significance of information (McCombs et al., 1997). As information spreads throughout social media, it is fairly easy to influence their agenda, especially since anyone can create the so-called content, moreover, false rumours tend to "diffuse significantly farther, faster, deeper and more broadly than the truth in all categories of information" (Wang et al., 2019). Social media infrastructures rely on networks of friends, interest groups, and political views to create social bubbles that cluster online communities into filter bubbles. As result, they distort the democratic information exchange. Society's vulnerability to false information is a significant aspect of the issue under consideration. According to research, public opinion is both gullible and indiscriminate towards false rumours (Ong and Cabañes, 2018).

The most general and perhaps the most appropriate term to describe the above-mentioned phenomena is propaganda. It has a range of negative connotations, mainly associated with World War II and the Cold War era. As such, it is the proper one to capture the issue of modern-world problems with misinformation, disinformation, and so-called fake news. These terms refer to an entire persuasion agenda – a set of manipulative actions by which we, as individuals and as society, are confronted and influenced. Nevertheless, in many official documents, such as the EU Code of Practice on Disinformation, the current general term in use is disinformation. As a result, the semantic coverage of these terms need to be further clarified.

In the literature, when discussing social media behaviour that poses a threat to society as a whole, it is common to distinguish between disinformation and fake news. This distinction is ambiguous mostly because there is no accepted definition of false news. Thus, there are various categories of news that are not accurate or destructive, but spread successfully for a variety of reasons. When incorrect information is disseminated with the purpose to cause harm, it is referred to as *disinformation. Misinformation*, on the other hand, is defined as false information that is disseminated without malicious intent. It denotes news items characterised by journalistic faults, whereas disinformation is the deliberate reporting of an untrue incident with the purpose to stir conflict. The third kind, *malinformation*, refers to circumstances in which genuine information is made public in order to inflict harm; often involving private confidential materials. The concept of *fake news* can be used to refer to all these kinds of news. Despite the fact that there is no commonly acknowledged definition, the phrase is used more colloquially than scientifically, and the phenomenon itself definitely exists. The Atlantic Council's Digital Forensic Research Lab[1] defines fake news as "deliberately presenting false information as news" and as such falls under the category of disinformation, which is defined as "deliberately spreading false information." According to another definition, fake news is "fabricated material that resembles news media content in form but not in organisational method or aim" (Lazer et al., 2018). The problem is not only the imprecision of the term, but also its history and context. Donald Trump, who made Twitter his primary means of communication and marketing, exploited this concept to discredit any negative content about himself regardless of its source or context (Woolley and Guilbeault, 2017). As a result, in the colloquial sense, fake news is a false rumour or slander – as none of these notions is accurate (Wang et al., 2019), they should not be used to analyse the phenomena known as disinformation in the EU. Even though it represents only one of the three separate phenomena mentioned above, it is far more widespread than the more appropriate term propaganda. To summarise, disinformation, as a popular general phrase, encompasses disinformation, misinformation, the so-called fake news, malinformation, as well as all types of information in media that we perceive to be intentionally inaccurate or misleading (Monaco and Nyst, 2018). Thus, it is a series of concerted efforts intended to influence and shape the opinions and views of the general public usually with malicious intent.

---

1   https://medium.com/dfrlab/fake-news-defining-and-defeating-43830a2ab0af

3   The Dangers of Disinformation

The top-down nature of the media, infrastructure, individual capacity to disseminate knowledge to large audiences, literacy rates, technology, and even ways of verifying information have all historically impeded the flow of information. Theoretically, all of these challenges have been overcome by the Internet and the services built around it, but the latter have significantly disrupted communication and given rise to new, more serious challenges and threats.

Disinformation and fake news thrive in these circumstances, because social media have made it possible for anybody to reach large audiences and disseminate incorrect information under the guise of factual news. Additionally, algorithms that drive social media platforms produce echo chambers or environments in which a person is exposed only to facts or viewpoints that mirror and support their own. Three factors make disinformation dangerous: using social media (because of their nature), fomenting social mistrust, and causing emotional disturbance (our behavioural determinants).

User engagement lies at the core of the design and integration of our involvement in social media activities. The business model of social media networks is simple: on a general level, their objective is to sell advertising time and space; whereas on a more in-depth level, they gather data on our behaviour (also known as behavioural surplus). As a result, the algorithms behind those platforms push people to share news, and in order to do so, they tailor the materials to users with this purpose in mind (Wylie, 2019; Zuboff, 2020).

Two mechanisms are at play in the virtual world. On the one hand, research findings on the adaptive mechanisms of the human mind are exploited to produce content that will naturally draw our attention in order to increase user engagement rates in social media. We have evolved to pay more attention to threats, and thus shocking information that stirs up unpleasant feelings also grabs our attention more quickly and effectively (Wylie, 2019).

On the other hand, man as a collective being feels a natural need to belong, be a member in a group, fears isolation and rejection. As a result, we often adopt the group's viewpoint and repeat it creating a 'spiral of silence' in the flow of information: instead of speaking our minds, for fear of being rejected, we repeat what we believe is accepted by a group to which we want to belong (Sharot 2018). The narrative and perception of reality are thus imposed and interpreted as the topic under debate (Donsbach et al., 2014).

The second component is mistrust. There is growing scepticism in Western countries of political and economic elites, as well as established institutions of public life such as the mainstream media, the state, and scientists. Under these conditions, the emerging populism enhances people's sense of marginalisation and suspicion of established institutions. As a result, extremist movements arise and conspiracy theories spread, providing a fertile ground for deception (Eatwell and Goodwin, 2018).

The third element again appeals to our nature. We are all susceptible to emotions which, in turn, affect our actions. We react differently when we are influenced by powerful emotions, and frequently act against our best interests in ways that we would otherwise reject (Kahneman, 2013). These behavioural mechanisms can be exploited against us: strong emotions, particularly rage and indignation, reduce the need for rational explanation and foster punitive attitudes. This process can be used to immunise target groups against opposing arguments for misinformation purposes (Wylie, 2019). Furthermore, our emotions influence our capacity to engage in dialogue. As online debate progresses, we tend to radicalise our beliefs, which reflects our urge to belong. On the Internet, we tend to conduct discussions within groups chosen by us, creating echo chambers that promote the polarisation of viewpoints. As a result, we skew knowledge dissemination toward like-minded peers. The nature of online debate, which typically seeks to win the argument, leads to misconceptions and polarisation of opinions (Cinelli et al., 2021). Thus, such 'discussions' offer an excellent channel for spreading false information and dividing society (Sharot, 2018).

Due to the aforementioned characteristics of social media and our behavioural determinants, disinformation on the Internet presents a threat to both society and the entire institutional base of the democratic law-governed state, as stated in the EU Code of Practice on Disinformation. The worldwide nature of social media is an essential aspect of this issue. As a component of hybrid warfare, disinformation can thus be utilised to achieve goals on a local, state, and international level. The military aspect of disinformation in the age of social media was openly recognised by Russian general Valeriy Gerasimov in 2013, and was further expanded by colonel S.G. Chekinov and lieutenant General S.A. Bogdanov. The so-called Gerasimov doctrine highlights the potential for propaganda and the possibilities for exploiting data acquired from open communication platforms. This principle underlies the infamous Russian hybrid warfare efforts (Giles, 2016; Wylie, 2019).

The process of 'democratisation' of the media landscape by social media ushered in new tensions and challenges both to the state and society. The key aspect of this 'democratisation' and a true game changer proved to be the elimination of gatekeepers, whose job in the traditional media is not only to determine what qualifies as news but also to ensure its quality in terms of both style and content. In short, in a democratic society, the gatekeepers of information both set the agenda and protect the public from misinformation.

This kind of work has become much more challenging in the Internet age, and the national state's influence is much more limited. The principal actors and, to some extent, gatekeepers are large, multinational corporations (to mention only Facebook and Google), which function as both markets and actors by establishing guidelines for online communication and by facilitating the exchange of ideas and information through their platforms. They control the flow of information, determine the agendas and, as such, are much more powerful and influential than individual national players, especially if the latter are small or medium-sized countries, like the v4.

There are several reasons why disinformation is so dangerous and is considered to be a very effective tool of hybrid warfare and a social threat. Disinformation may be used for the following purposes:

1. To deliberately manipulate society (interfere with consensus building, manipulate public opinion, build an atmosphere of distrust, polarise society);

2. To politically destabilise the state (by spreading rumours and false information, undermining public strategies and policies, and attempts to destabilize the political situation).

Manipulation through disinformation may be achieved by spreading fabricated stories or by creating infoshum. The former can take on various shapes and pursue various objectives. It can be used to create consensus, defame prominent personalities like journalists, scientists, or politicians, divide the public, and undermine trust in government agencies and official channels of communication. These actions may be pursued in order to destabilise a national economy or parts of it, weaken the state structures (international disinformation) or competition (domestic disinformation), and even suppress political opponents (Monaco and Nyst, 2018; Ong and Cabañes, 2018; Woolley and Guilbeault, 2017; Wylie, 2019).

The latter, sometimes referred to as info noise, can be defined as meaningless information that may overwhelm legitimate communication systems and make it difficult to discriminate between what is true and what is not. Finding relevant information is made considerably more difficult by the overabundance of such noise, half-truths, and rumours, moreover, in this context it is extremely challenging to disprove false and unreliable material ("Bullshit, the Noisy Conqueror of the Information Space" 2020; Lavin 2018; Wylie 2019).

3.1 International Disinformation

As was already mentioned, disinformation and the actors behind it can be foreign or domestic. Foreign influence has the potential to foment strife, widen social gaps, and interfere with elections. The most extensive research has been done on Russia's cyberwarfare efforts (Aro, 2019; Szicherle et al., 2019; Woolley and Guilbeault, 2017). Russian propaganda channels, such as Sputnik, RT, and pro-Russian social media accounts, are known to deliberately spread false information (Szicherle et al., 2019).

Russia interfered in UK politics by using Twitter accounts to undermine the validity of the Scottish referendum. Both RT and Sputnik promoted Brexit, spreading anti-EU sentiments and misleading information. This was pushed further by social media, reaching an estimated 134 million potential impressions, which was more than UK websites campaigning for Brexit (Bayer et al., 2019). Russia also deployed its cyberwarfare capabilities to meddle in US and EU elections (Aro, 2019; Szicherle et al., 2019; Wardle and Derakhshan, 2017; Woolley and Guilbeault, 2017; Wylie, 2019).

Disinformation is also used for military purposes. The most recent operations of this kind that received some attention occurred during the war in Syria (Higgins, 2021) or the most recent Israel-Hamas conflict in Gaza (Kossoff, 2021). Although a lot of fake news was generated by both sides at the time (BBC, 2021) the Israeli operation was arguably the most significant. According to a news release from the Israeli Defense Forces (IDF), Israel intended to advance into Gaza with troops amassed on the border. As a result, local Hamas members withdrew into a vast system of underground tunnels known as The Metro. The tunnels and everyone in them were destroyed shortly afterwards by Israeli bombs. In fact, there no invasion had been intended. Although the IDF attributed the misunderstanding to a translation error, it was likely a premeditated attempt to lure Hamas fighters into the tunnels (Kossoff, 2021).

3.2   *Domestic Disinformation*

It is unclear how much disinformation comes from foreign actors and how much comes from home sources in the EU, but in the US, the majority of accounts that distribute misleading information are domestic (Monaco and Nyst, 2018; Woolley and Guilbeault, 2017).

Several incidents involving fake news in the US have been publicised, but one of the most infamous was the so-called Pizzagate, which occurred in the run-up to the 2016 presidential elections. It is noteworthy because it was the first instance of the concept of fake news gained traction in popular discourse. Conspiracy theories circulating on social media and the Internet alleged that a Democratic Party donor's pizza parlour was the hub of a paedophile ring run by Hilary Clinton and that children were abused in its basement. Protesters began to gather in front of the restaurant. Some of them were invited inside, the owner demonstrated that there was actually no basement on the premises, but it had little effect. The story was spread by alt-right Trump supporters and was even used as a propaganda tool in Turkey (BBC 2016). A man armed with a rifle entered the restaurant and began to search it to rescue the children. Pizzagate was a seminal moment in the rise of the QAnon conspiracy theorists as well,[2] who, in turn, played a major role in the Capitol riots (Wylie, 2019).

Domestic disinformation may be used to gain voter support, reduce support for political opponents, conceal an issue, introduce a topic into public debate with the intent to attract and/or distract the public, or discredit someone. Domestic disinformation may originate in official circles – there are well-documented incidents of the so-called state-sponsored trolling aimed at consolidating support or creating online hate and harassment campaigns to intimidate and suppress political opposition or those who criticise government policy. State authorities may engage in such practices on four levels of commitment, namely (Monaco and Nyst, 2018):

1. State executed – disinformation campaign originates directly from the state apparatus and is state-funded;
2. State directed – disinformation campaign is directed and state-sponsored, but not executed by the state apparatus;
3. State incited – state instigates disinformation campaign and profits from it, but it is not directly or formally associated with it. State participation is limited to supporting a specific attack;
4. State leveraged – involves a kind of game of appearances, in which independent opinion centres lend credibility and create support for government action, which later relies on them to justify and legitimise its position.

3.3   *Economic Disinformation*

Not all instances of fake news and disinformation are political in nature. Companies can and do use it to discredit their competition or gain an advantage by portraying themselves as better than they actually are.

In 2020, thousands of Americans received packages containing mysterious seeds from China. Their recipients denied having ordered anything from there, so speculations began that it was an attack on the US by attempting to introduce invasive species into the country via home gardens. Others claimed that China was checking for authentic addresses for absentee mail-in ballots to manipulate elections. The Department of Agriculture ruled that there was no evidence of any malicious intent; it was most likely merely an e-commerce practice known as brushing, which involves creating false feedback

---

2   https://www.theatlantic.com/magazine/archive/2020/06/qanon-nothing-can-stop-what-is
    -coming/610567/

on e-commerce sites to mislead buyers about the quality of a firm or service. Since a lot of such websites only accept feedback from orders that can provide shipping proof, some firms send items of little value to random addresses and using the shipping details subsequently post positive feedback on their profiles. Seeds are excellent for this purpose. The seed scandal put a spotlight on this business practise of spreading misinformation, but the story became much more interesting, as conspiracy theories about China's alleged terrorist activities spread. The economic disinformation campaign led to a surge in anti-China sentiments; the country was even accused of meddling in the 2020 US elections, the results of which were questioned by conspiracy theorists and the alt-right, fuelled by disinformation and Donald Trump himself. In the end, the mystery of the seeds was solved. Many people took up gardening during the COVID-19 pandemic and ordered seeds from companies that they had no idea were Chinese. Due to the pandemic-induced interruption in worldwide trade, orders were delayed by several months, by which time people had forgotten having purchased the seeds (Heath, 2021).

4   Tools of Disinformation

A variety of evolving digital campaigning tools are employed to carry out mass propaganda operations. The most common ones include interactive advertisements, live-streamed footage, memes, hashtags, and personalised messaging (Woolley and Guilbeault, 2017). They can be used to persuade people, consolidate their beliefs, or change their views in order to affect voter turnout. They may also be deployed to more sinister ends, such as sow confusion, fear or panic, give a false impression of online support, attack and discredit the opposition, and spread illegitimate news reports (Bayer et al., 2019; Monaco and Nyst, 2018; Ong and Cabañes, 2018; Wylie, 2019).

Social media platforms are essential instruments for spreading propaganda and disinformation. Probably the most popular and best-understood are trolls, followed by bots and cybots. All three are involved in what is known as networked disinformation. Apart from deception, their activities include signal encryption and unstable virality. They are invariably part of broader tactics and campaigns, the goal of which can be the adoption of a specific political agenda, engendering confusion, or operations similar to hybrid warfare (Monaco and Nyst, 2018; Ong and Cabañes, 2018; Pomerantsev, 2019; Wylie, 2019).

Trolls are people who distribute false information on social media sites, such as Facebook and Twitter, typically while remaining anonymous and using several accounts. One common tactic employed by trolls is to hire others to run phoney accounts. They may include paid influencers with a financial incentive to act, and unpaid volunteers who support a given cause (Ong and Cabaes, 2018). They are unlikely to cause much damage individually, but when they strike in large groups, they form the so-called click armies capable of major disinformation campaigns. The most notorious ones include the St Petersburg-based Internet Research Agency (Agientstwo Internet-Issledowanij), a gang of Russian trolls that has allegedly participated in worldwide disinformation campaigns including the 2016 US elections (Pomerantsev, 2019), and the Chinese 50 Cent Army/50 Cent Party responsible for strategic distraction in Chinese social media by vociferously touting pro-government opinions (King et al., 2017). The latter is an example of a troll farm that operates mainly in its country of origin, whereas the former acts mostly abroad, but both are examples of state-sponsored trolling (Monaco and Nyst, 2018). The operations of these organisations are not limited to disinformation; they also serve as a tool to silence journalists and NGOs which are suspected of stirring up trouble for the authorities. Their activities include death and rape threats, accusations of treason, collusion with foreign intelligence agencies, disclosure of confidential information such as home addresses or telephone numbers as well as urging others to commit acts of violence against the named persons. They may also involve black public relations campaigns designed to slander, intimidate and/ or silence the targeted individuals (Ong and Cabañes, 2018; Woolley and Guilbeault, 2017; Wylie, 2019). Organised trolling is known as networked disinformation (Ong and Cabañes 2018). When comparing the activities of Russian trolls during the US election campaign and the Brexit referendum with those described by troll networks in the Philippines (Ong and Cabaes, 2018), we may notice that they have a lot in common in terms of design and characteristics.

Other tools used by disinformation agents include bots and automated agents or computer software that pretends to be human. Both are designed to amplify troll activity by publishing a huge number of comments in order to saturate a given community with content that serves the purposes of their creators. Bots are very common in mainstream social media, are usually short-lived, and are used to spread disinformation content created by trolls with a view to creating the impression of massiveness and popularity of specific in order to 'manufacture consensus' online (Taibbi, 2021; Woolley and Guilbeault, 2017, 2017). Cybots are more advanced versions of bots controlled by their masters. When a user responds to content published by a cybot, a human operator takes control of the cybot's account to continue the conversation. This kind of action prolongs the bot's life; otherwise, when its real identity is revealed, it is often removed (Taibbi, 2021).

5   Institutional Measures in the EU to Combat Online Propaganda and Disinformation

As instruments of hybrid warfare, disinformation and propaganda pose a persistent threat to society and the democratic order in the European Union. The European Commission, which is the primary institution at this level that handles the issue in question, has devised and begun implementing the following policies:

1.   2020: the European Democracy Action Plan: making EU democracies stronger by improving the Code of Conduct on Combating Disinformation (*Communication on the European Democracy Action Plan*, 2020; European Commission, 2020), and

2.   2018: the Code of Practice on Disinformation: the first large scale advertising industry agreement to address the spread of disinformation. It is a voluntary, self-regulation guideline designed to combat disinformation that has been recognised by major online platforms, including prominent social networks and advertisers, such as Facebook, Google, Microsoft, and Twitter (European Commission, 2018, 2021).

Another relevant institution in this context is the European External Action Service's Strategic Communications and Information Analysis Division (AFF-GEN.7), where a new unit named the East StratCom Task Force was established (2015) to address the issue of Russia's ongoing disinformation campaigns (East StratCom Task Force, 2021).

In 2014, a group of European NATO countries – including Estonia, Germany, Italy, Latvia, Lithuania, Poland, and the United Kingdom – created a unit specifically tasked with combatting disinformation, known as the NATO Strategic Communications Centre of Excellence (NATO StratCom COE).

The European External Action Service's East StratCom Task Force launched the EUvsDisinfo special online project in 2015 to assist a wide audience in destroying disinformation and give the public a means of recognising the threat of disinformation. EUvsDisinfo aims to anticipate, address, and respond to ongoing misinformation tactics by the Russian Federation that have an impact on the European Union, its Member States, and those in the shared neighbourhood (EuvsDiSiNFO, 2020).

These institutional responses reflect the efforts of democratic countries to counter modern propaganda warfare. They necessitate international support, trust, and cooperation among political and business actors, and must be carefully crafted so as not to jeopardise the inherently democratic values of free speech, unlimited access to information, social control, and the absence of state censorship of information.

6   Disinformation in the Visegrád Group

The Visegrád countries are especially interesting as a group of young democracies with a communist past and a strong populist wave that has recently started to undermine their ties and relations with other EU Member States. However, it should be noted that during the ongoing COVID-19 pandemic, anti-vaccination disinformation operations inspired or directly originating from outside the EU, mainly from Russia, have been observed across the EU as a whole (UEvsDiSiNFO, 2021a, 2021b).

Public authorities in the Visegrád countries appear to be aware of the dangers of disinformation. What is their current preparedness level, what actions have been taken at public policy level, and how advanced and established are counter-disinformation initiatives? We attempted to answer these questions in anonymised interviews with government officials, representatives of non-governmental organisations, and academic experts in individual countries.

6.1   *Czech Republic*

The Czech Republic has implemented a state-wide system of coordinated strategic communication. The Ministry of Defence was tasked with developing such a system under the National Security Audit (Ministerstvo vnitra R, 2016); as a result, the National Strategy for Combating Hybrid Action was approved in 2021 (Národní Strategie pro Čelení Hybridnímu Působení, 2021).

These texts provide important insights into how the Czech Republic views the problem of disinformation in the context of contemporary communication. Although organised cyberattacks and information warfare are becoming a greater concern across Europe, the Czech Republic has so far only been marginally impacted. There are some areas where interventions are required, such as when the right to unrestricted access to information is exercised without proper consideration for security issues. Decision-makers are aware of the need to improve or develop competencies in the area of threats related to disinformation at the level of strategic documents; however, building a system to improve the coordination of activities for the evaluation of hybrid threats still poses a significant challenge. This difficulty stems from the necessity to establish communication infrastructure and e-government technologies for use in maintaining internal order and security, state security, and crisis management. A significant finding from government papers is the idea of education system reforms intended to supplement educational programmes with topics such as security education and improving civic and media literacy (Cz_5_5).

The key strategic goals that the Czech Republic should pursue in the area of combating hybrid warfare (National Strategy for Combating Hybrid Action 2021) include the following:

1. To increase the capacity of the state and society to withstand sustained, intensive hybrid action without suffering substantial negative effects, as well as to quickly repair any damage and return to a fully functional state (resilient society, resilient state, resilient critical infrastructure);

2. To improve supra-ministerial coordination and inter-ministerial collaboration in the area of hybrid operations in the Czech Republic.

"In the context of the interviews, it is worth paying attention to the issue of legal norms. Czech legislation does not recognise the terms 'disinformation' or 'propaganda,' hence the scope of the crime of 'disinformation' or 'propaganda' is not defined in Czech criminal law either" (Cz_5_5).

Apart from civilian efforts, the Cyber Forces and Information Operations Command/KySIO is responsible for systematic surveillance of the information environment, including misinformation, for the Czech Army (Ministerstvo obrany ČR, 2020).

Non-governmental fact-checking organisations that fight disinformation are a part of the solution (Cz_5_2). An excellent example of one of these groups that engages in international cooperation is the International Fact-Checking Network, which serves as a safety net for national fact-checking NGOs (such as demagog.cz). The Elves (cesti-elfove.cz), whose motto is "Fighters against foreign disinformation efforts on the Czech Internet," is another intriguing and distinctive Czech group that combats trolls and propaganda. A unique feature of *Cesti elfove* is their anonymity; members of this group conceal their identities for security reasons due to the nature of the threats with which they are dealing (Skoupá, 2018). As many activists fighting disinformation and online trolls have found, the lack of anonymity poses a serious risk of personal attacks (Aro, 2019; Ong and Cabañes, 2018).

These organisations are not only independent, but also unrelated to the actions of governmental institutions (Cz_5_5). Understandably, they are distinct entities for a variety of reasons, but the fact that the state is unwilling to collaborate with them should be noted as an evident shortcoming.

The key Czech authorities, institutions, and agencies in charge of state security on the Internet are as follows: The Centre Against Terrorism and Hybrid Threats at the Ministry of the Interior (CTHH, cthh.cz), (2) National Cyber and Information Security Agency (NÚKIB, nukib.cz), separate from The Supreme Audit Office (NKÚ, nku.cz), (3) Cyber Forces and Information Operations (KySIO) at the Ministry of Defense (army.cz).

6.2   *Hungary*

The Hungarian example is especially interesting, as the country has openly embraced authoritarianism under the current Prime Minister Viktor Orbán and his populist Fidesz party. The media have been consolidated and subordinated to their interests. The Central European Press and Media Foundation KESMA, a government-affiliated foundation, controls most of the traditional media and there are almost no independent media (Hu_5_2, Hu_5_5, Hu_5_6). The former are known to be actively engaged in spreading fake news (Hu_5_1, Hu_5_3).

One of the major problems is associated with echo chambers on social media. The credibility of public institutions started to deteriorate as did public trust in institutions and the state (Hu_5_3). In the case of Hungary, this process has rapidly accelerated in recent years in no small part due to the politicisation of the mainstream media – institutions associated with the ruling party acquired control of radio stations and press publications operating on the market (Hu_5_6). All of this has eroded popular trust in the administration and contributed to the escalation of the conflict between supporters and opponents of the existing regime (Hu_5_1). This division reduces the state's ability to perform public tasks that require public trust, such as vaccinations in the pandemic era, mass migrations or disinformation on the Internet sponsored from abroad.

The propagation of disinformation works both ways, especially in countries whose leaders question democratic norms and take an authoritarian stance. In the case of Hungary, the state – captured by the ruling party Fidesz – is in charge of creating and disseminating propaganda operations to gain political capital (Hu_5_3, Hu_5_4, Hu_5_5). In consequence, the state does not have the capital of social trust needed to confront the issue of internet propaganda and disinformation, nor is it ready to do so as an active player and beneficiary of such actions (Hu 5 1). Hungary's authorities do not collaborate with other countries to ensure information security and combat disinformation; on the contrary, many charges have been levelled against Hungary's ruling party for exploiting conspiracy theories to discredit political opponents (Hu_5_1, Hu_5_2, Hu_5_4, Hu_5_5). It should be noted that Fidesz, the Hungarian ruling party, has been known for embracing Russian and Chinese foreign policies and information warfare (Hu_5_3).

The National Media and Infocommunication Authority is the primary government agency in Hungary in charge of state security on the Internet, but the experts consulted opine that given the organisation's lack of action during the process of media consolidation that eroded media pluralism, its activities should be viewed as very limited and sham (Hu_5_3, Hu_5_4).

6.3   *Poland*

In comparison with the other Visegrád Group countries, Poland has a comprehensive and advanced apparatus for detecting and combating disinformation on the Internet (Pl_5_2, Pl_5_3). In this area, both official institutions and independent non-governmental organisations are active, and Poland is involved in international, primarily EU-led, cooperation to prevent hybrid warfare. Poland's Martyna Bildziukiewicz heads EU's East Stratcom Task Force – a unique organisation that functions under the aegis of the European External Action Service, or the EU's diplomatic corps (Pl_5_2).

There are both national institutions such as NSAK, a state-owned research institute supervised by the Chancellery of the Prime Minister, and dedicated ministerial cells responsible for monitoring disinformation from their perspectives, affiliated with the Ministry of the Interior and the Ministry of National Defense. However, since their actions are barely coordinated, focus on the internal needs of individual ministries, and are not communicated to the public, they do not constitute an effective instrument for combating disinformation (Pl_5_3).

Apart from public bodies, non-governmental organisations also engage in efforts intended to identify and unmask false information. The best-known is the fact-checking Demagog association, which belongs to the International Fact-Checking Network (IFCN), and oko.press – a portal dedicated to fact-checking and conducting journalistic investigations. It should be noted, however, that formal cooperation between public entities and NGOs in the area of identifying and combating online disinformation is lacking (Pl_5_1, Pl_5_3).

In Poland, the rule of right-wing populist parties has resulted in a progressive deterioration of democratic state institutions. The media's independence was hampered by the purchase of press publications by a state-owned corporation – the main domestic petrochemical company Orlen – which took over a considerable portion of the local press market and turned it into a government propaganda mouthpiece (Pl_5_1).

Like in Hungary, the Polish government and its affiliated media outlets employ propaganda and false information to further their political goals, including suppressing and discrediting the opposition (Pl_5_1). A paradoxical situation compelled Poland's current leaders to address the issue of disinformation and propaganda as potential state destabilizers and a component of hybrid warfare. Political parties have used and continue to exploit social media for their purposes, frequently spreading misinformation (Pl_5_2). Therefore, it may be claimed that the ruling party should be motivated to maintain the status quo, because a war on misinformation could adversely affect it. However, in 2021, due to a leak of numerous e-mails from the account of one of the prominent politicians – Michał Dworczyk, head of the Chancellery of the Prime Minister – the party itself became the target of online attacks, which forced it to take action in this area (Pl_5_1). Furthermore, the situation at the Polish-Belarusian border due to the flood of migrants and the corresponding disinformation internet campaign have underscored the magnitude of the disinformation threat and the need for coordinated countermeasures. The international environment is a major factor distinguishing the situations of Poland and Hungary, both of which have autocratic ruling parties. The Hungarian administration is openly pro-Russian, whereas in Poland, the authoritarian Russian regime is viewed as a threat due to historical experience and proximity.

6.4   Slovakia

From the perspective of the state, the main issue is the polarisation of public opinion. Part of the problem is the tension between the strong, independent media scene dominated by socially liberal and centre-left and underrepresented conservative views – this imbalance of representation drives a serious problem of polarisation in society and growing distrust between the conservative and liberal parts of society (Sk_5_1, Sk_5_2). This offers an opportunity for foreign disinformation to erode trust and spread conspiracy theories about the different parts of the political spectrum The strength of social and alternative media as well as the penetration of the Internet have only made it worse in recent years. The rise of far-right and even far-left parties demonstrates a new political orientation toward both extremes of the political spectrum, with sources including China, Russia, and non-state extremist groups from Western Europe and the United States. (Sk_5_2).

The cooperation of the state with NGOs in ensuring information security and combating disinformation is very limited and at best based on personal connections and initiatives of individuals in ministerial departments or the civil service who have been active in specific areas (Sk_5_2). Assistance for such collaboration is occasionally provided in the form of EU subsidies, which are frequently used by public organisations to enable cooperation with qualified partners in specific areas of security or monitoring the misinformation scene.

As far as monitoring and assessing disinformation risks are concerned, state-directed processes are extremely weak and insufficient (Sk_5_1). Numerous NGOs – for example, GLOBSEC with its digital security and disinformation focus – try to perform these functions. Another example of an autonomous actor in Slovakia is the Agence France-Presse (AFP) – a news agency, part of the International Fact-Checking Network – which debunks disinformation and hoaxes on Facebook. Although such groups should be considered of utmost importance, their operations do not fall under the purview of a national system or plan to combat internet propaganda and disinformation. This is an example of bottom-up social initiative that, whilst effective, falls short of completely compensating for the absence of state action.

Even though disinformation is a fundamental problem that exacerbates social polarisation and distrust of governmental institutions, the latter should not respond by monitoring or even curtailing free speech (Sk_5_1), since efforts to that effect may result in a backlash, escalation of distrust, and lend credence to conspiracy theories. Instead, it should be more transparent and honest in public debate, which would increase trust in the mainstream sources of information and decrease the support for fringe sites and portals (Sk_5_2). Previous state activities in this area should be considered fragmentary and unsystematic with key initiatives being undertaken at the level of individual ministries, of which the most active are the Ministry of the Interior and the Ministry of Justice followed by the Ministry of Informatisation and Regional Development responsible for the inter-ministerial agenda (Sk_5_1, Sk_5_3). The spread of disinformation, which has intensified in the Central European digital arena over the last ten years, has not been adequately addressed by either the current or previous administrations. The political elites, who are frequently suspicious of disinformation since it may be easily utilised as a tool for political games, are a contributing factor to the issue. As populist politicians seek political support from believers in these sentiments, whether it is the pro-Russian narrative or specific anti-intellectual and anti-elitist conspiracies, they tailor their policy and narratives accordingly (Sk_5_1, Sk_5_3). This is especially dangerous in Slovakia, the country most conspiracy theory- and misinformation-prone in the Visegrád Group (Hajdu and Klingová 2020). It should also be noted that there is no formal collaboration between Slovakia and the other V4 countries in information security and combating disinformation (Sk_5_1).

7   Conclusion

The analysis of the situation in the Visegrád countries presented above leads to two groups of conclusions: those that are specific to these nations and those that are more general in nature.

The responses of these countries to the threats posed by disinformation have a number of features in common. First, the V4 governments are ambivalent about disinformation. They use it cynically as a political tool, therefore their efforts to prevent disinformation are necessarily selective. Accordingly, domestic counter-disinformation efforts are limited, as is collaboration with other countries and international organisations. Furthermore, there is little to no collaboration between governments and independent national and international anti-disinformation NGOs. The absence of a history of intersectoral cooperation and the 'novelty' of the danger are two contributing factors to mistrust and lack of cooperation in this area.

The perception of what actually constitutes disinformation and whether it really is something harmful that requires action depends on the subjective impression of social reality anchored in values and political views on international political economy. Differences in what governments consider as disinformation worth combating are due to the varying levels to which their countries are integrated into the international political economy. Geopolitical alliances, which affect the international standing of a given country and correlate with the interests of the ruling parties, are also important.

The mainstream media in those countries have a clear leftist and neoliberal bias. Consequently, by failing to represent a full spectrum of views, they contribute to building polarisation strategies and provide a breeding ground for alternative 'independent' sources of information.

Looking from a broader perspective, the modern era is shaped by technological advancement, the Fourth Industrial Revolution defines our lifestyles, the way we work, communicate, and perceive the world we live in in the early 21st century. However, the institutional framework – governments, legal norms, and rules – comes from the 20th century. This is only natural – the more fundamental and embedded an institution, the slower the process of its transformation (Alt, 2000).

Despite their various benefits, artificial intelligence, automation, and increasingly sophisticated marketing tools pose a growing threat to information security. According to a study, "experts estimate that bot traffic now makes up over 60% of all traffic online – up nearly 20% from two years prior (Bayer et al. 2019)."[3] This trend will only increase and become more automated.

With more advanced techniques to harvest data and circumvent rules, big data collections will continue to be an issue in the future, as seen in the case of Cambridge Analytica (Wylie, 2019).

Numerous websites fact-check news and their sources, whereas initiatives, such as those taken by Facebook, flag false information and unreliable sources. Fact-checking is being used more frequently to determine whether news is reliable as a result of the rise in fake news. Although studies suggest that flags on false news stories increase people's likelihood to accept them, this may prevent

---

3   www.europarl.europa.eu/RegData/etudes/STUD/2019/608864/IPOL_STU(2019)608864
    _EN.pdf

fake information from spreading further.[4] In some cases, the social media sites that serve as the main vehicles for the dissemination of false information ban users who do so.

By formulating action plans, conducting research, and distributing information, the EU and international organisations such as NATO are poised to take pre-emptive action. For example, the East StratCom Task Force of the European Council set up a dedicated website known as EUvsDisinfo.[5]

The term 'imagology,' coined by the celebrated author Milan Kundera, refers to the notion that our beliefs impact the social world in which we live. Robert J. Shiller, a recipient of the Nobel Prize in economics, developed this concept further (Shiller 2019). From the perspective of the state and society as a whole, the way in which technology is transforming our communication is fraught with risk. If what we believe may become reality, we bear a heavy responsibility for the thoughts and ideas we share.

From the perspective of the state, an important factor is the rapidly expanding uncontrolled information flow. Other countries and international business organisations control important communication channels and can decide not only what is conveyed but also who is permitted to communicate. They may therefore use specific imagological tools to construct a reality that is at odds with governmental aims, undercuts popular faith in the state, or leads to social unrest.

From the societal perspective, the unregulated and boundless world of social media also presents a threat. Exposure to overabundance of information which is difficult to verify, echo chambers and social bubbles leads to emotional exhaustion, polarisation, and foments distrust both in public institutions and other people.

The main challenges include identifying information and how it is disseminated, ensuring its quality, and determining where disinformation ends and outright propaganda war begins. The ability to manage online platforms is a source of concern for the state since it involves the sovereignty and agency of public institutions towards commercial players. Democracy necessitates social control, which is based on open access to knowledge, but this comes with inherent risks. On the other hand, where there is control, there are also doubts about freedom of expression and access to information.

It appears that current best practices in this respect are insufficient. State agencies, private tech corporations, international institutions and the media

---

4 https://news.mit.edu/2020/warning-labels-fake-news-trustworthy-0303
5 https://euvsdisinfo.eu/about

thus need to agree upon a range of media standards to ensure reliability of data circulating online.

As part of a comprehensive strategy to combat disinformation, states should collaborate with one another, the media, the non-profit sector, and the business sector. To monitor the sources and patterns of fake news, national and international policies must collaborate with government organisations for the sake of national security. Tech companies must be much stricter with disinformation – currently, fake news stories generate a lot of traffic, hence there is not enough incentive for social media platforms to police their content. Furthermore, journalists must clearly distinguish between facts and opinions by double-checking their sources and confirming facts.

Both governments and the media must re-establish trust to discourage people from seeking information from alternative sources. Education must be prioritised, with digital skills and literacy, including media literacy, being integrated into primary and secondary curricula to effectively teach people to seek out sources of information and promote the habit of checking it. Changes must involve not only critical thinking in the context of the media, such as the press or television, but also verifying information obtained from friends, acquaintances, particularly the messages uncritically shared via social media.

Disinformation is nothing new and will continue to exist, but its reach and delivery techniques have evolved. Only by the combined efforts of the media, government, and business can it be overcome, or at the very least kept at bay.

Bibliography

Alt, J. E. (2000). Time, Transition, and Institutional Change: Concluding Comment. *Journal of Institutional and Theoretical Economics* (JITE), 156(1), 300–305.

Aro, J. (2019). *Putin's Trolls*. IG Publishing.

Bayer, J., Bitiukova, N., Szakács, J. and Alemanno, A. (2019). *Disinformation and propaganda – impact on the functioning of the rule of law in the EU and its Member States.* Policy Department for Citizens' Rights and Constitutional Affairs Directorate General for Internal Policies of the Union. www.europarl.europa.eu/RegData/etudes/STUD/2019/608864/IPOL_STU(2019)608864_EN.pdf.

BBC (2016, December 2). The saga of 'Pizzagate': The fake story that shows how conspiracy theories spread. *BBC Trending.* www.bbc.com/news/blogs-trending-38156985.

BBC (2021, May 16). Israel-Palestinian conflict: False and misleading claims fact-checked. *BBC News.* www.bbc.com/news/57111293.

Bevan, S. and Jennings, W. (2019). The Public Agenda: A Comparative Perspective. In: S. Bevan and W. Jennings, *Comparative Policy Agendas* (pp. 219–242). Oxford University Press. https://doi.org/10.1093/oso/9780198835332.003.0025.

Bullshit, the noisy conqueror of the information space (2020). EUvsDiSiNFO. https:// euvsdisinfo.eu/bullshit-the-noisy-conqueror-of-the-information-space/.

Chaffey, D. (2021, July 23). Global social media statistics research summary 2021. *Smart Insights.* www.smartinsights.com/social-media-marketing/social-media-strategy/ new-global-social-media-research/.

Cinelli, M., De Francisci Morales, G., Galeazzi, A., Quattrociocchi, W. and Starnini, M. (2021). The echo chamber effect on social media. *Proceedings of the National Academy of Sciences, 118*(9), e2023301118. https://doi.org/10.1073/pnas.2023301118.

Communication on the European democracy action plan (2020). European Commission. https://eur-lex.europa.eu/legal-content/EN/TXT/?uri=CELEX:52020DC0790.

Eurostat (2021, June 30). *Do you participate in social networks?* https://ec.europa.eu/ eurostat/web/products-eurostat-news/-/edn-20210630-1.

Donsbach, W., Salmon, C. T. and Tsfati, Y. (Eds.). (2014). *The spiral of silence: New perspectives on communication and public opinion.* Routledge.

East StratCom Task Force (2021, April 28). *Questions and Answers about the East StratCom Task Force.* https://eeas.europa.eu/headquarters/headquarters-homepage/2116/-questions-and-answers-about-the-east-stratcom-task-force_en.

Eatwell, R. and Goodwin, M. J. (2018). *National populism: The revolt against liberal democracy.* Pelican an imprint of Penguin Books.

European Commission (2018). *EU Code of Practice on Disinformation.* European Commission. https://ec.europa.eu/newsroom/dae/document.cfm?doc_id=54454.

European Commission (2020, December 3). *European Democracy Action Plan: Making EU democracies stronger.* https://ec.europa.eu/commission/presscorner/detail/en/ ip_20_2250.

European Commission (2021, August 6). Code of Practice on Disinformation. *Shaping Europe's Digital Future.* https://digital-strategy.ec.europa.eu/en/policies/code-practice-disinformation.

EuvsDiSiNFO (2020). *To Challenge Russia's Ongoing Disinformation Campaigns: The Story of Euvsdisinfo.* https://euvsdisinfo.eu/to-challenge-russias-ongoing-disinformation-campaigns-the-story-of-euvsdisinfo/.

Giles, K. (2016). *Handbook of Russian information warfare.* Research Division NATO Defense College.

Hajdu, D. and Klingová, K. (2020). *Voices of Central and Eastern Europe: Perceptions of democracy and governance in 10 EU countries.* GLOBSEC.

Heath, C. (2021, July 15). *The truth behind the Amazon mystery seeds. Why did so many Americans receive strange packages they didn't think they'd ordered?* The Atlantic. www.theatlantic.com/science/archive/2021/07/unsolicited-seeds-china-brushing /619417/.

Higgins, E. (2021). *Eliot Higgins.* Bloomsbury Publishing.

Kahneman, D. (2013). *Thinking, fast and slow* (1st pbk. ed). Farrar, Straus and Giroux.

King, G., Pan, J. and Roberts, M. E. (2017). How the Chinese Government Fabricates Social Media Posts for Strategic Distraction, Not Engaged Argument. *American Political Science Review, III*(3), 484–501. https://doi.org/10.1017/S0003055417000144.

Kossoff, J. (2021, May 15). Israel accused of tricking major news outlets into reporting a fake Gaza invasion to lure Hamas fighters into tunnels that were targeted for massive airstrikes. *Business Insider*. www.businessinsider.com/gaza-israel-used-media-reports-lure-hamas-fighters-into-tunnels-2021-5?IR=T.

Krastev, I. (2013). In *Mistrust We Trust. Can Democracy Survive When We Don't Trust Our Leaders?*, TED Books.

Lavin, T. (2018, November 19). How the Russian concept of "info-noise" can help American outlets cover Trump. *Media Matters for America*. www.mediamatters.org/donald-trump/how-russian-concept-info-noise-can-help-american-outlets-cover-trump.

Lazer, D. M. J., Baum, M. A., Benkler, Y., Berinsky, A. J., Greenhill, K. M., Menczer, F., Metzger, M. J., Nyhan, B., Pennycook, G., Rothschild, D., Schudson, M., Sloman, S. A., Sunstein, C. R., Thorson, E. A., Watts, D. J. and Zittrain, J. L. (2018). The science of fake news. *Science, 359*(6380), 1094–1096. https://doi.org/10.1126/science.aao2998.

McCombs, M. E., Shaw, D. L. and Weaver, D. H. (Eds.). (1997). *Communication and democracy: Exploring the intellectual frontiers in agenda-setting theory*. Lawrence Erlbaum Associates.

Ministerstvo obrany ČR (2020). *Velitelství Kybernetických Sil a Informačních Operací*. www.acr.army.cz/struktura/generalni/kyb/velitelstvi-kybernetickych-sil-a-informacnich-operaci-214169/.

Ministerstvo vnitra ČR (2016). *Audit národní bezpečnosti*. Ministerstvo vnitra ČR, odbor bezpečnostní politiky a prevence kriminality.

Národní strategie pro čelení hybridnímu působení (2021) (testimony of Ministry of Defense).

Monaco, N. and Nyst, C. (2018). *State-Sponsored Trolling. How Governments Are Deploying Disinformation as Part of Broader Digital Harassment Campaigns*. Institute for the Future.

Ong, J. C. and Cabañes, J. V. A. (2018). *Architects of Networked Disinformation: Behind the Scenes of Troll Accounts and Fake News Production in the Philippines*. University of Massachusetts. https://doi.org/10.7275/2CQ4-5396.

Pomerantsev, P. (2019). *This is not propaganda: Adventures in the war against reality* (First Edition). PublicAffairs.

Ronkova, N. (2016). International legal framework for media. *Journal of Process Management. New Technologies, 4*(2), 57–63. https://doi.org/10.5937/JPMNT1602057R.

Sharot, T. (2018). *The Influential Mind: What the Brain Reveals About Our Power to Change Others*. Picador.

Shiller, R. J. (2019). *Narrative economics: How stories go viral and drive major economic events*. Princeton University Press.

Skoupá, A. (2018). Čeští "elfové" potírají dezinformace a propagandu. Jsou mezi nimi lékaři i vojáci. *Aktuálně.Cz*. https://zpravy.aktualne.cz/domaci/cesti-elfove-rusti-trollove-dezinformace-propaganda/r~93a60ad0db6b11e89de10cc47ab5f122/.

Szicherle, P., Lelonek, A., Mesežnikov, G., Syrovatka, J. and Štěpánek, N. (2019). *Investigating Russia's role and the Kremlin's interference in the 2019 EP elections*. Friedrich Naumann Foundation. www.politicalcapital.hu/pc-admin/source/documents/pc_russian_meddling_ep2019_eng_web_20190520.pdf.

Taibbi, M. (2021). *Hate Inc.: Why today's media makes us despise one another: with a new post-election preface.*

UEvsDiSiNFO (2021a, March 29). *Attacking the west, putting Russians in danger*. UEvsDiSiNFO. https://euvsdisinfo.eu/attacking-the-west-putting-russians-in-danger/.

UEvsDiSiNFO (2021b, April 28). *EEAS special report update: Short assessment of narratives and disinformation around the COVID-19 pandemic (update December 2020 – April 2021)*. UEvsDiSiNFO. https://euvsdisinfo.eu/eeas-special-report-update-short-assessment-of-narratives-and-disinformation-around-the-covid-19-pandemic-update-december-2020-april-2021/.

Wang, Y., McKee, M., Torbica, A. and Stuckler, D. (2019). Systematic Literature Review on the Spread of Health-related Misinformation on Social Media. *Social Science and Medicine, 240*, 112552. https://doi.org/10.1016/j.socscimed.2019.112552.

Wardle, C. and Derakhshan, H. (2017). *Information Disorder: Toward an interdisciplinary framework for research and policy making* (Council of Europe Report).

Woolley, S. C. and Guilbeault, D. (2017). *Computational Propaganda in the United States of America: Manufacturing Consensus Online*. University of Oxford. http://blogs.oii.ox.ac.uk/politicalbots/wp-content/uploads/sites/89/2017/06/Comprop-USA.pdf.

Wylie, C. (2019). *Mindf*ck: Cambridge Analytica and the plot to break America* (First edition). Random House.

Zuboff, S. (2020). *The age of surveillance capitalism: The fight for a human future at the new frontier of power* (First Trade Paperback Edition). PublicAffairs.

Internet Sources

https://medium.com/dfrlab/fake-news-defining-and-defeating-43830a2ab0af

www.theatlantic.com/magazine/archive/2020/06/qanon-nothing-can-stop-what-is-coming/610567/army.cz

www.europarl.europa.eu/RegData/etudes/STUD/2019/608864/IPOL_STU(2019)608864_EN.pdf

https://news.mit.edu/2020/warning-labels-fake-news-trustworthy-0303

https://euvsdisinfo.eu/about/

The Limited Yet Existing Agency of the Semi-periphery and the Case for Technological Re-Embedding: Conclusions

Michał Możdżeń

Karl Marx was the first to observe that the nature of technological revolutions directly reflects the way in which the international division of labour emerges and reproduces the centre-periphery divide (De Paula et al, 2020). The emerging technical paradigms offer the centre both the tools for long-term control over the supplies from the periphery and the objectives of accumulation that drive technological change. This process is not straightforward, as what constitutes the centre is not given once and for all due to discontinuities in path dependence (which entrenches the system, but may change in various windows of opportunity). As a result, control of new technology paradigms is fiercely contested, implying that it is political in nature, as illustrated by the ongoing confrontation between the United States and China over the technical frontier.

In a very general sense, national economic policies are constrained by the international division of labour (IDL) both in scope and direction, and any remaining autonomy can be used for one of two purposes: local capital accumulation or distributive policies (da Motta e Albuquerque, 2007). This becomes even more complicated by the quickly shifting and therefore hard to grasp social consequences of technological revolution. Their goals are dispersed and ambiguous, as highlighted by M. Frączek in his chapter devoted to socio-economic consequences and challenges of the Fourth Industrial Revolution.

With this in mind, we can see the difficulty in addressing the topic of how semi-peripheral players, such as CEE countries in general and the Visegrád countries (V4) in particular, might position themselves vis-à-vis current technological advancements. At least five important aspects define and limit their possible responses as well as the scope of agency:

1. The structural nature of economic dependence (place in GVCs);
2. Their political and institutional alignments (EU);
3. The global business cycle and its specific influence on their economic options;
4. The distributive consequences of the chosen economic model;

© MICHAŁ MOŻDŻEŃ, 2025 | DOI:10.1163/9789004711952_011

5. The capacity of governments to formulate and implement increasingly resilient and independent political agendas and to act as a part of the centre in some technological niches.

The openness of semi-peripheral CEE economies to trade combined with their strong and growing specialisation in producing intermediate inputs into the GVC (Geodecki and Grodzicki, 2015) produce a sort of path-dependent development trajectory on which technological leapfrogging independent of technical change downstream becomes difficult, at least in the most integrated sectors (such as the automotive one; cf. Grodzicki and Skrzypek, 2020), with local strategies focused on continuous and incremental technical upgrading.

EU membership, which imposes certain restrictions on the possibilities to act independently for both eurozone-aligned countries and those that only adhere to the club's rulebook, highlights the uniqueness of the development model of the CEE countries and their function as "Factory Europe" (Geodecki and Możdżeń, 2016). At the same time, it facilitates limited "transnational industrial policy" initiatives (Medve-Bálint and Šćepanović, 2019).

The nature of these relationships as well as the ability of semi-peripheral countries to pursue autonomous economic policies is complicated by the global business cycle. On the upswing, they enjoy greater financial independence, which 'loosens' the macroeconomic restriction and makes it easier to pursue their policies, which can, at least in theory, be geared towards technical advancement. On the other hand, during a downturn, the role of financial constraints increases. During recessions, however, the amount of FDI allows these countries to be more selective and execute technological upgrading by encouraging investment in areas with the best prospects (despite the reservation mentioned in 2 above).

Internal policies, which are inextricably associated with the dominant economic model of competing on labour costs, further limit the opportunities for active participation in the technological revolution that individual economies exhibit to varying degrees. The model's fundamentals (cost competition) allow for low wages and relatively substantial income inequality. This naturally puts pressure on the government to favour distributive measures against domestic capital accumulation during upswings and labour-intensive (therefore cost-sensitive) FDIs during downturns. The path-dependent nature of the process makes meaningful levels of internally generated technological upgrading difficult to attain.

Despite the fact that dependence on location in the IDL is occasionally viewed as an important component explaining state capacity, the latter remains one of the most commonly studied explanations for technological advancement (Acemoglu et al., 2016; Geodecki and Możdżeń, 2016; Reinsberg et al., 2019). Even though state capacity is endogenous to the workings of local political economy in general and to a specific policy's purpose, it continues to play an important role in developing technical edge in both the public and private sectors (Mazzucato, 2014).

Nevertheless, as the following chapters of the book show, there is a range of opportunities for independent action at the semi-periphery.

T. Geodecki argues that under the pressure of COVID-19-induced lockdowns, public administration was capable of deliberate and meaningful transformation. In general, however, he emphasises numerous reform paths to enable better deployment of state powers, such as faster digitisation and stronger partner links with the business sector. Regarding the first research question, this areas have seen the most conspicuous effects of globalisation and technological change.

B. Biga provides some compelling evidence that data sharing is hampered not only by an unwillingness to cooperate on the part of IT corporations but also by a lack of proactivity on the part of government.

While individual reforms face similar external constraints, M. Oramus and M. Kędzierski demonstrate that there are major differences in the quality of data sharing protocols and e-government services.

As chapters 5, 6 and 7 argue in the context of the second research question all countries have seen extensive reforms in the areas of development of e-services, the management and regulation of data and information flows and open data policy. Overall they remain less developed in these areas compared to the richer western countries with stronger governments, with notable exceptions in particular e-services.

In the same chapters we can find many similarities in the reforms that are taking place, which enables us to give partially affirmative reply to the fourth research question on the convergence of the reform paths. However it seems that a lot of these reforms are to some extent indirectly coordinated by the EU policies, which runs counter to the ascertainment that a truly specific Visegrád path of public management and governance is emerging to meet the challenges of the Fourth Industrial Revolution.

The possibilities for stakeholder management, particularly for technologically active states, depend heavily on the use of appropriate management instruments, the most essential of which, according to A. Kozina, is the administration's openness to dialogue and negotiations.

One of the key prerequisites for both state capacity and social cohesion around chosen development goals involves building a transparent communication sphere. M. Żabiński and M. Hajba suggest that there are various methods available to governments to combat disinformation, but their effective implementation is hampered by partisan agendas whose promoters sometimes resort to fake news. In the context of the third research question, state capacity remains the obstacle of developing active and coherent response to to the effects of globalisation and technological change.

S. Mazur emphasises the role of active labour market and education policies in the process of building local resilience to technological shocks that are inextricably tied to global capital flows, which can make or break a particular semi-periphery. In his view, this necessitates the adoption of agile government practices.

Because of political idiosyncrasies and path dependence, the countries studied grapple with globalisation and technological advancement in similar, albeit not identical, ways. We argue, however, that:

a   More scope for international cooperation definitely exists, which would make it possible to partially overcome the challenges of dependence and the precarious position of the semi-periphery. This includes cooperation with countries similarly placed in the IDL and those that make up the global 'core' as long as their interests at least partly overlap. This is true of coordinated actions at the EU level with respect to global technology companies, the majority of which are headquartered outside the continent.

b   Investing in state capacity is a prerequisite for effective transformation in the face of technological development and the challenges it brings. In practice, this means improved technology regulation and absorption capacity as well as stronger labour market policies, which have become all but neglected due to the robust macroeconomic conditions in which CEE countries currently find themselves. A social contract that enables income and wealth redistribution across increasingly divided social groups in terms of the human capital available is also necessary, as is education that prioritises developing skills which allow society to harness the potential of both AI technologies and those that cannot be automated.

c   Some countries (e.g. Poland) mobilise SOE resources with a view to improving state capacity, which appears to be a workaround for the difficulty in mustering sufficient human resources due to its inability to compete for the best and brightest at the peak of the global business cycle. It must, however, be institutionally entrenched in the democratic process, which is problematic in the absence of effective social dialogue.

Another point concerns the popular conceptualisation of technological changes (revolutions) as something disembedded from the social fabric of political and economic systems in which they arise. Although technology, due

to its partly open nature, needs relatively few well-established cultural conditions to develop, it is inherently a social phenomenon.

a   Technology is not a given for any society, its adoption is culturally and
     economically conditioned, and social agency may overcome the 'inevita-
     ble' nature of technological megatrends;
b   Regulation that benefits society with very little harm to technology pro-
     viders is possible (see Chapter 7 on state capacity by B. Biga);
c   Considerable challenges arise locally when technology, as used by e.g.
     social media marketers, becomes advantageous for political entities that
     are also responsible for controlling its myriad negative consequences
     (see Chapter 9 by M. Żabiński and M. Hajba)
d   Yet, making internal use of government data and opening it to the public
     may be immensely valuable in identifying problems and leveraging data
     for use by society at large (see Chapter 8 by M. Oramus and Chapter 6 by
     M. Kędzierski)
e   This is not an easy task, especially when dealing with conflicting political
     and economic processes, in which technology is increasingly viewed as
     a source of competitive advantage, and which allows for greater techno-
     logical disembedding while simultaneously instrumentalising political
     institutions (see e.g. Biga et al., 2022).

Many challenges posed by the unfolding technological revolution have found
their way into the public agenda both on national and EU levels. As a result,
tech-companies are increasingly subject to regulation and taxation for public
purposes. Active state and international cooperation thus appears to be the
optimal approach to the growing concerns brought by current IT adoptions,
such as superhuman level AI with its enormous unknown computing power.

    All the preceding arguments represent a call for political action aimed at
social re-embedding of technology, which is a particularly difficult task for
countries with limited external autonomy and social cohesion coupled with a
correspondingly lower cultural capital in comparison with the core ones. However, in some instances the technology itself can be used to overcome some of
these barriers.

    To make a point rather than to speculate how this re-embedding could be
accomplished, we will conclude with a performance (Piazzoli, 2018) by citing
selected responses to two questions on related topics provided by ChatGPT
(see below). This exercise is not intended to demonstrate that new technologies can in any way replace critical, informed debate, but rather get a glimpse
of whether they may serve as tools to assist purposeful human action. The
responses provided by this recently developed language model are meant to
prompt the reader to ask questions such as:

- To what extent it is possible to engage technology in a struggle to overcome peripherality and what are its current limitations?
- Is it necessary to have background cultural competencies (i.e. the ability to ask a question with at least a rudimentary understanding of the relevant literature) to elicit an answer that goes beyond meaningless chatter? If so, to what extent is the latter possible even then?
- Would it not be ironic if we used cutting-edge technology developed at the heart of the global capitalist system to support thought and critical action based on theories that, by definition, see the technological frontier as a tool for maintaining the core-periphery divide, dependency, and colonialism?

Q1: Using arguments from critical political economy and STS research, explain how semi-peripheral countries may strive for social re-embedding of the latest technological revolution innovations, such as AI similar to yourself.
ChatGPT: Critical political economy and Science and Technology Studies (STS) offer valuable insights into how semi-peripheral countries can strive for social re-embedding of the latest technological revolution innovations, such as AI.

Firstly, critical political economy suggests that technology is not neutral but embedded in social relations, power structures, and economic interests. Thus, the development and deployment of AI should be guided by social objectives and democratic principles rather than market imperatives alone. Semi-peripheral countries can strive for social re-embedding of AI by adopting policies that promote domestic technological capabilities, public research and development, and a regulatory framework that safeguards the interests of citizens and workers.

Secondly, STS studies emphasize the co-construction of technology and society, suggesting that AI should be developed and deployed in collaboration with social actors, including civil society organizations, workers, and communities. Semi-peripheral countries can strive for social re-embedding of AI by involving a diverse set of stakeholders in the decision-making process, ensuring that the development and deployment of AI align with social needs, values, and aspirations.

Thirdly, critical political economy and STS studies highlight the importance of redistributive policies to address the potential negative impacts of AI, including displacement of workers, widening inequalities, and concentration of power in the hands of tech giants. Semi-peripheral countries can strive for social re-embedding of AI by adopting policies that redistribute the benefits and risks of AI across society, including progressive taxation, social protection, and worker participation in decision-making.

To achieve social re-embedding of AI technologies, semi-peripheral countries can also draw on the concept of "technological democracy," which emphasizes the importance of inclusive participation in the development and use of technology. This can involve developing new forms of technology governance that prioritize participation, transparency, and accountability. By involving diverse stakeholders in the governance of technology, semi-peripheral countries can ensure that the development and use of AI technologies are aligned with their social and environmental objectives (Author' note: the paragraph above was added after the question was asked a second time).

In summary, critical political economy and STS studies suggest that semi-peripheral countries can strive for social re-embedding of the latest technological revolution innovations, such as AI, by adopting policies that promote domestic technological capabilities, involve a diverse set of stakeholders in the decision-making process, and redistribute the benefits and risks of AI across society.

Q2: What are the main constraints to the semi-periphery actively pursuing technology re-embedding?

ChatGPT: Semi-peripheral countries face a number of constraints that can limit their ability to actively pursue technology re-embedding. Some of the main constraints include:

1. Limited access to resources: Semi-peripheral countries may have limited access to the resources needed to develop and implement new technologies. This can include access to funding, research facilities, and skilled labour.

2. Dependence on dominant economic structures: Semi-peripheral countries may be dependent on dominant economic structures that prioritize profit over social and environmental objectives. This can make it difficult for these countries to prioritize technology re-embedding efforts that align with their social and environmental objectives.

3. Lack of political autonomy: Semi-peripheral countries may have limited political autonomy and may be subject to external political pressures that limit their ability to pursue technology re-embedding efforts.

4. Limited technological infrastructure: Semi-peripheral countries may lack the technological infrastructure needed to support the development and implementation of new technologies. This can include access to high-speed internet, advanced computing systems, and other critical technologies.

5. Cultural barriers: Semi-peripheral countries may face cultural barriers that limit their ability to adopt and implement new technologies. This can include differences in language, values, and social norms.

6. Lack of technical expertise: Semi-peripheral countries may lack the technical expertise needed to develop and implement new technologies. This can make it difficult for these countries to effectively participate in the global technology market.

7. Overall, these constraints can limit the ability of semi-peripheral countries to actively pursue technology re-embedding. To overcome these constraints, these countries may need to develop new partnerships and collaborations with other countries, invest in education and training programs to develop technical expertise, and prioritize the development of critical infrastructure and resources needed to support the development and implementation of new technologies.

∴

Postscript

When we began writing this book, the political situation in Eastern Europe did not yet imply that we, the authors of this monograph, would soon not only witness but also indirectly suffer the impacts of Russia's full-scale war in Ukraine. As a result, we did not incorporate such a possibility in the research plan, and this viewpoint is not evident in the reported findings. However, by focusing on the nature and specifics of the technological change occurring over a longer time horizon, as well as the impact it is having on the sphere of public management and governance in the Visegrád countries, we suspected that the might trigger new processes directly related to the phenomena discussed in this monograph, which already are much more apparent today.

The signs of ongoing hybrid warfare, which essentially involves the blurring of boundaries between military personnel and civilians as well as between armed conflict and peacekeeping, were evident well in advance of 24 February 2022. Russia's invasion of Ukraine had a variety of , mostly negative effects on the world, chief among them being a new wave of refugees, a food crisis, decreased energy security, rising prices and inflation, as well as the consolidation of NATO.

The war's worldwide repercussions are all being felt by the Visegrád countries. But due to their close proximity and economic ties with Ukraine and Russia, they have also been confronted with a number of unique challenges for the state and economic processes, the citizens and the non-governmental sector. The consequences of these challenges have already manifested themselves as more profound changes in the sphere of public management and governance. The most significant of these include:

- An overall increase in the operating costs of central and local government systems responsible for providing public services (housing, education, health care, social assistance and welfare, employment and labour market) as a result of the influx of Ukrainian refugees and their inclusion in their respective social security systems;
- The need to increase the number of places in educational institutions to enable the launch of programmes tailored to the specific needs of migrants;
- The need to ensure the availability of health care services for refugees, which involves adapting the infrastructure and resources;
- Integrating refugees into the labour market by launching vocational training courses, job search support, and dissemination of labour market information;
- As the need for social benefits and refugee relief rises, social welfare services become even more stretched;
- The need to develop effective technologies and systems to ensure digital security in response to cyberattack threats;
- The need to create administrative databases and services in Ukrainian (rapid integration of refugee data to improve the delivery of public services);
- The need to implement new negotiation and dispute resolution procedures in response to the crises caused by the deregulation of access to markets and services for Ukrainian operators (e.g. agricultural produce exports, freight transport, including cabotage);
- The need to develop new policies in the areas of social integration and multiculturalism, promoting the social inclusion of Ukrainian refugees and reducing the risk of culturally motivated tensions;
- Activation of the civic sector, which played a key role in assisting refugees during the early months of the war, with a view to securing its long-term participation in public governance processes.

All of these outcomes have significant consequences for the public finance sector and local labour markets. The long-term impact of Russia's invasion of Ukraine on the public management and governance spheres of the Visegrád countries is currently difficult to fathom and will undoubtedly require more in-depth research and analysis.

Bibliography

Acemoglu, D., Moscona, J. and Robinson, J. A. (2016). State Capacity and American Technology: Evidence from the Nineteenth Century. *The American Economic Review*, 106(5), 61–67. www.jstor.org/stable/43860988

Biga, B., Możdżeń M., Oramus M. and Zygmuntowski, J.J. (2022). Data Governance. The State, the Market, and the Commons in the Era of the Fourth Industrial Revolution, In: S. Mazur (Ed.), *Industrial revolution 4.0. Economic foundations and practical implications* (pp. 221–240). Routledge.

da Motta e Albuquerque, E. (2007). Inadequacy of technology and innovation systems at the periphery. *Cambridge Journal of Economics, 31*(5), 669–690. www.jstor.org/stable/23601646

De Paula, J. A., De Deus, L. G., Da Gama Cerqueira, H. E. A. and Da Motta E Albuquerque, E. (2020). New starting point(s): Marx, technological revolutions and changes in the centre-periphery divide. *Brazilian Journal of Political Economy, 40*(1), 100–116. https://doi.org/10.1590/0101-31572020-3023

Geodecki, T. and Grodzicki, M. (2015). Jak awansować w światowej lidze gospodarczej? Kraje Europy Środkowo-Wschodniej w globalnych łańcuchach wartości. *Zarządzanie Publiczne, 3*(33)/2015, 16–40. https://doi.org/10.15678/zp.2015.33.3.02

Geodecki, T. and Możdżeń, M. (2016). Polityka przemysłowa na rzecz podniesienia konkurencyjności gospodarki, In: T. Geodecki (Ed.), *Polityka wsparcia konkurencyjności gospodarki. Wybrane aspekty*, Polskie Wydawnictwo Ekonomiczne.

Grodzicki, M. and Skrzypek, J. (2020). Cost-competitiveness and structural change in value chains – vertically-integrated analysis of the European automotive sector. *Structural Change and Economic Dynamics, 55*, 276–287. https://doi.org/10.1016/j.strueco.2020.08.009

Mazzucato M. (2013) The Entrepreneurial State: Debunking Public vs. Private Myths in Risk and Innovation, Anthem Press

Medve-Bálint, G. and Šćepanović, V. (2020). EU funds, state capacity and the development of transnational industrial policies in Europe's Eastern periphery. *Review of International Political Economy, 27*(5), 1063–1082. https://doi.org/10.1080/09692290.2019.1646669

Reinsberg, B., Kentikelenis, A., Stubbs, T. and King, L. (2019). The World System and the Hollowing Out of State Capacity: How Structural Adjustment Programs Affect Bureaucratic Quality in Developing Countries. *American Journal of Sociology, 124*, 1222–1257.

List of Experts Participating in IDIS

Country	Research area[a]	Interviewee short characteristic	Code
Czech Republic	1	University professor, economist	Cz_1_1
Czech Republic	1	HR employee in a non-profit organisation	Cz_1_2
Czech Republic	1	High-ranking official in an employers' organisation	Cz_1_3
Czech Republic	1	Professor of technical engineering	Cz_1_4
Czech Republic	1	Senior official, Ministry of Labour and Social Affairs	Cz_1_5
Czech Republic	2	Entrepreneur, printing industry	Cz_2_1
Czech Republic	2	High-ranking official in an employers' organisation	Cz_2_2
Czech Republic	2	Investor in new technology start-ups	Cz_2_3
Czech Republic	2	Former director of a technological centre in a mail company	Cz_2_4
Czech Republic	3	Senior official, Brno City Council	Cz_3_1
Czech Republic	3	Senior official, Ministry of Finance	Cz_3_2
Czech Republic	3	Data specialist, Ministry of Health	Cz_3_3
Czech Republic	4	Investor in new technology start-ups	Cz_4_1
Czech Republic	4	Senior official, South Moravian Region, Brno	Cz_4_2
Czech Republic	4	High-ranking official in an employers' organisation	Cz_4_3
Czech Republic	4	Manager in a vocational school, Brno	Cz_4_4
Czech Republic	4	Professor of social science, Masaryk University	Cz_4_5
Czech Republic	5	Senior official, Brno City Council	Cz_5_1
Czech Republic	5	Senior official, Ministry of Finance	Cz_5_2
Czech Republic	5	IT manager, Ministry of Health	Cz_5_3
Czech Republic	5	Professor of political science, Masaryk University	Cz_5_4
Czech Republic	5	Professor of political science, Masaryk University	Cz_5_5
Czech Republic	5	Senior official, Ministry of the Interior	Cz_5_6
Hungary	1	Businessperson, e-learning expert, digital developer	Hu_1_1
Hungary	1	Deputy editor of an economic media outlet	Hu_1_2
Hungary	1	Expert in digital technologies, entrepreneur	Hu_1_3
Hungary	1	Financial analyst	Hu_1_4
Hungary	1	AI and machine learning developer	Hu_1_5
Hungary	1	Researcher in financial think tank, journalist	Hu_1_6
Hungary	1	Academic teacher, Corvinus University, expert in digital education	Hu_1_7

© MOŹDŻEŃ AND ZAWICKI, 2025 | DOI:10.1163/9789004711952_012

Country	Research area[a]	Interviewee short characteristic	Code
Hungary	2	Economist and researcher, Hungarian Academy of Sciences	Hu_2_1
Hungary	2	Professor Emeritus, Széchenyi István University	Hu_2_2
Hungary	2	Senior manager in a multinational corporation	Hu_2_3
Hungary	2	Senior official in a business cluster	Hu_2_4
Hungary	3	Analyst in a public policy think tank	Hu_3_1
Hungary	3	Advisor to the President of Hungary	Hu_3_2
Hungary	3	Member of Parliament	Hu_3_3
Hungary	4	Financial analyst	Hu_4_1
Hungary	4	Researcher in an economic think tank	Hu_4_2
Hungary	4	Former Member of Parliament, entrepreneur	Hu_4_3
Hungary	4	Senior manager in an economic think-tank	Hu_4_4
Hungary	5	Senior manager in a public policy think tank	Hu_5_1
Hungary	5	Advisor to the President of Hungary	Hu_5_2
Hungary	5	Analyst in a public policy think tank	Hu_5_3
Hungary	5	Journalist	Hu_5_4
Hungary	5	Senior manager in a political think tank	Hu_5_5
Hungary	5	Former Member of Parliament, entrepreneur	Hu_5_6
Hungary	6	Senior manager in a public policy think tank	Hu_6_1
Hungary	6	Senior official, Győr City Council	Hu_6_2
Hungary	6	Government appointee	Hu_6_3
Poland	1	Manager, Regional Labour Office, Kraków	Pl_1_1
Poland	1	Manager in a trade union	Pl_1_2
Poland	1	Senior official in an employers' association	Pl_1_3
Poland	1	Professor of social science, University of Wrocław	Pl_1_4
Poland	2	Manager in a private company, former senior official in one of government ministries	Pl_2_1
Poland	2	Member of Parliament, former senior official in one of government ministries	Pl_2_2
Poland	2	Staff member in a local employers' association	Pl_2_3
Poland	2	Entrepreneur, investor in new technology start-ups	Pl_2_4
Poland	3	Digital activist	Pl_3_1
Poland	4	Senior official, Ministry of the Interior and Administration	Pl_4_1
Poland	4	Professor of economics, University of Gdańsk	Pl_4_2
Poland	4	Former senior local government official, City of Sanok, social activist, academic teacher	Pl_4_3

Country	Research area[a]	Interviewee short characteristic	Code
Poland	4	Senior local government official, City of Jarosław	Pl_4_4
Poland	5	Digital activist	Pl_5_1
Poland	5	Advisor, Chancellery of the Prime Minister	Pl_5_2
Poland	5	Former senior cabinet official, Chancellery of the Prime Minister	Pl_5_3
Poland	6	Senior official in the Łukasiewicz Research Network, former senior official in the Ministry of Science and Higher Education	Pl_6_1
Poland	6	Expert in legal and European matters in a public policy think tank	Pl_6_2
Poland	6	Advisor in the Ministry of Digital Affairs	Pl_6_3
Slovakia	1	Analyst in an economic think tank, former economic journalist	Sk_1_1
Slovakia	1	Macroeconomist in a commercial bank, former economic editor of a weekly journal	Sk_1_2
Slovakia	1	Advisor to the State Secretary in the Ministry of Economy of the Slovak Republic	Sk_1_3
Slovakia	2	Secretary of the National Union of Employers	Sk_2_1
Slovakia	2	Economist and Expert on the Topics of Money, Currency and Digital Transformation	Sk_2_2
Slovakia	2	Economist, analyst, columnist, journalist, advisor, economist in a consulting firm	Sk_2_3
Slovakia	2	State Secretary in the Ministry of Economy of the Slovak Republic	Sk_2_4
Slovakia	3	Marketing manager in an employment portal	Sk_3_1
Slovakia	3	Executive director in a public policy and economic think tank	Sk_3_2
Slovakia	3	Director and economist in an economic think tank, academic teacher	Sk_3_3
Slovakia	3	Senior official responsible for information technologies, City of Bratislava	Sk_3_4
Slovakia	4	Former Senior official in the Ministry of Labour	Sk_4_1
Slovakia	4	Analyst in the Slovak Business Agency	Sk_4_2
Slovakia	4	Manager, Faculty of Economics, Matej Bel University	Sk_4_3
Slovakia	4	Senior Analyst in an economic think tank	Sk_4_4
Slovakia	5	Entrepreneur, former Member of Parliament	Sk_5_1

Country	Research area[a]	Interviewee short characteristic	Code
Slovakia	5	Academic teacher, legal scholar, Comenius University in Bratislava	Sk_5_2
Slovakia	5	Business, economic, and policy analyst and researcher	Sk_5_3
Slovakia	6	Senior analyst in a socio-economic think-tank	Sk_6_1
Slovakia	6	Member of Parliament	Sk_6_2
Slovakia	6	Senior analyst in an economic think-tank	Sk_6_3

[a]Legend

Research areas

1. Key economic and social challenges resulting from the Fourth Industrial Revolution
2. Technological upgrading and industrial policy in the European globalised semi-peripheral economies
3. Management and regulation of data and information flows
4. Key relationships between the state and its stakeholders during the Fourth Industrial Revolution
5. Communication management – the nation state towards narratives and fake news
6. The potential and limits of hierarchical public management in the face of globotics

Index

Printed in the United States
by Baker & Taylor Publisher Services